The Microsoft® Net[work For] Dummies,® 2nd Edition

S0-BEC-907

Cheat Sheet

Buttons on the Navigation Bar

Button	What It Does
	Displays or hides the Internet toolbar
	Goes back to the previous page
	Returns to the page where you were before you went back
	Downloads a fresh copy of the current page
	Stops downloading the current page
	Accesses your list of favorite places
	Accesses the MSN Help page

Buttons on the Internet Toolbar

Button	What It Does
	Increases or decreases the size of text displayed in the page
	Prints the current page
	Saves the current page to a disk file
	Copies the current page to the Clipboard so you can paste it into another program
	Changes the character set for international pages

World Wide Web Catalogs (Search Services)

AltaVista	http://www.altavista.com
Excite	http://www.excite.com
Infoseek	http://www.infoseek.com
Lycos	http://www.lycos.com
Yahoo!	http://www.yahoo.com

IDG BOOKS WORLDWIDE

...For Dummies: #1 Computer Book Series for Beginners

COMPUTER
BOOK SERIES
FROM IDG

The Microsoft® Network For Dummies, 2nd Edition

Cheat Sheet

Important Stuff About My Account

My member ID: _____

My password: **DO NOT WRITE IT HERE!!!!**

My e-mail address: _____

Tips for Parents

- Place reasonable limits on MSN and Internet usage.

- Do not enable access to Adult content if kids will be using your account unsupervised.

- Be involved. Learn for yourself how MSN and the Internet work.

- Instruct your kids in the proper use of MSN and the Internet (see Chapter 25).

- Report any inappropriate conduct or content to MSN.

Abbreviations and Smileys

Abbreviation or Smiley	What It Means
BTW	By the way
FWIW	For what it's worth
IMHO	In my humble opinion
IOW	In other words
LOL	Laughing out loud
OIC	Oh, I see
BRB	Be right back
AFK	Away from keyboard
PMJI	Pardon me for jumping in
ROFL	Rolling on the floor laughing
TTFN	Ta ta for now (quoting Tigger)
TTYL	Talk to you later
<g>	Grin
<bg>	Big grin
<vbg>	Very big grin
:-)	Just kidding
;-)	Wink
:-(	Bummer

Important Keyboard Shortcuts

Keyboard Shortcut	What It Does
Ctrl+A	Selects everything
Ctrl+C	Copies the selected text or graphic to the Clipboard
Ctrl+X	Cuts the selected text or graphic to the Clipboard
Ctrl+V	Pastes the contents of the Clipboard at the current location of the cursor
Ctrl+B	Formats the selection in boldface
Ctrl+I	Formats the selection in italics
Ctrl+U	Underlines the selection
Ctrl+F	Brings up the Find dialog box so you can search the current page for a word or phrase
Ctrl+P	Prints the current page
Ctrl+S	Saves the current page as a disk file

...For Dummies: #1 Computer Book Series for Beginners

THE MICROSOFT® NETWORK FOR DUMMIES®

2ND EDITION

THE MICROSOFT® NETWORK FOR DUMMIES®

2ND EDITION

by Doug Lowe

IDG BOOKS WORLDWIDE

IDG Books Worldwide, Inc.
An International Data Group Company

Foster City, CA ♦ Chicago, IL ♦ Indianapolis, IN ♦ Southlake, TX

The Microsoft® Network For Dummies® 2nd Edition

Published by
IDG Books Worldwide, Inc.
An International Data Group Company
919 E. Hillsdale Blvd.
Suite 400
Foster City, CA 94404
www.idgbooks.com (IDG Books Worldwide Web site)
www.dummies.com (Dummies Press Web site)

Library of Congress Catalog Card No.: 97-71813

ISBN: 0-7645-0160-7

Printed in the United States of America

10 9 8 7 6 5 4 3 2 1

1DD/RY/QY/ZX/IN

Distributed in the United States by IDG Books Worldwide, Inc.

Distributed by Macmillan Canada for Canada; by Transworld Publishers Limited in the United Kingdom; by IDG Norge Books for Norway; by IDG Sweden Books for Sweden; by Woodslane Pty. Ltd. for Australia; by Woodslane Enterprises Ltd. for New Zealand; by Longman Singapore Publishers Ltd. for Singapore, Malaysia, Thailand, and Indonesia; by Simron Pty. Ltd. for South Africa; by Toppan Company Ltd. for Japan; by Distribuidora Cuspide for Argentina; by Livraria Cultura for Brazil; by Ediciencia S.A. for Ecuador; by Addison-Wesley Publishing Company for Korea; by Ediciones ZETA S.C.R. Ltda. for Peru; by WS Computer Publishing Corporation, Inc., for the Philippines; by Unalis Corporation for Taiwan; by Contemporanea de Ediciones for Venezuela; by Computer Book & Magazine Store for Puerto Rico; by Express Computer Distributors for the Caribbean and West Indies. Authorized Sales Agent: Anthony Rudkin Associates for the Middle East and North Africa.

For general information on IDG Books Worldwide's books in the U.S., please call our Consumer Customer Service department at 800-762-2974. For reseller information, including discounts and premium sales, please call our Reseller Customer Service department at 800-434-3422.

For information on where to purchase IDG Books Worldwide's books outside the U.S., please contact our International Sales department at 415-655-3200 or fax 415-655-3295.

For information on foreign language translations, please contact our Foreign & Subsidiary Rights department at 415-655-3021 or fax 415-655-3281.

For sales inquiries and special prices for bulk quantities, please contact our Sales department at 415-655-3200 or write to the address above.

For information on using IDG Books Worldwide's books in the classroom or for ordering examination copies, please contact our Educational Sales department at 800-434-2086 or fax 817-251-8174.

For press review copies, author interviews, or other publicity information, please contact our Public Relations department at 415-655-3000 or fax 415-655-3299.

For authorization to photocopy items for corporate, personal, or educational use, please contact Copyright Clearance Center, 222 Rosewood Drive, Danvers, MA 01923, or fax 508-750-4470.

is a trademark under exclusive license to IDG Books Worldwide, Inc., from International Data Group, Inc.

About the Author

Doug Lowe lives in sunny Fresno, California — where the motto is, "At least it's a dry heat" — with his wife Debbie, daughters Rebecca, Sarah, and Bethany, and female Golden Retrievers Nutmeg and Ginger. He works full-time creating outstanding literary works such as *The Microsoft Network For Dummies* and wonders why he hasn't yet won a Pulitzer Prize or had one of his books made into a movie staring Harrison Ford so he can retire. Doug really believes that Harrison Ford would be excellent as the Dummies Guy and thinks John Kilkullen's people should call Harrison's people real soon before someone else steals the idea.

ABOUT IDG BOOKS WORLDWIDE

Welcome to the world of IDG Books Worldwide.

IDG Books Worldwide, Inc., is a subsidiary of International Data Group, the world's largest publisher of computer-related information and the leading global provider of information services on information technology. IDG was founded more than 25 years ago and now employs more than 8,500 people worldwide. IDG publishes more than 275 computer publications in over 75 countries (see listing below). More than 60 million people read one or more IDG publications each month.

Launched in 1990, IDG Books Worldwide is today the #1 publisher of best-selling computer books in the United States. We are proud to have received eight awards from the Computer Press Association in recognition of editorial excellence and three from *Computer Currents'* First Annual Readers' Choice Awards. Our best-selling ...For Dummies® series has more than 30 million copies in print with translations in 30 languages. IDG Books Worldwide, through a joint venture with IDG's Hi-Tech Beijing, became the first U.S. publisher to publish a computer book in the People's Republic of China. In record time, IDG Books Worldwide has become the first choice for millions of readers around the world who want to learn how to better manage their businesses.

Our mission is simple: Every one of our books is designed to bring extra value and skill-building instructions to the reader. Our books are written by experts who understand and care about our readers. The knowledge base of our editorial staff comes from years of experience in publishing, education, and journalism — experience we use to produce books for the '90s. In short, we care about books, so we attract the best people. We devote special attention to details such as audience, interior design, use of icons, and illustrations. And because we use an efficient process of authoring, editing, and desktop publishing our books electronically, we can spend more time ensuring superior content and spend less time on the technicalities of making books.

You can count on our commitment to deliver high-quality books at competitive prices on topics you want to read about. At IDG Books Worldwide, we continue in the IDG tradition of delivering quality for more than 25 years. You'll find no better book on a subject than one from IDG Books Worldwide.

John Kilcullen
CEO
IDG Books Worldwide, Inc.

Steven Berkowitz
President and Publisher
IDG Books Worldwide, Inc.

Eighth Annual Computer Press Awards ➤ 1992

Ninth Annual Computer Press Awards ➤ 1993

Tenth Annual Computer Press Awards ➤ 1994

Eleventh Annual Computer Press Awards ➤ 1995

IDG Books Worldwide, Inc., is a subsidiary of International Data Group, the world's largest publisher of computer-related information and the leading global provider of information services on information technology. Sixty million people read one or more International Data Group publications each month. International Data Group's publications include: **ARGENTINA:** Buyer's Guide, Computerworld Argentina, PC World Argentina; **AUSTRALIA:** Australian Macworld, Australian PC World, Australian Reseller News, Computerworld, IT Casebook, Network World, Publish, Webmaster; **AUSTRIA:** Computerwelt Osterreich, Networks Austria, PC Tip Austria; **BANGLADESH:** PC World Bangladesh; **BELARUS:** PC World Belarus; **BELGIUM:** Data News; **BRAZIL:** Annuário de Informática, Computerworld, Connections, Macworld, PC Player, PC World, Publish, Reseller News, Supergamepower; **BULGARIA:** Computerworld Bulgaria, Network World Bulgaria, PC & MacWorld Bulgaria; **CANADA:** CIO Canada, Client/Server World, ComputerWorld Canada, InfoWorld Canada, NetworkWorld Canada, WebWorld; **CHILE:** Computerworld Chile, PC World Chile; **COLOMBIA:** Computerworld Colombia, PC World Colombia; **COSTA RICA:** PC World Centro America; **THE CZECH AND SLOVAK REPUBLICS:** Computerworld Czechoslovakia, Macworld Czech Republic, PC World Czechoslovakia; **DENMARK:** Communications World Danmark, Computerworld Danmark, Macworld Danmark, PC World Danmark, Techworld Denmark; **DOMINICAN REPUBLIC:** PC World Republica Dominicana; **ECUADOR:** PC World Ecuador; **EGYPT:** Computerworld Middle East, PC World Middle East; **EL SALVADOR:** PC World Centro America; **FINLAND:** MikroPC, Tietoverkko, Tietoviikko; **FRANCE:** Distributique, Hebdo, Info PC, Le Monde Informatique, Macworld, Reseaux & Telecoms, WebMaster France; **GERMANY:** Computer Partner, Computerwoche, Computerwoche Extra, Computerwoche FOCUS, Global Online, Macwelt, PC Welt; **GREECE:** Amiga Computing, GamePro Greece, Multimedia World; **GUATEMALA:** PC World Centro America; **HONDURAS:** PC World Centro America; **HONG KONG:** Computerworld Hong Kong, PC World Hong Kong, Publish in Asia; **HUNGARY:** ABCD CD-ROM, Computerworld Szamitastechnika, Internetto online Magazine, PC World Hungary, PC-X Magazin Hungary; **ICELAND:** Tolvuheimur PC World Island; **INDIA:** Information Communications World, Information Systems Computerworld, PC World India, Publish in Asia; **INDONESIA:** InfoKomputer PC World, Komputek Computerworld, Publish in Asia; **IRELAND:** ComputerScope, PC Live!; **ISRAEL:** Macworld Israel, People & Computers/Computerworld; **ITALY:** Computerworld Italia, Macworld Italia, Networking Italia, PC World Italia; **JAPAN:** DTP World, Macworld Japan, Nikkei Personal Computing, OS/2 World Japan, SunWorld Japan, Windows NT World, Windows World Japan; **KENYA:** PC World East African; **KOREA:** Hi-Tech Information, Macworld Korea, PC World Korea; **MACEDONIA:** PC World Macedonia; **MALAYSIA:** Computerworld Malaysia, PC World Malaysia, Publish in Asia; **MALTA:** PC World Malta; **MEXICO:** Computerworld Mexico, PC World Mexico; **MYANMAR:** PC World Myanmar; **NETHERLANDS:** Computer! Totaal, LAN Internetworking Magazine, LAN World Buyers Guide, Macworld Netherlands, Net, WebWereld; **NEW ZEALAND:** Absolute Beginners Guide and Plain & Simple Series, Computer Buyer, Computer Industry Directory, Computerworld New Zealand, MTB, Network World, PC World New Zealand; **NICARAGUA:** PC World Centro America; **NORWAY:** Computerworld Norge, CW Rapport, Datamagasinet, Financial Rapport, Kursguide Norge, Macworld Norge, Multimediaworld Norge, PC World Ekspress Norge, PC World Nettverk, PC World Norge, PC World ProduktGuide Norge; **PAKISTAN:** Computerworld Pakistan; **PANAMA:** PC World Panama; **PEOPLE'S REPUBLIC OF CHINA:** China Computer Users, China Computerworld, China InfoWorld, China Telecom World Weekly, Computer & Communication, Electronic Design China, Electronics Today, Electronics Weekly, Game Software, PC World China, Popular Computer Week, Software Weekly, Software World, Telecom World; **PERU:** Computerworld Peru, PC World Profesional Peru, PC World SoHo Peru; **PHILIPPINES:** Click!, Computerworld Philippines, PC World Philippines, Publish in Asia; **POLAND:** Computerworld Poland, Computerworld Special Report Poland, Cyber, Macworld Poland, Networld Poland, PC World Komputer; **PORTUGAL:** Cerebro/PC World, Computerworld/Correio Informático, Dealer World Portugal, Mac*In/PC*In Portugal, Multimedia World; **PUERTO RICO:** PC World Puerto Rico; **ROMANIA:** Computerworld Romania, PC World Romania, Telecom Romania; **RUSSIA:** Computerworld Russia, Mir PK, Publish, Seti; **SINGAPORE:** Computerworld Singapore, PC World Singapore, Publish in Asia; **SLOVENIA:** Monitor; **SOUTH AFRICA:** Computing SA, Network World SA, Software World SA; **SPAIN:** Communicaciones World Espana, Computerworld Espana, Dealer World Espana, Macworld Espana, PC World Espana; **SRI LANKA:** Infolink PC World; **SWEDEN:** CAP&Design, Computer Sweden, Corporate Computing Sweden, Internetworld Sweden, it.branschen, Macworld Sweden, MaxiData Sweden, MikroDatorn, Nätverk & Kommunikation, PC World Sweden, PCaktiv, Windows World Sweden; **SWITZERLAND:** Computerworld Schweiz, Macworld Schweiz, PCtip; **TAIWAN:** Computerworld Taiwan, Macworld Taiwan, NEW ViSiON/Publish, PC World Taiwan, Windows World Taiwan; **THAILAND:** Publish in Asia, Thai Computerworld; **TURKEY:** Computerworld Turkiye, Macworld Turkiye, Network World Turkiye, PC World Turkiye; **UKRAINE:** Computerworld Kiev, Multimedia World Ukraine, PC World Ukraine; **UNITED KINGDOM:** Acorn User UK, Amiga Action UK, Amiga Computing UK, Apple Talk UK, Computing, Macworld, Parents and Computers UK, PC Advisor, PC Home, PSX Pro, The WEB; **UNITED STATES:** Cable in the Classroom, CIO Magazine, Computerworld, DOS World, Federal Computer Week, GamePro Magazine, InfoWorld, I-Way, Macworld, Network World, PC Games, PC World, Publish, Video Event, THE WEB Magazine, and WebMaster; online webzines: JavaWorld, NetscapeWorld, and SunWorld Online; **URUGUAY:** InfoWorld Uruguay; **VENEZUELA:** Computerworld Venezuela, PC World Venezuela; and **VIETNAM:** PC World Vietnam.

3/24/97

Dedication

To Debbie, Rebecca, Sarah, and Bethany.

Author's Acknowledgments

I'd like to thank project editor Kathy Cox who put up with many missed deadlines and still managed to whip this book into shape. Thanks also to copy editors Patricia Pan and Jill Brummett, proof editor Stephanie Koutek, and technical editor Allen Wyatt for many excellent corrections and suggestions.

I'd also like to thank the crew who helped with the first edition: Pam Mourouzis, Tammy Castleman, and Pam Hazelrigg.

Publisher's Acknowledgments

We're proud of this book; please send us your comments about it by using the IDG Books Worldwide Registration Card at the back of the book or by e-mailing us at feedback/dummies@idgbooks.com. Some of the people who helped bring this book to market include the following:

Acquisitions, Development, and Editorial

Project Editor: Kathleen M. Cox

Acquisitions Editor: Michael Kelly

Associate Permissions Editor: Heather H. Dismore

Copy Editors: Jill Brummett, Patricia Pan

Technical Editor: Allen Wyatt, Discovery Computing, Inc.

Editorial Manager: Mary C. Corder

Editorial Assistant: Donna Love

Production

Project Coordinator: Regina Snyder

Layout and Graphics: Lou Boudreau, Cameron Booker, J. Tyler Conner, Todd Klemme, Drew R. Moore, Heather Pearson, Brent Savage, Kate Snell

Proofreaders: Renee Kelty, Carrie Voorhis, Joel K. Draper, Nancy C. Price, Robert Springer,

Indexer: Liz Cunningham

Special Help

Stephanie Koutek, Proof Editor; Pamela Mourouzis, Senior Project Editor; Tamara Castleman, Senior Copy Editor

General and Administrative

IDG Books Worldwide, Inc.: John Kilcullen, CEO; Steven Berkowitz, President and Publisher

IDG Books Technology Publishing: Brenda McLaughlin, Senior Vice President and Group Publisher

Dummies Technology Press and Dummies Editorial: Diane Graves Steele, Vice President and Associate Publisher; Judith A. Taylor, Product Marketing Manager; Kristin A. Cocks, Editorial Director; Mary Bednarek, Acquisitions and Product Development Director

Dummies Trade Press: Kathleen A. Welton, Vice President and Publisher

IDG Books Production for Dummies Press: Beth Jenkins, Production Director; Cindy L. Phipps, Manager of Project Coordination, Production Proofreading, and Indexing; Kathie S. Schutte, Supervisor of Page Layout; Shelley Lea, Supervisor of Graphics and Design; Debbie J. Gates, Production Systems Specialist; Robert Springer, Supervisor of Proofreading; Debbie Stailey, Special Projects Coordinator; Tony Augsburger, Supervisor of Reprints and Bluelines; Leslie Popplewell, Media Archive Coordinator

Dummies Packaging and Book Design: Patti Sandez, Packaging Specialist; Lance Kayser, Packaging Assistant; Kavish + Kavish, Cover Design

◆

The publisher would like to give special thanks to Patrick J. McGovern, without whom this book would not have been possible.

◆

Contents at a Glance

Cartoons at a Glance

By Rich Tennant

page 7

page 67

page 233

page 309

page 289

page 125

page 177

Fax: 508-546-7747 • E-mail: the5wave@tiac.net

Table of Contents

Introduction

● ●

*Y*our coworkers are doing it. Your neighbors are doing it. Heck, even your dog is probably doing it. These days, everybody is *going online,* what ever that means. According to the latest polls, the whole world is quickly jumping aboard the so-called Information Superhighway.

Now Microsoft is in on the online revolution. It started a few years back with a modest online service called The Microsoft Network, also known as MSN. The original version of MSN was slightly cumbersome to use, but nevertheless people signed up by the millions. Now Microsoft has thoroughly revamped MSN to make it the splashiest, easiest to use, most energetic, and best looking online service available. To use the service, all you have to do to is click the MSN icon on your desktop.

Well, so goes the official party line. In reality, there's more to joining the online revolution than clicking an icon. Although Microsoft has done its best to make MSN an inviting place, venturing online is still a daunting experience. If you've never been online before, you have a lot to learn. Visiting MSN is much like visiting a foreign country: You have to learn how to get around, speak the language, and honor the local customs.

When you get right down to it, MSN is nothing more exciting than a computer program. Like any computer program, MSN has its own commands to learn, menus to traverse, icons to decipher, nuances to discover, and quirks to work around. Bother.

Oh — I can't forget to mention the Internet. Access to the Internet is one of the highly touted features of MSN. But if you think MSN is tough to get around in, wait until you land in the Internet. What a sprawling mess! The Internet is everything you've heard, except easy to use.

Good news! You've found the right book. Help is here, within these humble pages.

This book is your friendly guide to the Information Superhighway. It talks about MSN and the Internet in everyday terms. No lofty prose here. The language is friendly. You don't need a graduate degree in computer science or telecommunications to get through this book. I have no Pulitzer ambitions for this book. Maybe one of these days I'll write a 1,000-page novel about the Civil War, but not today.

I may take a carefully aimed potshot at the hallowed and sacred institutions of online computerdom throughout this book, just to spice things up. If that doesn't work, I may throw in an occasional lawyer joke.

My goal is to bring the lofty precepts of The Microsoft Network and the Internet down to earth where you can touch them and squeeze them and say, "What's the big deal? I can do that!"

About This Book

This is not the kind of book you pick up and read from start to finish, as if it were a cheap novel. Do not take it with you on vacation! If I ever see you reading it at the beach, I'll kick sand in your face. This book is more like a reference — the kind of book that you can pick up, turn to any page, and start reading whenever you get the urge to learn something about MSN or the Internet.

Each chapter is divided into self-contained chunks, all related to the theme of the chapter. For example, the chapter on using electronic mail (e-mail) contains nuggets such as:

✔ Sending electronic mail

✔ Receiving electronic mail

✔ Using the address book

✔ Sending attachments

✔ Adding a signature

You don't have to memorize anything in this book. It's a *need-to-know* tool. You pick it up when you need to know something, learn what you need to know, and then put it down and get on with your life.

How to Use This Book

This book works like a reference. Start with the topic you want to learn about, and look for it in the table of contents or index to get going. The table of contents is detailed enough that you can find most of the topics you'll look for. If you can't find a topic, turn to the index, where you'll find even more detail.

After you find your topic in the table of contents or index, turn to the pages and read as much or as little as you need or want. Then close the book and get to work.

On occasion, this book directs you to use specific keyboard shortcuts to get things done. When you see something like

Ctrl+Z

it means to hold down the Ctrl key while pressing the Z key and then release both keys at the same time. You don't type the plus sign.

Sometimes I'll tell you to use a menu command, like this:

File⇨Open

This line means to use the keyboard or mouse to open the File menu and then choose the Open command. (The underlined letters are the keyboard hot keys for the command. To use them, first press the Alt key. In the preceding example, you would press and release the Alt key, press and release the F key, and then press and release the O key.)

Whenever I describe a message or information you see on-screen, it will look like this:

Are we having fun yet?

Anything you are instructed to type appears in bold like so: Type **puns** in the text box. You type exactly what you see, with or without spaces.

Another little nicety about this book is that when you are directed to click one of those little toolbar buttons that are found everywhere in MSN, a picture of the button appears in the margin. This way, you can see what the button looks like to help you find it on your screen.

This book rarely directs you elsewhere for information. Almost everything you need to know about using MSN is here. However, two other books may come in handy from time to time. The first book is *Windows 95 For Dummies*, by Andy Rathbone (IDG Books Worldwide, Inc.). This book helps when you're not sure how to perform a Windows 95 task, such as copying a file or creating a new folder. Then there's *The Internet For Dummies,* 4th Edition, by John R. Levine, Carol Baroudi, and Margaret Levine Young (IDG Books Worldwide, Inc.). This book helps if you decide to venture into the dark recesses of the Internet.

What You Don't Need to Read

Much of this book is skippable. I've carefully placed extra-technical information in self-contained sidebars, and clearly marked them so that you can give them a wide berth. Don't read this stuff unless you just gotta know and feel really lucky. Don't worry; I won't be offended if you don't read every word.

Foolish Assumptions

I'm going to make only three assumptions about you:

- ✔ You use a computer.
- ✔ You use Windows 95.
- ✔ You use or are thinking about using MSN.

Nothing else. I don't assume that you're a computer guru who knows how to change a controller card or configure memory for optimal usage. Such computer chores are best handled by people who like computers. Hopefully, you are on speaking terms with such a person. Do your best to keep it that way.

How This Book is Organized

Inside this book, you'll find chapters arranged into seven parts. Each chapter is broken down into sections that cover various aspects of the chapter's main subject. There is a logical sequence to the chapters, so you can read them in order — if you're crazy enough to read this entire book. You don't have to read them in order, however. You can flip open the book to any page and start reading.

Here's the lowdown on what's in each of the seven parts:

Part I: Welcome to the New Microsoft Network

In this part, you get the basics of using MSN. This is a good place to start if you're clueless about what The Microsoft Network is, let alone how to use it.

Part II: The Sites and Sounds of MSN

This part is sort of a tour guide for the more interesting online locations to be found on MSN. You'll find out how to use one of the best online news services, MSNBC, and about many other fancy online programs available on MSN.

Part III: Reach Out and Electronically Touch Someone

This part explains how to use e-mail, which enables you to exchange messages with any other MSN member or, for that matter, anyone who is connected to just about any online service in existence, including CompuServe, America Online, Prodigy, and the Internet itself. Plus, you find out about the MSN online chat services and how to exchange ideas with other MSN users via bulletin boards.

Part IV: Great Stuff to Do on The Microsoft Network

The chapters in this part describe four of the most useful online services on MSN: Investor, which lets you track your personal finances online; Expedia, an online travel service; the Plaza, an online shopping mall; and Cinemania, an online database of movie reviews.

Part V: Internet Excursions

The chapters in this part show you how to access the Internet from MSN. You'll learn what the Internet is, how to access Internet newsgroups (the Internet equivalent to the MSN bulletin boards), and how to surf the World Wide Web.

Part VI: Customizing Your MSN Journey

In this part, you find what you need to know in order to control the plethora of options and settings to customize your MSN experience. An entire chapter is devoted to the topic of limiting access to offensive material on MSN and the Internet so that you can make MSN a safer place for your kids.

Part VII: The Part of Tens

This wouldn't be a ...*For Dummies* book if it didn't include a collection of chapters with lists of interesting snippets: Ten Microsoft Network Commandments, Ten Things That Often Go Wrong, and so on.

Glossary

There's so much techno-babble thrown about when discussing online services that I decided to include an extensive glossary of online terms called "Good Terms to Know", free of charge.

Icons Used in This Book

As you read this wonderful prose, you'll occasionally see the following icons. They appear in the margins to draw your attention to important information.

Watch out! Some technical drivel is about to come your way. Cover your eyes if you find technical information offensive.

Danger! Danger! Danger! Stand back, Will Robinson!

Pay special attention to this icon — it lets you know that a particularly useful tidbit is at hand, perhaps a shortcut or a way of using a command that you may not have considered.

Activate your brain cells. This icon points out stuff that's good to remember.

Where to Go From Here

Yes, you can get there from here. With this book in hand, you're ready to charge full speed ahead into the strange and wonderful world of MSN. Browse through the table of contents and decide where you want to start. Be bold! Be courageous! Be adventurous! Above all else, have fun!

Part I

Welcome to the New Microsoft Network

The 5th Wave

By Rich Tennant

AFTER THE INITIAL MERGER OF TWO COMPANIES COMES THE DELICATE PROCESS OF SELECTING A DOMINANT ONLINE SERVICE.

SOMEONE SAY "GO".

In this part . . .

The new MSN is one of the hottest online services around. If you've tried the old MSN and didn't like it, try it again. Microsoft has thoroughly revamped its online service and spiced it up with cool multimedia features and useful services. Plus, you get full access to the Internet. What more could you want from an online service?

Still, MSN takes some figuring out if you want to get the most from the service. The chapters in this part are where you find out things that help you get the most out of MSN.

If this is your first experience with online services, or if you're a seasoned online veteran, these chapters will provide you with a gentle introduction to MSN. You'll discover what MSN is, how to sign up for the service, and how to find your way around once you get in to the service. Happy surfing!

Chapter 1

Introducing The Microsoft Network

. . . .

In This Chapter

▶ Identifying The Microsoft Network

▶ Finding out what The Microsoft Network isn't

▶ Putting The Microsoft Network to work

▶ Finding out what The Microsoft Network has to offer

. . . .

I know the story. You just finished the latest issue of *Newsweek* and found out that 35 trillion people signed up to use the Internet this year. And of course, you're the only person left on the planet who isn't yet online, and the average 4-year-old knows more about computers than you do. So now you want to jump aboard the "Information Superhighway" — whatever that is — and become a part of the Information Revolution.

Make sure your seat tray is in the upright and locked position and fasten your seat belts. You're in for the ride of your life.

What The Microsoft Network Is

The Microsoft Network (or MSN for short) is an online service run by Microsoft, the company that brings you the software you love to hate, such as Windows 95, Word, and Excel.

So what exactly is an online service?

Simply put, an online service is a computer service that you subscribe to for a monthly fee. In exchange for your hard-earned cash (or, more likely, your hard-earned plastic), the online service enables you to connect your computer to other computers over the telephone. You can exchange electronic messages with other users, retrieve news and reference information, and access convenient services such as checking airline schedules or purchasing concert tickets.

The Microsoft Network is not the only online service. In fact, MSN was a latecomer to the online service world when Microsoft introduced MSN as a part of Windows 95 back in (you guessed it) 1995. Several other online services, most notably America Online and CompuServe, had already been around for years and had millions of users each. However, Microsoft rightfully felt that it could become a major player in the online service game by starting its own service. Thus, The Microsoft Network was born.

In early 1997, Microsoft unveiled an all-new version of The Microsoft Network, which the company calls the New Microsoft Network, or sometimes MSN 2. The New Microsoft Network is compatible with the Internet's World Wide Web. This consistency enables you to go from an area on MSN to one on the Web without any special effort. In fact, when you use MSN, it is sometimes hard to tell whether you're in an MSN area or an area of the Web.

The original version of MSN is now called MSN Classic. By the middle of 1997, Microsoft expects to have completely eliminated MSN Classic. As a result, this book focuses exclusively on the New Microsoft Network. Figure 1-1 shows the opening screen of the New Microsoft Network. (If you are a current user of MSN Classic and would like to switch to MSN 2, you can find instructions for doing so in Chapter 2.)

Figure 1-1:
The New
Microsoft
Network.

What Can You Do with The Microsoft Network?

So big deal. The Microsoft Network is one more thing that shows up on your monthly credit card bill. What can you *do* with MSN to justify the monthly expense? Plenty, actually. Following are just a few of the possibilities:

- Stay in touch with friends and colleagues throughout the world via electronic mail, which is much faster and cheaper than regular mail.

- Meet new people and make new friends.

- Get the latest sports scores.

- Do your homework.

- Do your kids' homework.

- Read an online magazine (sometimes called an *e-zine*).

- Stay abreast of the latest developments in just about any area of interest, such as what's happening with the next space shuttle mission.

- Find free games and other programs for your computer, in case you don't have enough real work to do.

- Retrieve electronic pictures that you can display on your computer, ranging from classic works of art to images beamed from the Hubble space telescope.

- "Talk" electronically with users around the world, from Austria to Zimbabwe.

- Read an online book (though it's still hard to curl up by the fire on a rainy night with an online book).

- Get help with computer problems.

- Access the so-called Information Superhighway, the famous Internet, just in case the MSN offerings don't keep you busy.

- And more! (*Lots* more!)

What The Microsoft Network Is Not

I want to clear up a few misunderstandings about The Microsoft Network before going much further. Following are some of the things MSN is not:

- ✔ It is not a general-purpose network that allows you to connect the various computers in your office so that you can share printers or exchange files with your coworkers. Windows 95 has that type of networking capability built in, but you don't need to sign up for The Microsoft Network to get it. Check out my book *Networking For Dummies* (IDG Books Worldwide, Inc.) for more information about setting up this type of network.

- ✔ It is not the Internet. You can access the Internet from The Microsoft Network, but The Microsoft Network is not the same thing as the Internet.

- ✔ It is not a sneaky plot that allows Microsoft to creep into your computer and snoop around your hard disk, looking for personal information about you, such as your credit card numbers or what kind of software you use. This fallacy likely has the same roots as rumors started by the same people who believe Bill Gates (the Chairman of Microsoft) secretly runs the White House and once tried to purchase the Vatican.

- ✔ It is not the only remaining information service. Prior to the grand opening of The Microsoft Network, the existing players in the online services game, such as CompuServe and America Online, complained bitterly that Microsoft would gain an unfair competitive advantage if it were allowed to include MSN in Windows 95. You'd think that the day after MSN came online, all the other online services would have just shriveled up and died. That hasn't happened, of course, and it isn't likely to happen anytime soon. MSN is an excellent online service that is getting better every month, but it's not the only online service you can use.

- ✔ It isn't the only information service you can access by using Windows 95. Even though Windows 95 comes with the software that you need to tap into The Microsoft Network, you can still access CompuServe, America Online, and other information services with Windows 95.

All the Information Superhighway puns in one convenient location

Ever since Al Gore coined the phrase Information Superhighway to refer to the Internet and other online information services, one bad Information Superhighway pun after another began to appear. I grew tired of those jokes long ago, so when I first learned that I was going to write a book about The Microsoft Network, I decided right away that I would bundle all the Information Superhighway puns I could think of in one convenient location near the start of the book and then make a solemn promise to not let them appear anywhere else in the book.

So here I go:

✔ **On-ramp:** Refers to the means of accessing the online world. CompuServe, America Online, Prodigy, and The Microsoft Network are all on-ramps to the Information Superhighway. These services allow you to connect your computer to other computers over phone lines so that you can converse with other computer users, access information stored in computer databases, and otherwise peruse the online world.

✔ **Speed bumps, speed limbs, road blocks, and detours:** Refer to the simple fact that the Information Superhighway isn't an easy drive. Traversing the roadways typically requires more computer savvy than the average computer user has, which explains why the Information Superhighway

is still largely a gathering place for nerds. One of the main reasons The Microsoft Network is successful is that it is considerably easier to use than most on-ramps.

✔ **Road construction:** Refers to the fact that the Information Superhighway isn't finished. Major portions of it are still under construction, not the least of which is the Microsoft Network itself.

✔ **Roadkill:** Refers to victims of the Information Superhighway, those poor souls who tried to become a part of the Information Superhighway but bailed before they figured it out.

✔ **Rush hour:** Refers to the sluggishness with which online services respond during peak hours, not to a daily online chat with Rush Limbaugh.

✔ **Toll road:** Refers to the fact that the Information Superhighway isn't free. Many online services charge a fixed amount each month (usually $10–30), plus additional charges for hourly usage. The more you use the service, the more you pay. The Microsoft Network is no exception.

Now that I've gotten that out of my system, I promise not to lay any more Information Superhighway puns on you for the rest of the book.

What You Get with The Microsoft Network

One of the things you come to realize after your first few minutes exploring the Microsoft Network is that it is huge. And not only is it huge, it gets bigger every day. Fortunately, exploring MSN can be fun. New discoveries are never more than a few mouse clicks away, and you never know what's around the corner.

The following sections describe the basic types of services that are available through the Microsoft Network.

Online news and information

When you first connect to MSN, one of the first things you notice is six online channels that serve as host to various online programs. (These channels appear back in Figure 1-1.) It's almost as if Microsoft was creating a cable television system instead of an online service.

One of the best-known MSN online programs is MSNBC. MSNBC is a joint effort of Microsoft and broadcasting giant NBC to create an online news service that delivers up-to-the-minute news right to your computer screen.

In addition to MSNBC, The Microsoft Network sports 30 other online programs, including *Entertainment Tonight* and off-beat programs such as *Mungo Park* and *Duckman Presents*. I explain everything you need to know about online channel surfing in Chapter 4.

Electronic mail

Electronic mail, or just e-mail, is one of the main reasons many people bother to use online information services at all. With electronic mail, you can compose a message on your computer and have it delivered almost instantly to any other computer user who is also connected to The Microsoft Network. Actually, the recipient of your mail doesn't have to be signed up for MSN; you can send e-mail to just about anyone connected to the Information Superhighway, whether through CompuServe, America Online, Prodigy, or the Internet. (Strictly speaking, all e-mail to users of other information services goes through the Internet on its way to the other service. But you don't have to know about the Internet to send mail to folks who use other services.)

Usually cheaper and delivered almost instantaneously, e-mail has many advantages over conventional mail. In e-mail's early days, one disadvantage was that e-mail only let you send plain-text messages. With MSN, however, you can send imaginatively formatted messages to other MSN users. You can use different fonts; emphasize text with bold, italics, and color; and even include simple pictures in your mail. You can also send any kind of file, such as a program file, a picture, a sound, or even a video clip, as an attachment.

Unfortunately, fancy formatting in e-mail messages is useful only when you're sending e-mail to other MSN users. The moment the message leaves MSN on its way to another information service such as CompuServe or America Online, the fonts, bold, italics, color, and other fancy formats are stripped away.

Both e-mail and bulletin boards are mail systems, and, just like regular mail, they have built-in delays. After you post a message, you have to wait for the intended recipient to log on to The Microsoft Network, retrieve the message, and then send you back a reply message. The mail may be delivered instantly, but the delay between when the mail is delivered and when the recipient actually reads it and responds can range from several hours to several days, or maybe even several weeks if the recipient happens to be on vacation.

For more information about using e-mail, turn to Chapter 10.

Bulletin board systems

Bulletin board systems (BBSs) are similar to e-mail — with a crucial difference. While e-mail is for personal, private communication between two individuals, bulletin boards are places where many individuals can exchange messages with one another about specific topics. The Microsoft Network has bulletin boards for a wide variety of interests, ranging from specific types of computer software and hardware to politics and current events to sports and hobbies. Plus, new bulletin boards form all the time as MSN grows and members express interest in new subjects. You find more information about using bulletin boards in Chapter 12.

Online chat

Chat gives more immediate satisfaction than e-mail. Chat is more like the phone system: It allows you to communicate directly with other users who are logged on to MSN at the same time that you are. When you communicate with someone in a chat, the message you type is immediately sent to the other user. He or she instantly sees your message and types a reply, which you see right away. Back and forth, tit for tat, give and take. Chat isn't restricted to just two users; many users can talk at the same time, somewhat like a conference call.

Like bulletin boards, chat areas are organized according to subject matter. You find chat areas all over MSN, with topics ranging from politics to history to archaeology to Windows 95.

Downloading files

The Microsoft Network is chock full of files just waiting to be copied to your computer. All sorts of files are available, ranging from computer games to accounting programs to complete transcripts of the Gettysburg Address. The process of copying one of these files from The Microsoft Network to your computer is called *downloading,* which I cover in detail in Chapter 12.

Essential services

The Microsoft Network is host to dozens of companies that provide products and services available directly via the network. If you can buy it, you can probably buy it over MSN. There's an online travel service called *Expedia,* an online automobile purchasing service called *CarPoint,* and an online shopping mall called the *Plaza* that hosts several stores, including *1-800-Flowers* and *Tower.*

MSN also includes several reference services that you can use to look up interesting facts. For example, Microsoft's own *Cinemania* movie database is available online to MSN users, as is the online encyclopedia *Encarta,* also from Microsoft. You can track your investments online using a service called *Microsoft Investor.*

The Internet

As if the services available on The Microsoft Network weren't enough, MSN also allows you to access information that is available on the Internet, the world's largest and oldest information network. You can access thousands of additional bulletin boards via the Internet (in Internet lingo, bulletin boards are known as *newsgroups*). You can also access the popular *World Wide Web* (WWW).

Internet access is a major benefit of using The Microsoft Network, so I devote several chapters to it. Take a look at Chapters 17–20 if you're interested in accessing the Internet via The Microsoft Network.

Chapter 2

Signing Up and Getting Connected

- -

In This Chapter

▶ Gearing up to join The Microsoft Network

▶ Signing up for MSN

▶ Installing MSN (if it isn't already on your computer)

▶ Connecting to MSN after you've signed up

▶ Changing your password, checking your bill, and other tasks

- -

*B*efore you can use The Microsoft Network, you must sign up for the service. When you apply, MSN creates an account, which keeps track of who you are and, most importantly, how much you owe Microsoft for the privilege of using The Microsoft Network.

Signing up for most online networks can be a project, but the MSN sign-up routine is easy. All it takes is a few points here and a few mouse clicks there, and you're in. This chapter shows you how.

What You Need to Use The Microsoft Network

Here is a list of what you need before you can join The Microsoft Network:

✔ **A computer:** The Microsoft Network is an online computer system, so naturally you need a computer to access it. At the present time, only IBM-compatible computers may access MSN; Macintosh users are out of luck. (Microsoft said it plans to enable Macintosh users to access MSN in the near future, though.)

You don't have to have the most powerful Pentium multimedia computer to access MSN. Any computer that can run Windows 95 can access MSN. For best results, make sure you have at least 8MB of random access memory (RAM).

✔ **A modem:** A modem is a device that enables your computer to connect to other computers via a telephone line. The modem may be internal, which means that it is physically contained within your computer's case, or external, which means that the modem lives in its own case and connects to your computer via a cable.

Modems are rated by their speed, using a measurement called baud. Although you can connect to MSN with a 14,400-baud modem, your MSN experience is much more satisfying if you use a modem rated at 28,800 baud. You can purchase a 28,800-baud modem for well under $100.

✔ **A telephone line:** The modem must connect to a phone line to work. You don't have to have a special computer-type phone line; your normal voice phone line can work. However, be warned that whenever you connect your computer to MSN, you can't use the phone line for anything else. If you try calling home and the phone is busy for hours, don't automatically assume that it's your teenager talking — it could be your spouse using MSN.

✔ **Windows 95:** MSN is available only to users of Windows 95. In fact, the capability to connect to MSN may be the main reason many computer users switch to Windows 95. (Microsoft has said that it will offer MSN to Macintosh users in the near future but has no plans to offer MSN to users of Windows 3.1.)

✔ **A credit card:** Sigh!

Signing Up

Before you can use The Microsoft Network, you must sign up. Signing up is the electronic equivalent of raising your hand and saying, "Yes, Bill Gates, I would like to use The Microsoft Network! Here is my name, address, phone number, mother's maiden name, credit card number, and deed to the house. Sign me up!"

Microsoft has done everything it can think of to make signing up for MSN as easy as possible. The following steps show you how to sign on to The Microsoft Network:

1. Get an MSN CD-ROM disk.

Because Microsoft wants everyone on the planet to sign up for MSN, the MSN software itself is free. As a result, you shouldn't have much trouble locating a copy of the MSN CD-ROM. Microsoft routinely stuffs these disks into the back of computer magazines, and most computer stores will give you one if you ask politely. If you already have an Internet connection, you can request the CD from the Microsoft Web site (www.Microsoft.com). If all else fails, try calling Microsoft at 800-426-9400.

Your Windows 95 desktop may already have an MSN icon sitting on it. However, that icon probably belongs to the older version of The Microsoft Network. To get signed up with the newest version of the MSN, you should use the CD instead of the desktop MSN icon.

2. Put the MSN CD-ROM disk in your CD drive, printed side up.

When you insert the disk, the MSN Startup CD program automatically starts up.

3. Click Next.

This leads you to the MSN Setup program, shown in Figure 2-1.

Figure 2-1:
The MSN
Setup CD
program.

4. If the MSN Setup program tells you to quit any other programs that happen to be running (see Figure 2-2), do so now.

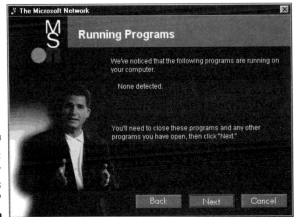

Figure 2-2:
Any other
programs
running?

MSN Setup should not be run while any other programs are running. Use the Alt+Tab keyboard combination to switch to any other programs that are running, then quit those programs by choosing the File⇨Exit command.

5. **Click Next.**

The Setup program asks what country you want to set up MSN for, as shown in Figure 2-3.

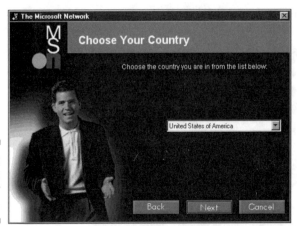

Figure 2-3:
Selecting
your
country.

6. **Select the country you are in and click Next.**

The Setup program displays the rules you must obey when using MSN.

7. **Read the rules.**

Use the scroll bar to scroll through the rules so you can read them all. Unfortunately, the rules appear to have been written by Microsoft's legal department, which means you can't understand them no matter how many times you read them. For a concise explanation of the rules, see the sidebar "What the rules really mean."

8. **Click I Agree.**

Unless, of course, you disagree, in which case you can click I Disagree. Microsoft doesn't allow disagreeable people on MSN, however, so if you want to use The Microsoft Network, you have to click I Agree. When you do so, the MSN Setup program displays the dialog box shown in Figure 2-4. The dialog box informs you that MSN is going to copy a bunch of files onto your hard drive and lets you know how much hard drive space these files take up.

What The Rules really mean

The Rules, officially known as "The Official MSN Member Agreement," spell out what you agree to when you sign up for MSN. You need to read the rules carefully, but because lawyers wrote them, only lawyers can understand them. Basically, the rules say the following:

✔ You agree to behave yourself.

✔ You agree to pay your bill.

✔ Microsoft agrees to nothing.

One important point that is buried deeply within The Rules is that you must be 18 years old or older to join. Minors can use the network, but only adults can sign up officially. (Of course, Microsoft has no way of verifying that the person signing up really is 18 or over. However, be warned that if you are under 18, you must have your parents sign up for you.)

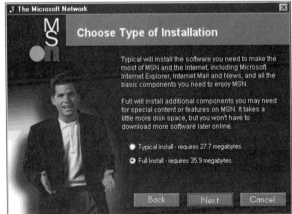

Figure 2-4: Choose your installation

9. Select Typical Install or Full Install.

Notice that a Typical Install requires less disk space than the Full Install option. If you have loads of disk space on your computer, go ahead and select Full Install. But if you are tight on space, pick Typical instead. This will save you about 8MB.

10. Click Next.

The screen shown in Figure 2-5 appears.

Figure 2-5:
Are you
ready to
rumble?

11. **Take a deep breath and then click Next.**

    The MSN Setup program will begin to copy all of the necessary files
    from the CD-ROM drive to your hard disk. This will take a few minutes,
    so be patient. The MSN Setup program will display a progress dialog
    box to let you know how things are progressing.

12. **When MSN Setup informs you that it needs to reboot your computer,
    click the Restart button.**

    Your computer will be restarted. After a moment, the MSN Setup
    program will automatically resume, displaying a dialog box announcing
    its presence.

13. **Click Next to continue with the Setup process.**

    The MSN Setup program whirs and spins for a moment and then
    displays the dialog box shown in Figure 2-6.

14. **Click Next.**

    The MSN Setup program starts another program called the Internet
    Connection Wizard, which uses your modem to connect to the Internet
    using a special toll-free 800 number and then lets you choose from one
    of several pricing plans.

    Note: For the following steps (Steps 15 through 26), the exact sequence
    of screens you see may vary. Don't be alarmed if the screens you see
    vary from the screens shown in these steps. Just follow the instructions
    on the screen and you'll be fine.

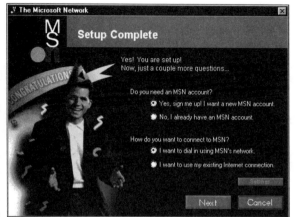

Figure 2-6:
MSN Setup
offers
several
signup
options.

If you already have an Internet connection with another Internet Service Provider, you can sign up to access MSN from your existing Internet connection. To do so, check off the option that says Sign up for MSN but use my existing Internet Connection.

If you already have an MSN account and are just upgrading to the new Microsoft Network, check the "I already have an MSN account" option. The MSN setup program copies the new MSN files to your computer but doesn't create a new MSN account for you.

15. Select the connection option you want to use and then click Next.

MSN allows you to connect to The Microsoft Network through Microsoft's own phone numbers, or you can connect through your existing Internet Service Provider. Or if you have a special high-speed ISDN connection, you can connect through that by clicking the "I want to use an ISDN terminal adapter to connect to MSN and the Internet" option shown in Figure 2-7. (If you don't know what ISDN is, you probably aren't using ISDN, so don't worry about this option.)

When you click Next, the screen shown in Figure 2-8 appears, offering you one of three pricing plans for MSN.

16. Select the pricing option you want and then click Next.

As I write this, Microsoft offers three pricing plans for MSN:

- $6.95 per month, which allows you to use the network for up to five hours each month, with additional hours costing $2.50 each

- $69.95 for a full year's access with five hours per month; again, with each extra hour you use costing $2.50

- $19.95 per month for unlimited access, with no additional hourly charge

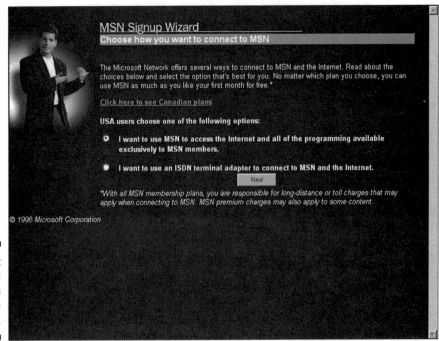

Figure 2-7:
MSN
Signup asks
if you are
using ISDN.

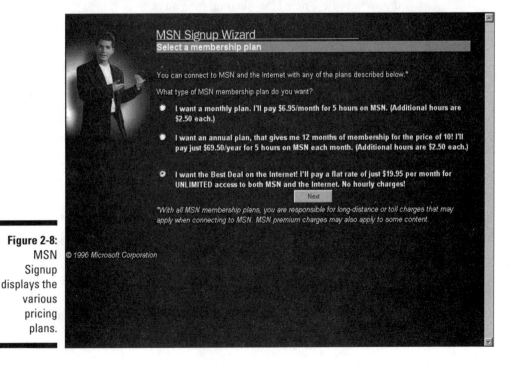

Figure 2-8:
MSN
Signup
displays the
various
pricing
plans.

Although the first two options may seem the cheapest, they can actually be the most expensive. For example, if you use MSN 15 hours in one month, you end up paying $31.95 under the first plan. If you use it 30 hours, your bill is a whopping $69.45 under the same plan. That's why I always recommend the $19.95 plan.

When you click Next, the screen shown in Figure 2-9 appears.

17. Type your name and address information and click Next.

The screen shown in Figure 2-10 appears, listing the various membership plans and prices that are available for The Microsoft Network. If you wish, you can review the plans and change the plan you selected.

18. Choose a different pricing plan if you've changed your mind already. Then scroll to the bottom of the display and click Next.

The screen shown in Figure 2-11 will be displayed.

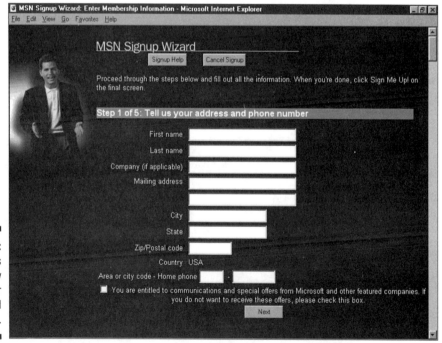

Figure 2-9: MSN wants to know your name and address.

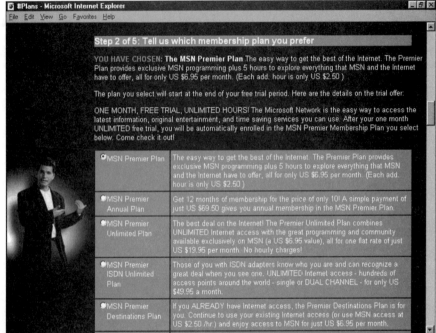

Figure 2-10:
MSN Setup
displays the
various
pricing
plans.

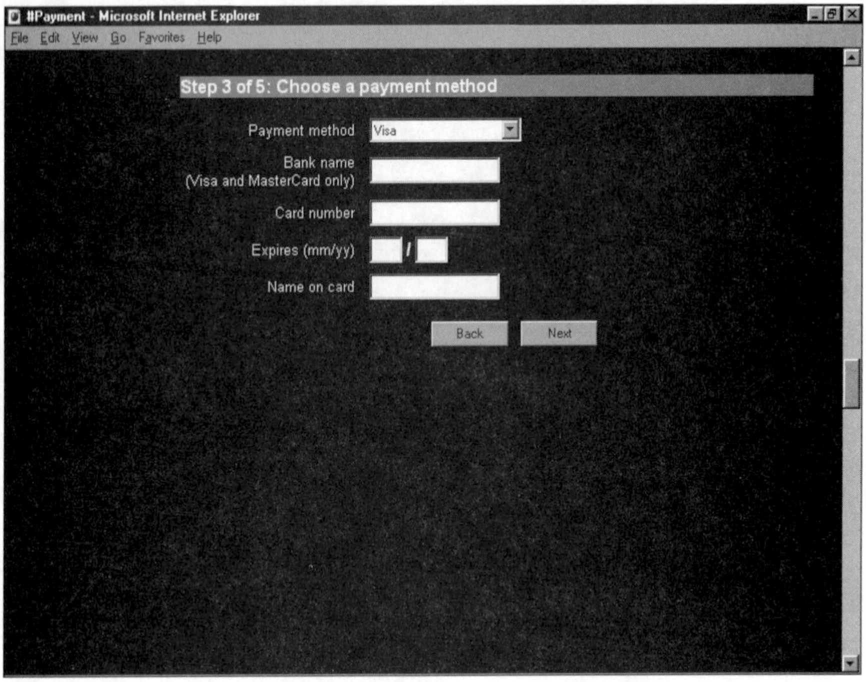

Figure 2-11:
MSN asks
for your
credit card
information.

19. Select the type of credit card you want to use from the Payment Method list box. Then type the credit card information in the dialog box fields.

The sign-up process is the only time you should ever give your credit card number as a part of joining MSN. If anyone claiming to be a Microsoft representative asks you to send your credit card information via electronic mail, contact MSN Member Services immediately. You are being scammed by an electronic con artist! (I've never heard of this happening on MSN, but it has happened on other online services and is bound to happen on MSN sooner or later. This scam is similar to the one in which you receive a phone call saying that you have won some valuable prize, and all you have to do is give your credit card number for "verification purposes.")

20. Click Next.

The screen shown in Figure 2-12 appears, asking if you agree with the rules. This is all very annoying, of course, because you already agreed to the rules back in Step 8.

21. Click I Agree and then click Next.

You may have to scroll the screen down to locate the Next button. When you click it, you see the screen shown in Figure 2-13.

Figure 2-12:
MSN makes
you agree
to the rules
again.

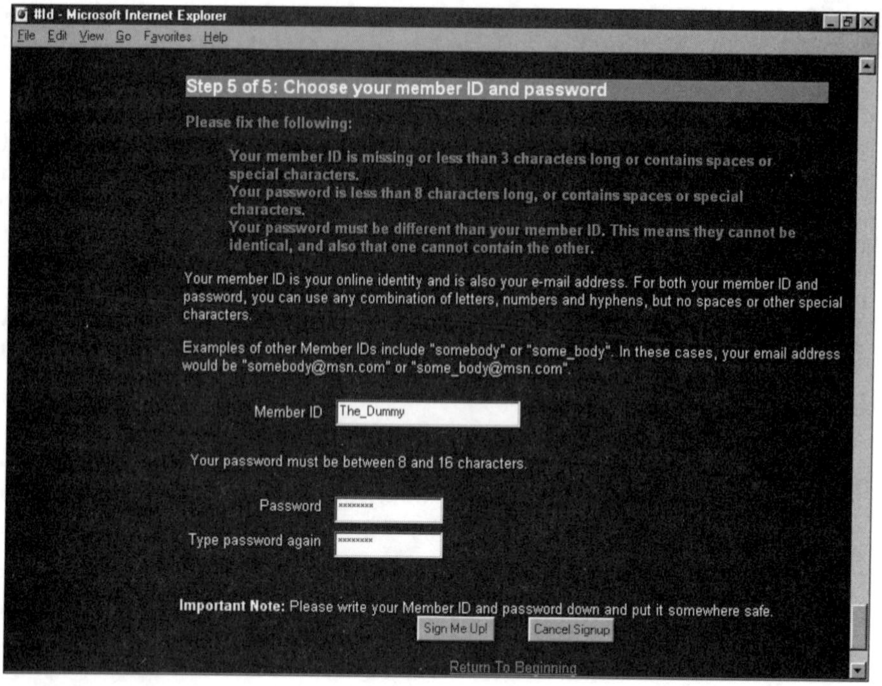

#ld - Microsoft Internet Explorer

File Edit View Go Favorites Help

Step 5 of 5: Choose your member ID and password

Please fix the following:

> Your member ID is missing or less than 3 characters long or contains spaces or special characters.
> Your password is less than 8 characters long, or contains spaces or special characters.
> Your password must be different than your member ID. This means they cannot be identical, and also that one cannot contain the other.

Your member ID is your online identity and is also your e-mail address. For both your member ID and password, you can use any combination of letters, numbers and hyphens, but no spaces or other special characters.

Examples of other Member IDs include "somebody" or "some_body". In these cases, your email address would be "somebody@msn.com" or "some_body@msn.com".

Member ID   The_Dummy

Your password must be between 8 and 16 characters.

Password   ********

Type password again   ********

Important Note: Please write your Member ID and password down and put it somewhere safe.

[Sign Me Up!]   [Cancel Signup]

Return To Beginning

Figure 2-13: MSN asks you to enter a member ID and password.

22. **Type the name you would like other MSN users to know you by in the Member ID field.**

    This name does not have to be your real one. You can make up a silly name such as Godzilla, Luke_Skywalker, Fred_Flintstone, Maniac, Gonzo, or whatever. (Of course, you can use your real name, but many users prefer to hide behind a nickname.)

    Your member name cannot include spaces, but you can use the underscore or hyphen character to separate words. Also, each MSN user must have a unique name. As a result, MSN will tell you to come up with something more original if someone has already claimed "Godzilla" as a member ID.

23. **Type a password in the Password field.**

    The password is a secret code that allows you and only you to access MSN by using your member ID. While other users are allowed to know your member ID, only you can know your password.

    Choosing a good password and keeping it a secret is very important. If your password gets out, anyone can log in to MSN using your member ID and password and pretend to be you. That can be not only annoying but also expensive. For some sage advice about passwords, see the sidebar "Sage advice about passwords." (Clever title, eh?)

Sage advice about passwords

Your password is the only protection you have against unscrupulous users accessing MSN by using your member ID, which can become expensive as they rack up connect time and other charges. Here are some tips for keeping your password secret:

✔ Don't use obvious passwords, like your last name, your kid's name, or your dog's name. Don't pick passwords based on your hobbies, either. I have a friend who is into boating, and he uses the name of his boat as his password. Anyone who knows about his interest in boating could guess his password after a few tries.

✔ Use unusual words. I like to use words from Chaucer's "Canterbury Tales" because the spelling is so weird. For example, Chaucer's spelling of "Opinion" is "Opynyoun" — perfect for a password.

✔ A random combination of letters and numbers makes for a good password. For example, no one would guess B49H20CD243928Q.

✔ Write your password down, but keep it in a secure location. You'll be in a pickle if you forget your password. I keep mine in my Day Timer.

24. Click Sign Me Up!

You are signed up for MSN. If there is a problem with any of the information you've entered, MSN informs you of the error and asks you to re-enter the appropriate information. Problems could include choosing an ID that another member is using already or signing up without giving a valid credit card number.

If all the information you entered is acceptable, the screen shown in Figure 2-14 appears.

25. Click Continue.

The MSN Setup program then downloads the latest MSN files to your computer so that your computer is configured to run properly with the latest version of MSN. You may see a dialog box similar to the one shown in Figure 2-15. If so, select "Open it" and click OK.

You may also see a dialog box similar to the one in Figure 2-16. If so, click Yes.

When the configuration is finished, you see a dialog box similar to the one shown in Figure 2-17.

26. Click OK.

You're done!

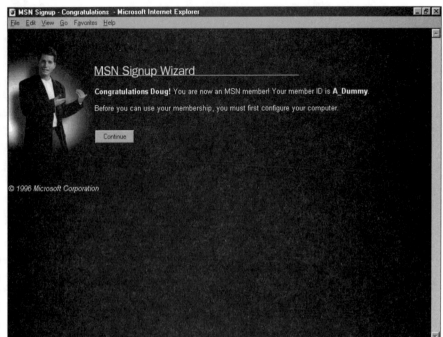

Figure 2-14:
Congratu-
lations! You
made it.

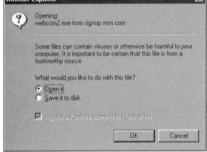

Figure 2-15:
MSN may
ask your
permis-
sion to
download
some
important
files.

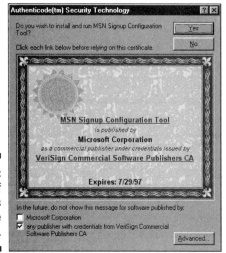

Figure 2-16:
Click Yes if
you see this
Certificate
dialog box.

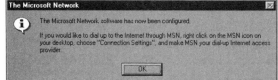

Figure 2-17:
Whew!

Connecting to MSN after You Join

Here is the procedure for connecting to The Microsoft Network after you
sign up. This procedure should become a familiar one:

MSN

1. **Double-click the MSN icon that appears on your desktop.**

   The Sign In dialog box appears, as shown in Figure 2-18.

2. **If necessary, type your member ID and password in the Member ID
   and Password fields.**

   Your password doesn't appear on-screen as you type it; instead, an
   asterisk appears for each character you type. This procedure protects
   your password from snoopy neighbors.

3. **Click the Connect button,**

   MSN calls the phone numbers that were saved when you signed up.
   When the connection is complete, the MSN home page appears, and
   you can begin exploring MSN. Refer to the next chapter for a guided
   tour of MSN, suitable for getting your feet wet the first time you sign in.

Figure 2-18:
The Sign-In
dialog box.

If you tire of typing your password every time you sign in, check the Remember my password checkbox. Then MSN automatically provides your password when the Sign-In dialog box appears. This feature is convenient (I use it myself), but you may not want to use it if your computer is in an unsecured location where unauthorized users can get to it. They can't read your password, but they can sign in using your member ID.

The Settings button lets you fiddle with unmentionable settings that you shouldn't mess with unless you are having trouble accessing The Microsoft Network. Put on your safety goggles before venturing into this land of dialing properties and modem settings.

If for some reason the Setup program doesn't configure a phone number which your computer can use to access MSN, click the Settings button and then click the Phone Book button and choose the phone number closest to your location. (Be sure you don't pick a long-distance number. If you do, your phone bills will skyrocket!)

Changing Your Password

Changing your password once in a while is not a bad idea. It helps foil those who would attempt to access The Microsoft Network without paying for it by stealing someone else's member ID and password. Here's the procedure:

1. **Double-click the Microsoft Network icon, type your member ID and password (if necessary), and click Connect.**

   Your computer dials The Microsoft Network computers, and eventually the familiar MSN home page appears.

2. **Point the mouse at the question mark icon that appears in the upper-right corner of the MSN window to reveal the Member Services menu; then choose the Check or Change Your Account command.**

   The Check or Change Your Account page appears, as shown in Figure 2-19.

3. **Click Password in the list of options that appears on the left edge of the page.**

   The Change Your Password page appears, as shown in Figure 2-20.

4. **Type your current password and then type your new password twice in the fields indicated.**

   As a security precaution, the passwords do not display as you type them.

5. **Click OK.**

   The next time you sign in, you must use the new password.

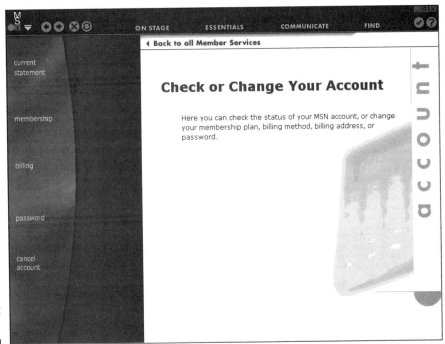

Figure 2-19:
The Check
or Change
Your
Account
page.

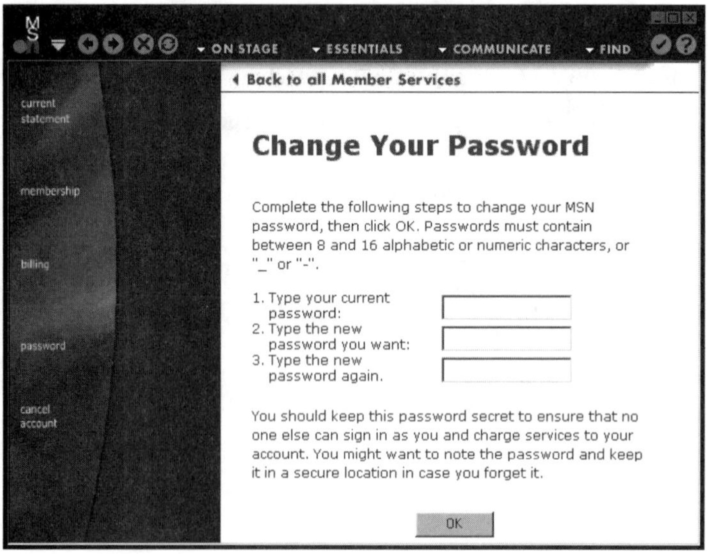

Figure 2-20:
The Change
Your
Password
page.

Checking Your Bill

If you're curious about your current charges, connect to The Microsoft Network and choose the Check or Change Your Account command from the Member Services menu. You can access this menu by clicking the question mark in the upper-right corner of the MSN window. Doing so brings up the Check or Change Your Account page that you see back in Figure 2-19. In addition to allowing you to change your password, this page lets you review the status of your MSN account.

In particular, the following options are available from the Check or Change Your Account page:

✓ **Current Statement:** Lets you check the amount you currently owe to Microsoft. You can view a quick summary, or you can view detailed account charges.

✓ **Membership:** Displays your current membership plan and allows you to change plans if you wish.

✓ **Billing:** Allows you to change your billing address or payment method.

✓ **Password:** Lets you change your password. See the section "Changing Your Password," for more information about using this option.

✓ **Cancel account:** Allows you to cancel your MSN account.

Disabling Call Waiting

If your phone has call waiting — the feature that creates an annoying beep when someone tries to call you while you are talking on the phone — be forewarned that this feature can wreak havoc on online connections. Fortunately, The Microsoft Network can automatically disable call waiting for you. Follow these steps to tell MSN that you want call waiting disabled when you are using the network:

1. Right-click the MSN icon on your desktop and choose the Connection Settings command.

The Connection Settings dialog box appears, as shown in Figure 2-21.

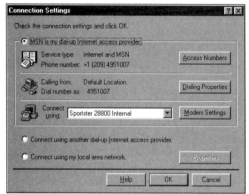

Figure 2-21:
The
Connection
Settings
dialog box.

2. Click the Dialing Properties button.

The Dialing Properties dialog box appears.

3. Click the checkbox that says This location has call waiting.

4. Select the code to disable Call Waiting in the listbox.

The listbox provides the most common codes: *70, 70#, and 1170. If your phone uses a different code, just type the code in the field. (The phone book provided by your phone company should list the code used to disable call waiting.)

5. Click OK to return to the Connection Settings dialog box, and then click OK again.

You're done!

Chapter 3

Getting Around The Microsoft Network

• •

In This Chapter

▶ Understanding the MSN Program Viewer screen

▶ Touring the sites: On Stage, Essentials, Communicate, and Find

▶ Following links

▶ Going back

▶ Stopping long downloads

▶ Refreshing pages

▶ Leaving the MSN Program Viewer

• •

*T*his chapter is an introduction to finding your way around The Microsoft Network. The more you work with MSN, the more familiar with it you become and the more adept you get at moving around. Your first few experiences with MSN can be confusing, however, so don't be intimidated. Jump right in. You'll find your feet in no time.

Don't be afraid to click anywhere you want. The best way to learn how to get around MSN is to start clicking.

The MSN Program Viewer

Each time you connect to The Microsoft Network, a program called the MSN Program Viewer starts. The exact contents of the Program Viewer window may vary each time you connect, but it usually resembles Figure 3-1.

Across the top of the MSN Program Viewer window is the Navigation bar, which contains all of the controls you need to use to get around MSN. The following paragraphs describe the various controls located on the Navigation bar:

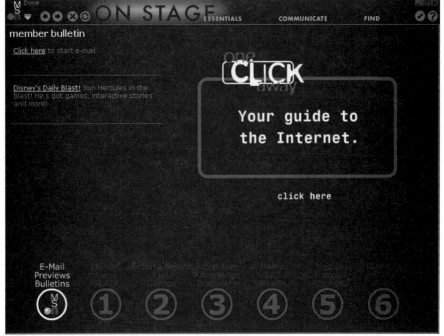

Figure 3-1:
The MSN
Program
Viewer
and its
changeable
window.

✔ **Site headings:** The central portion of the Navigation bar contains four *site headings* that you can click to go to the four main parts of The Microsoft Network: On Stage, Essentials, Communicate, and Find. When you click on one of these site headings, the home page for the site heading you clicked appears, and the site heading itself enlarges. For example, in Figure 3-1, the On Stage site heading appears enlarged. (I have more to say about the four MSN sites later in this chapter.)

✔ **Site heading arrows:** The down-pointing arrows next to each of the site headings contain menus that list the options available at each site. To summon these menus, just point the mouse at the down arrow for a few moments; you don't have to click.

✔ **Back button:** Moves you back to the most recently displayed page.

✔ **Forward button:** Moves you forward to the page you most recently moved back from.

✔ **Stop button:** Stops the current download. See the section "Stopping a Long Download," later in this chapter, for an explanation of how to use this button.

✔ **Reload button:** This button downloads again the page that you currently have on display. You reload a page so that any changes you've made since you first accessed the page show up. See the section "Reloading a Page," later in this chapter, for more information.

✔ **OnMSN:** This control indicates that you are connected to MSN. The *O* in the word *On* flashes whenever the Program Viewer is busy downloading information from MSN. The *O* stops flashing when the current page finishes downloading.

You can click the OnMSN control to display the Program Viewer's Control menu, which includes commands that let you move, size, minimize, maximize, and close the Program Viewer window.

✔ **Reveal Internet Toolbar:** Click this button to display a toolbar that contains additional controls. Figure 3-2 shows this toolbar. As you can see, when the Internet Toolbar is on display, the arrow in the Reveal Internet Toolbar control points upward instead of downward. Click the arrow again to hide the Internet Toolbar.

Figure 3-2:
The Internet
Toolbar.

The following paragraphs briefly describe the controls that are available on the Internet Toolbar:

- **Explorer:** Click this button to summon an Options dialog box that enables you to control various aspects of MSN's operation.

- **Font Size:** Increases the size of text displayed in the Program Viewer window.

- **Print:** Prints the current page.

- **Save:** Saves the current page to a disk file.

- **Copy:** Copies the current page to the Clipboard so you can paste it into another program.

- **Character set:** Lets you change the character set when viewing Web pages in different languages.

- **Address:** Allows you to enter the address of an Internet site you wish to visit.

- **Enter:** Clicking the Enter button is the same as pressing the Enter key.

Oh, the Places You'll Go!

The MSN Program Viewer is actually a special version of the popular Web browser program from Microsoft, Internet Explorer. The main function of the MSN Program Viewer is to let you view the various pages that make up The

Microsoft Network. To view all those pages, you need to know how to get around — that is, how to *navigate* so you can go from one MSN page to another. The following sections explain the MSN navigation features.

The MSN home pages

The Microsoft Network actually consists of four major sites, each with its own home page. These home pages serve as starting points for your explorations into the various MSN sites. To get to a site's home page, all you have to do is click one of the four site headings, which appear across the top of the MSN Program Viewer Navigation bar.

The four MSN sites are:

- **On Stage:** The On Stage site is like an Internet version of cable TV. The site consists of six *channels,* each of which carries Internet programs related to various topics, such as news and current events or sports. These Internet programs are not programs in the sense of computer programs such as Lotus 1-2-3 or Microsoft Word. Instead, they are programs in the sense of *Happy Days* and *Laverne and Shirley.* In other words, they are more like TV shows than computer programs.

  On Stage is such a major portion of MSN that I devote an entire chapter to it. In Chapter 6, you find your way around On Stage and get an overview of the programming available on the various On Stage channels. (The programming varies, so by the time you read this, new "shows" may be available.)

  On Stage also happens to be the default start page for MSN, so the On Stage home page automatically displays when you sign in. You can get to On Stage at any time by clicking On Stage in the Navigation bar. Refer to Figure 3-1 for a glimpse of the On Stage home page.

- **Essentials:** Essentials is the site for accessing reference information or online services such as making airline reservations, tracking the stock market, or buying a car. Figure 3-3 shows the Essentials home page. I cover all of this essential stuff in detail in Chapter 7.

- **Communicate:** The Communicate home page is your gateway to interacting with other MSN users. Three primary methods of communicating in MSN consist of:

  - **Electronic mail,** in which you can send and receive private messages to other users

  - **Bulletin boards,** where you can post messages that other MSN users interested in similar topics can read and respond to

  - **Chat,** where you can hold online conversations with other MSN users

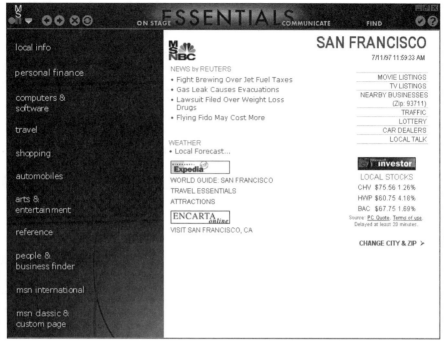

Figure 3-3:
Essentials
stuff on
MSN.

For more detail on these communication features, which are the heart and soul of MSN, take a look at Chapters 10 through 20 of this book. Figure 3-4 shows the Communicate home page.

✔ **Find:** If you're lost, use the MSN Find feature by pointing to Find on the Navigation bar and then clicking Search by Word or Phrase. Doing so takes you to the Find page. On this page, you can search MSN or the entire Internet for pages related to specific words (such as "Bengal tiger" or "softball"), browse the subject index for all of MSN, or check the calendar of upcoming MSN events. Figure 3-5 shows the Find page.

Using the menus

Each of the main MSN sites listed at the top of the Navigation bar has a menu, which you can access simply by pointing at the down arrow next to the site heading. These menus enable you to access specific pages within sites without having to first access the site's home page.

Figure 3-4:
Communi-
cate.
The MSN
communi-
cation
home page.

Figure 3-5:
The Find
page.

You can also use the following keyboard shortcuts to access the site menus:

Alt+O   On Stage

Alt+E   Essentials

Alt+C   Communicate

Alt+F   Find

To choose a menu item, click the menu item with the mouse. You can also use the up- or down-arrow keys to highlight the menu item you want to select and then press Enter.

Many of the menus have submenus. An arrow at the end of the menu item indicates a submenu. To access a submenu, just point at a menu item that has a submenu arrow. The submenu instantly appears. For example, Figure 3-6 shows the On Stage menu with one of its submenus displayed.

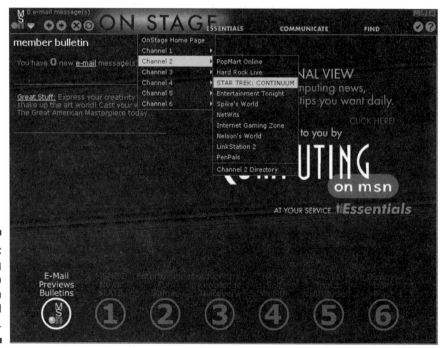

Figure 3-6:
Burrowing deep into MSN with menus and submenus.

Follow the links

A *link* is a bit of text or a graphic on an MSN page that, when clicked, leads you to another page. The new page can be another MSN page, or the link can lead to a page outside of MSN on the Internet.

Two types of links are available: text links and graphic links. Text links are easy to spot because they have an underline and appear in an alternate color. Text links are usually blue, but you can change the color if you wish. See Chapter 21 for more information. Figure 3-7 shows an MSN page with a text link. The underlined text (Check out which computer baseball games hit a homerun) that you see near the middle of the page is a link. Click it to display the entire article.

 Graphic links are harder to find than text links. When you point the mouse at a graphic link, the mouse pointer changes from an arrow to a pointing finger. In addition, some links change appearance when you point at them. Take a look at what happens when you point the mouse at one of the channel numbers that appear at the bottom of the On Stage home page. The channel number changes appearance, and the names of the programs that are available on the channel appear.

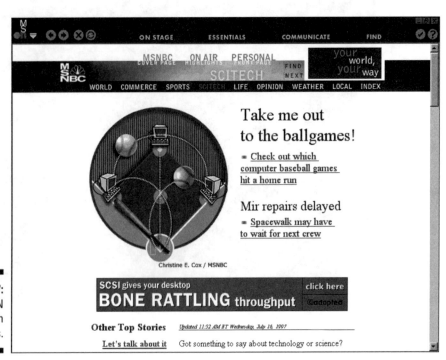

Figure 3-7:
An MSN
page with
text links.

Some links are hard to find. For example, did you notice the musical note that appears to the right of Channel 6 back in Figure 1-1? If you click the note, the music that automatically plays when you view the On Stage home page stops. Click it again to restart the music.

Yes, you can go back

Exploring MSN can be kind of like exploring the woods. You see a link that looks promising, so you take it. The page the link leads to has other links that look promising, so you pick one and take it — and so on, until pretty soon you're lost. You should have marked your path with bread crumbs.

Fortunately, the MSN Program Viewer enables you to retrace your steps easily. Two of the buttons on the Navigation bar handle this purpose expressly:

The Back button moves backward along the path you've taken. The button retraces the links you've followed, only backwards. You can click it several times in a row if necessary to retrace your steps through several links.

The Forward button moves forward along your path. As long as you keep plowing ahead, this button stays grayed out — meaning you can't use it. However, after you begin to retrace your steps with the Back button, the Forward button becomes active. Clicking the Forward button takes you to the page where you were when you clicked the Back button.

Remember that you can always go directly to one of the MSN four home pages by clicking On Stage, Essentials, Communicate, or Find at the top of the Navigation bar.

Reloading a Page

The first time you access a page, the Program Viewer copies the entire page over the network from the MSN computers to your computer. Depending on the size and complexity of the page and the speed of your connection, this process can take a few seconds or a few minutes.

To avoid repeating this download, the Program Viewer saves the information for the page in a special area of your hard disk known as the *cache*. The next time you retrieve the same page, the page displays directly from this cache instead of being downloaded again from the MSN. Thus, the page appears more quickly.

However, what happens if the page has changed since the last time you downloaded it? Many MSN pages change frequently. Some pages change daily, some change almost hourly. For such pages, you can force Program Viewer to reload its view of the page. The page downloads again, so you have to wait for it. But at least you know the information is current.

To reload a page, all you have to do is click the Reload button and then twiddle your thumbs while Program Viewer downloads the page.

Note: The MSN Program Viewer resets the cache each time you start a new Program Viewer session. As a result, pages always download from the MSN computers rather than from the cache the first time you view the pages during an MSN session.

 You can also use the Reload button to replay an animation or a sound that you want to see or hear again. For example, if you stumble on a page that shows a neat animated spaceship flying across the screen, and you want to see the spaceship fly by again, just click the Reload button.

Stopping a Long Download

Every once in a while, you wander into an MSN page you wish you hadn't. The link that led you to the page may have looked interesting, but after you get there, the page isn't what you expected. According to Murphy's Law, that page is filled with complicated graphics and takes forever to download.

 Fortunately, you are not forced to sit there and wait while a long graphic that you don't want is downloaded. All you have to do is click the Stop button, and Program Viewer cancels the rest of the download. The portion of the page that has already made it to your computer continues to be on display, but anything that hasn't yet arrived does not display. You can then click the Back button to go back to the previous page.

Leaving the Program Viewer

After you finish exploring MSN, you can exit Program Viewer using any of the following techniques:

- ✔ Click the OnMSN icon in the upper-left corner of the Program Viewer window and then choose Close from the menu.
- ✔ Click the Close button, which you can find at the top-right corner of the Internet Explorer window. (It's the one marked with an X.)

 If you leave your computer connected to MSN for 20 minutes without doing anything, MSN will automatically disconnect you. (You can change the 20-minute disconnect period to any time period you wish by changing the MSN Options, available from the menu that appears when you click on the MSN icon in the Windows 95 taskbar.)

Chapter 4

Shortcuts and Time-Savers

· ·

In This Chapter

▶ Right-clicking with your mouse

▶ Building a list of your favorite Web pages

▶ Saving a picture as a graphic file

▶ Saving and printing pages

▶ Locating text on a page

▶ Saving your eyes by displaying text in a larger size

▶ Using the Quick View menu

· ·

*T*hink of this chapter as a bag of useful tricks that come in handy as you explore The Microsoft Network. Although these tricks are strictly optional, several of them are so helpful that you may find yourself using them every day.

Right-Clicking

Like just about everything else in Windows 95, the MSN Program Viewer puts the right-side mouse button to good use. When you click the right mouse button, a shortcut menu appears, as shown in Figure 4-1.

Figure 4-1:
Right-click
to call up
a shortcut
menu.

The commands that appear on this shortcut menu vary depending on what you were pointing to when you right-clicked. Table 4-1 summarizes the function of each command that may appear on the shortcut menu. Note that not all these commands appear in each shortcut menu; the exact mix of commands that appears depends on what type of object you right-click. For example, if you right-click a picture, you get a shortcut menu that includes commands for manipulating pictures. But if you right-click a text link, the picture commands don't appear. This type of menu support is called context-sensitive — you get a different menu depending on the context of your question.

I describe the proper use of many of these commands later in this chapter.

Table 4-1	Commands That Appear in Shortcut Menus
Command	*What It Does*
Open	Displays the page indicated by the link, the same as if you clicked the link
Open in New Window	Displays the link in a new window while leaving the current page open in the current window, allowing you to view both pages at once
Save Target As	Saves, as a file on your hard disk, the content of the page linked to by a hyperlink so you can access it later without connecting to MSN
Save Picture As	Saves a graphic image as a file on your hard disk
Set As Wallpaper	Uses a graphic image as your Windows 95 wallpaper
Copy	Copies the selected item to the clipboard
Copy Shortcut	Copies the address of a link to the clipboard
Add to Favorites	Adds the current page or shortcut to your Favorites folder
View Source	Displays the HTML source file for the current page in a separate window
Properties	Displays a Properties dialog box for the selected item
About Shockwave Flash 2.0	Displays information about the technology used to create animated MSN pages

Playing Favorites

The Microsoft Network offers hundreds of interesting destinations. However, when you get off of MSN and onto the Internet's World Wide Web, you find virtually *millions* of interesting pages to visit.

Exploring all of MSN and the Internet's pages just to see what's available can be fun, assuming you can live long enough. But after you see a few hundred or a few thousand pages, you may come to realize that not all pages are created equal. You soon settle on a few sites that are your personal favorites: They are the pages you return to over and over again.

The Favorites feature in MSN allows you to get to those few favorites as quickly as possible without having to navigate your way through link after link to get to them. The following sections describe how to use the MSN Favorites feature.

Adding a page to Favorites

To designate an MSN or Web page as one of your Favorites so that you can find it quickly later, use the following procedure:

1. **Browse your way to the page that you want to add to the list of favorite pages.**

 2. **Click the Favorites button and then select <u>A</u>dd to Favorites from the menu that appears.**

   The Add to Favorites dialog box appears, as shown in Figure 4-2.

Figure 4-2:
The Add to
Favorites
dialog box.

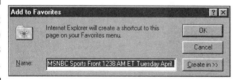

3. **Click the OK button.**

   The Web page is added to the Favorites menu.

 An alternate method for adding a page to the list of favorites is to find a page that has a link to the page you want to add. Right-click the link and then choose <u>A</u>dd to Favorites from the shortcut menu that appears. (Note that this tip works only for some links. If a shortcut menu does not appear when you right-click a link, use the Favorites button to add the page to Favorites.)

Going to one of your favorite places

After you add your favorite MSN and Web pages to the Favorites menu, you can call up the Favorites menu to quickly go to any of the pages it contains. Here's how:

1. **Click the Favorites button (it's the check-mark button, as shown in the margin).**

    The Favorites menu reveals your list of favorite places, as shown in Figure 4-3.

2. **Select the page you want, and off you go.**

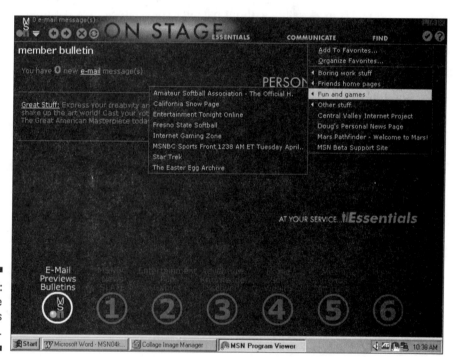

Figure 4-3:
The
Favorites
menu.

Using Favorites folders

If you keep adding pages to your Favorites menu, pretty soon the Favorites menu becomes so full of favorites that you can't find anything. To ease crowding on the Favorites menu, Program Viewer lets you create separate folders in which you can categorize your favorites.

Where do these Favorites folders come from? You create them yourself. To create a new Favorites folder, just click the New Folder button, type a name for the new folder, and click OK.

To add a page to a Favorites folder, follow these steps:

1. **Choose Favorites⇨Add to Favorites.**

   The Add to Favorites dialog box appears.

2. **Click the Create In button.**

   The Add to Favorites dialog box expands, as shown in Figure 4-4.

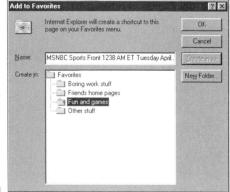

Figure 4-4:
Adding a
page to a
Favorites
folder.

3. **Select the folder to which you want to add the page.**

4. **Click OK.**

   The page is added to the folder you selected.

Organizing your Favorites

Eventually, your Favorites menu may fill up with pages that no longer hold your interest, are out of date, or just need to be better organized. When you reach that point, it's time to roll up your sleeves and reorganize your Favorites. Fortunately, MSN provides a command just for this purpose.

 To organize your Favorites, click the Favorites button and choose the Organize Favorites command (or choose Favorites⇨Organize Favorites from the menu bar). The Organize Favorites dialog box appears, as shown in Figure 4-5.

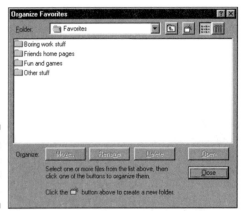

Figure 4-5:
The
Favorites
folder.

The buttons on this dialog box enable you to delete, rename, or move items in your Favorites menu.

- ✔ To delete a page or folder, select the page or folder and click the Delete button.

- ✔ To rename a page or folder, select the page or folder and click the Rename button. Type a new name for the page or folder and click OK.

- ✔ To move a page or folder, select the page or folder and click the Move button. Then select the folder you want to move the item to and click OK.

Saving a Picture

You can save many of the pictures you see on MSN and World Wide Web pages as graphic files on your local hard disk. To save a picture, all you have to do is follow these steps:

1. **Right-click the picture you want to save.**

   A shortcut menu appears.

   Note: If the shortcut menu does not appear, you cannot save the picture as a graphic file. Some pictures — mostly fancy animations or videos — just can't be saved. Sorry.

2. **Choose the Save Picture As command.**

   A standard Save As dialog box appears, as shown in Figure 4-6.

Figure 4-6:
The
Save As
dialog box.

3. **Find your way to the folder in which you want to save the file.**

4. **Type a new filename for the file if you don't like the one that is supplied.**

5. **Click the Save button.**

You can also choose to use the picture as your desktop wallpaper. Simply right-click the image and then choose the Set As Wallpaper command.

Beware of copyright protections when you save a graphic file. Many images, especially artwork, photographs, and company logos, are copyrighted. If you do save a graphic that is (or may be) protected by copyright law, be sure to get the owner's permission before you use the graphic. Check the Web site from which you want to obtain the graphic for the name of the copyright owner.

Finding Text on a Page

Sometimes you stumble across a large page of text that you know contains some useful tidbit of information, but you can't seem to locate the information you're trying to find. When this happens, you can use the Find command to locate specific text on the page. Simply follow these steps:

1. Choose Edit⇨Find (or press Ctrl+F).

The Find dialog box in Figure 4-7 appears.

2. Type the text that you want to find.

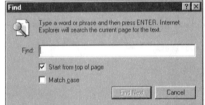

Figure 4-7:
The Find
dialog box.

3. Click Find Next.

MSN finds the first occurrence of the text on the current page. The Find dialog box remains active, so you can quickly find additional occurrences of the text.

4. Keep clicking Find Next until you find the text you want.

5. Click Cancel to dismiss the Find dialog box.

Keep in mind that the Find command searches for text only on the current page; it does not search other MSN pages for the text you're trying to find. To do that type of search, you must use the MSN Find page, which I describe in Chapter 8.

Printing a Page

Suppose you're exploring MSN one day, minding your own business, when you come across a page that lists a recipe for Stewed Possum. You say to yourself, "That sounds mighty tasty," so you decide you want to print a copy of the file so you can cook it for Sunday dinner this week.

No problem. Y'all just foller these steps:

 1. Click the Show Internet Toolbar button to reveal the Internet Toolbar.

2. Click the <u>P</u>rint button.

The Print dialog box appears, as shown in Figure 4-8.

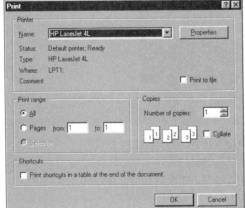

Figure 4-8:
The Print
dialog box.

3. Stare at the Print dialog box for a moment.

If you have more than one printer at your disposal, make sure you have the correct printer selected in the Name drop-down list. And if you want to print more than one copy of the page, change the Number of copies setting.

4. Click the OK button.

5. Wait a moment while your printer grinds and whirls.

Walk to your printer and collect the printed page.

You can also summon the Print dialog box by pressing Ctrl+P or by choosing <u>F</u>ile⇨<u>P</u>rint.

Saving a Page

If you want to save the contents of an entire MSN page, just follow this procedure:

1. Choose <u>F</u>ile⇨Save <u>A</u>s (or press Ctrl+S).

The Save As dialog box appears, as shown in Figure 4-9.

2. Select a suitable location for the file.

If the default location is not acceptable, you can browse your way to a better locale.

Figure 4-9:
The
Save As
dialog box.

3. **Type a name for the file you want to save in the File name field.**

4. **Choose the file type in the Save as type field.**

   You have two choices: HTML, which saves the page complete with formatting, and Plain Text, which saves the text without the formatting information.

5. **Click the Save button.**

As an alternative to saving the entire page as a text file, you can select the text you want to save and then press Ctrl+C to copy it. Then switch to a word processing program such as Microsoft Word, open an existing document or create a new document, and press Ctrl+V to paste the copied text into the document.

Making the Text Bigger

If you constantly find yourself squinting at The Microsoft Network, you may want to visit your ophthalmologist or get a larger monitor. In the meantime, however, you can bump up the size of the text used to display most of the MSN content. Here's how:

1. **Click the Show Internet Toolbar button.**

   The Internet toolbar appears.

2. **Click the Font Size button.**

   All of the text on the page jumps to a larger size.

To see what a difference the size can make, compare Figures 4-10 and 4-11. Figure 4-10 shows an MSN page displayed with normal text.

Figure 4-11 shows the same page after clicking the Font Size button to enlarge the text.

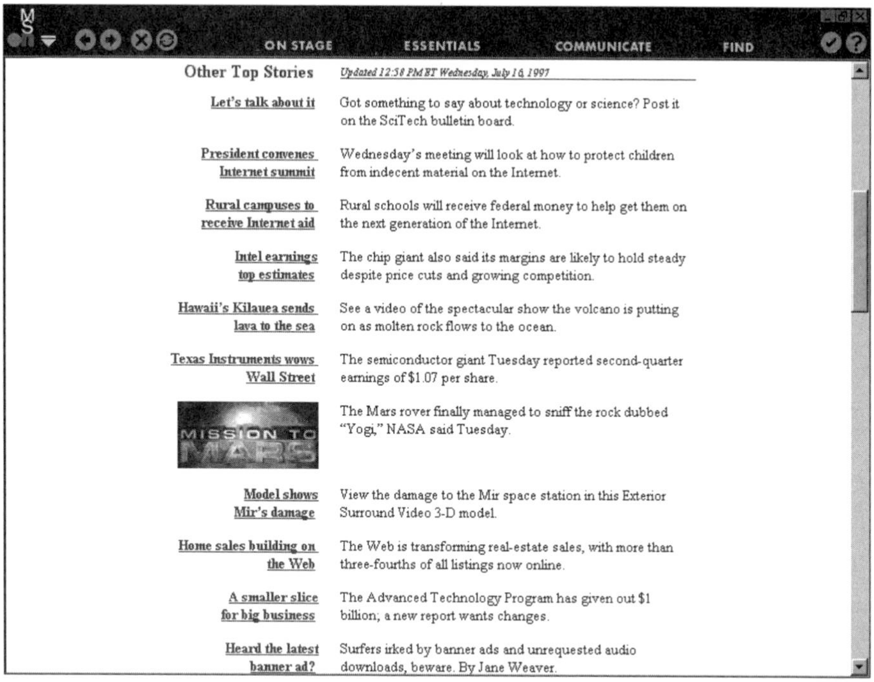

Figure 4-10:
A page with
normal text.

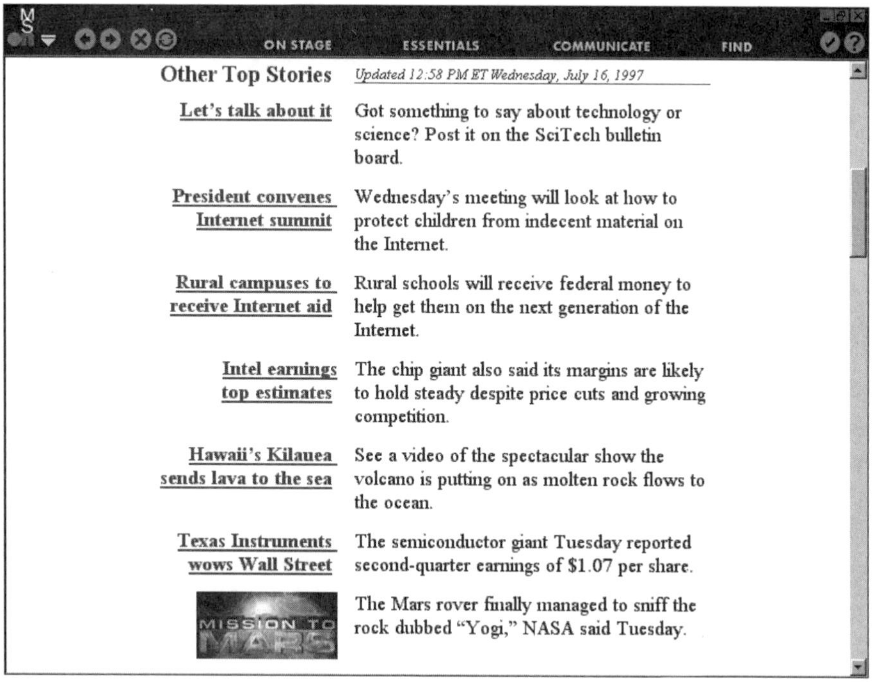

Figure 4-11:
A page with
bigger text.

If the text is still too small, click again to make it larger yet. MSN has five text sizes from which to choose. Repeatedly clicking the Font Size button cycles through the five sizes. After you get to the largest size, clicking the Font Size button once more returns you to the smallest size.

Using the MSN Quick View Menu

MSN

MSN sports a handy shortcut called the Quick View menu, which enables you to quickly access MSN features without first starting the MSN Program Viewer. Any time you are connected to MSN, the MSN Quick View icon appears (shown in the margin). If you click this icon, a menu will appear listing the most commonly used MSN features, as shown in Figure 4-12.

Note that many of the menu choices on the Quick View menu lead to additional menus. For example, if you point to On Stage, a separate menu of the On Stage channels will appear. If you then point to one of the channels, yet another menu will appear, listing all of the programs available on the channel you pointed to.

You don't have to run the MSN Program Viewer to use the Quick View menu. The MSN Quick View icon is always available in the taskbar whenever you are connected to MSN.

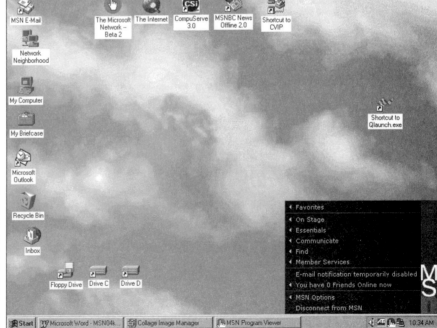

Figure 4-12: The MSN Quick View menu is a handy shortcut to most MSN features.

Chapter 5

Help! I Can't Get Online!

*T*he ideal way to use The Microsoft Network is to have an MSN expert sitting patiently at your side answering your every question with a straightforward response, gently but firmly correcting without insulting you when you make silly mistakes, and otherwise minding his or her own business. All you'd have to do is toss the expert an occasional cookie and let him or her outside once a day.

The next best thing is to learn how to use the MSN built-in help features. No matter how deeply you sink into the depths of The Microsoft Network, help is but a few keystrokes or mouse clicks away.

Summoning Help

MSN has an entire section devoted to providing online help for using MSN. To access this help, just follow these steps:

1. Click the Help button in the Program Viewer's Navigation bar.

The Help menu appears.

2. Choose the Help & Support option.

Program Viewer whirls and grinds for a moment and then displays the Welcome page shown in Figure 5-1.

Figure 5-1:
The
Welcome
page for
the MSN
online help.

Another way to get help is to press the F1 key. This takes you to the Member Services home page, from which you can easily access the MSN online help services.

Answering Common Questions

The MSN Help section is jam-packed with answers to the most common questions that arise when using MSN. To access these question/answer pages, follow these steps:

1. **From the Help Welcome page, click Frequently Asked Questions.**

   The Frequently Asked Questions page appears, as shown in Figure 5-2. As you can see, a list of subjects appears at the bottom of the page. (You have to scroll down the page to see the entire list.) The subjects include Accounts & Billing, Connecting to MSN, and others. For each subject, you find a list of one or more commonly asked questions.

2. **Click the questions you want answered.**

   MSN displays the answer, as shown in Figure 5-3, which answers the question: How do I configure Internet News?

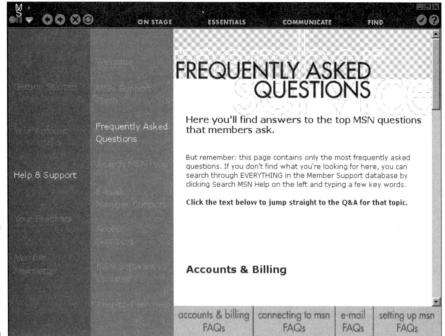

Figure 5-2: The Frequently Asked Questions page.

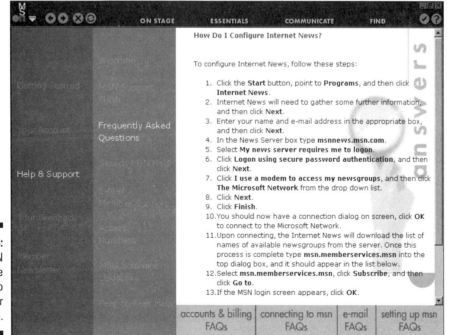

Figure 5-3: MSN displays the answer to your question.

3. **If you want to see the answer to another question, click the Back button.**

   You return to the list of questions that appeared in Step 1, where you can select another question. To change topics, just click one of the other topic headings.

4. **When you're done, return to the MSN content areas by clicking on one of the Site headings in the Navigation bar (On Stage, Communicate, Essentials, or Find).**

   You're done!

Searching for Help

If you're not sure which subject heading most likely contains the answer to a burning question, try searching for help using a keyword search.

The following procedure explains how:

1. **From the Help Welcome page, click Search for Help.**

   The Search MSN Help page appears, as shown in Figure 5-4.

2. **Type a word for which you want to search and then press Enter or click the Search button.**

   A list of questions that are related to the word you typed appears. For example, Figure 5-5 shows the questions that appear if you search for the word *keyboard*.

3. **Click the question you want to display.**

   The answer to the question appears.

If none of the questions that appeared as a result of your search is what you're looking for, then try again using a different keyword.

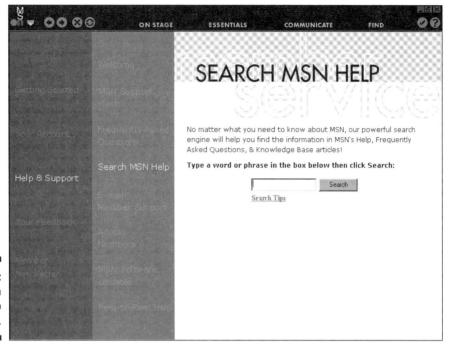

Figure 5-4:
The Search
MSN Help
page.

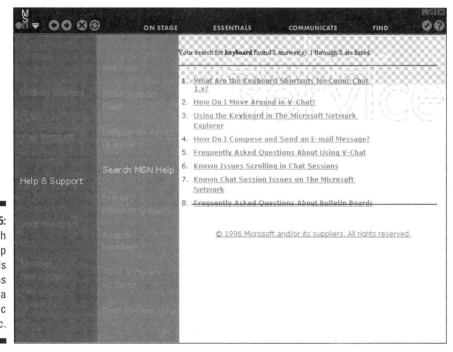

Figure 5-5:
Search
MSN Help
finds
questions
for a
specific
topic.

Using the MSN Support Newsgroups

If you can't find the answer to a question in the MSN Help, Browse, or Search areas, you can try posting the question to one of the MSN support newsgroups. Then check back the next day to see if another MSN user has answered your question.

To access the MSN support newsgroups, click Peer-to-Peer Help on the Help Welcome page. The Peer-to-Peer Help page appears, as shown in Figure 5-6.

The Peer-to-Peer Help page lists several newsgroups you can visit to ask questions about using MSN. The first three newsgroups are for general MSN questions. To keep these newsgroups more manageable, three of them are available for specific regions of the world. The other newsgroups are for programs you use in conjunction with MSN, such as Internet Explorer.

Figure 5-7 shows the window that appears when you choose the MSN – US & Canada newsgroup. To read one of the messages posted in this newsgroup, just double-click on the message title. To create your own message, click the New Message button.

For more information about using newsgroups, take a look at Chapter 20.

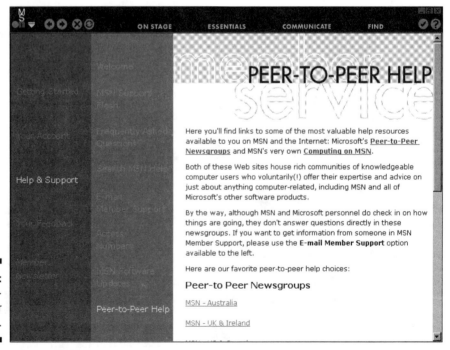

Figure 5-6:
The Peer-
to-Peer
Help page.

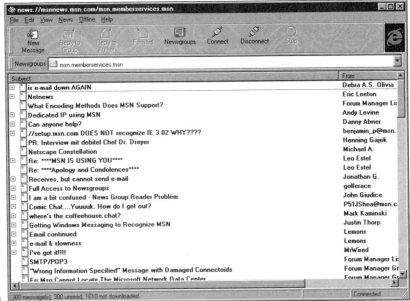

Figure 5-7:
An MSN
support
newsgroup.

Asking for Help

If you can't find an answer to your question in MSN Help or one of the Peer-to-Peer newsgroups, you can always send a message to the MSN support staff to see if they can help. Follow these steps:

1. **From the Help Welcome page, click E-Mail Member Support.**

   The page shown in Figure 5-8 appears.

2. **Click the area you need help with.**

   Your choices are: Customer Service, Technical Support, and Report a Problem with Another Member.

3. **Click Next.**

   A page similar to the one in Figure 5-9 appears. (The exact appearance of the page will vary depending on which area you chose in Step 2.)

4. **Fill in the blanks.**

   When you type your question, provide as much specific information as you can about the problem you're experiencing.

5. **If there is a Send button at the bottom of the page, click it. Otherwise, click the Next button and fill in whatever additional information MSN requests and then click the Send button.**

   That's all there is to it! You should get an answer to your e-mail message within 24 hours.

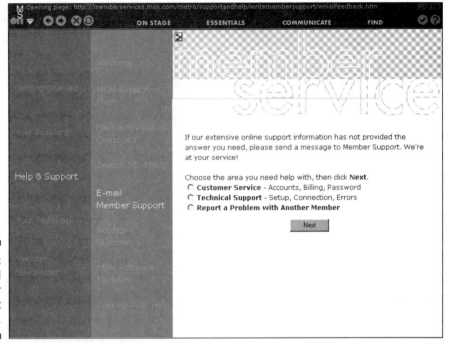

Figure 5-8:
The E-Mail
Member
Support
page.

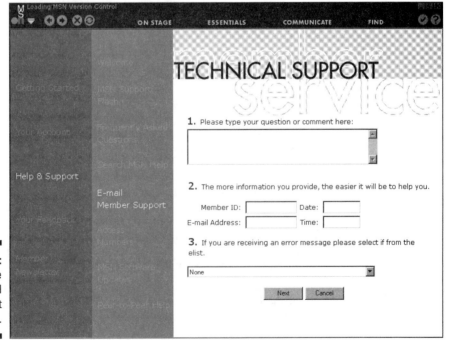

Figure 5-9:
The
Technical
Support
page.

Part II
The Sites and Sounds of MSN

The 5th Wave   By Rich Tennant

"...AND YOU'RE CLAIMING THAT THE SOURCE CODE USED FOR THE MICROSOFT CORP. GUI, WAS ACTUALLY AUTHORED BY YOU AS THE GUMBY USER INTERFACE?!"

In this part . . .

This is the part of the book where you discover all of the cool features, services, and programs that MSN has to offer. You read about how to find your way around the primo online news service, MSNBC, plus other programs you find in the OnStage area of MSN. Plus you dabble in the Essentials area and learn how to use MSN's excellent Find service to find interesting places both on MSN and on the Internet.

Chapter 6

Surfing the News at MSNBC

. . . .

In This Chapter

▶ Getting your news from MSNBC

▶ Personalizing your Front Page

▶ Using News Alert to hear about news as it happens

▶ Using News Offline to read news

▶ Setting up a news screen saver

. . . .

*M*SNBC, the result of a collaboration between Microsoft and media giant NBC, is one of the Internet's best news sites. You can tune in to MSNBC any time of the day or night to get up-to-the-minute news stories, sports scores, and commentary.

This chapter gives you an overview of how to use MSNBC. You figure out how to read stories in MSNBC, plus you find out how to use two advanced MSNBC features: News Alert and News Offline.

Tuning In to MSNBC

To view MSNBC, just click the Channel 1 icon at the bottom of the On Stage page. After a brief animated introduction, MSNBC comes to life, as shown in Figure 6-1.

MSNBC breaks out its news, much like a daily newspaper. The MSNBC sections include:

   ✔ **MSNBC Front Page:** Lists the top stories from each of the other sections at MSNBC

   ✔ **World:** Includes breaking stories from around the world

   ✔ **Weather:** So you can find out if it's raining in Paris

Figure 6-1:
Welcome to
MSNBC.

✔ **On Air Highlights:** Lists upcoming programs on the three NBC television channels: NBC, plus cable channels MSNBC and CNBC

✔ **Commerce:** Keeps you up to date on business news

✔ **Sports:** So you can get your daily fix

✔ **SciTech:** For the brainy types

✔ **Life:** Includes stories about health, lifestyles, and society

✔ **Opinion:** Features several prominent columnists

As Figure 6-1 shows, the top two or three stories from the Front Page appear on the MSNBC On Stage page. You can go directly to any of these stories by clicking on it. If you wait a few moments, the Front Page stories get replaced by the top three World stories, followed by Weather, On Air Highlights, and each of the other categories in turn. If you want a quick overview of the day's breaking stories, just stare at the MSNBC On Stage page for about two minutes.

Channel 1 also gives you access to Slate, an online magazine featuring opinion and analysis of politics, culture, and current events.

Getting around MSNBC

Although you can see the top three headlines from each category without leaving On Stage, you have to get into the MSNBC Front Page to see all that MSNBC has to offer. When you click Front Page, MSNBC obliges by displaying its Front Page, as shown in Figure 6-2. Although it isn't apparent in the figure, the Front Page lists the top stories from each of the MSNBC sections. Just scroll down the page to see each section's highlights. To read a story, click on the story's headline.

Notice that the top of the MSNBC Front Page consists of a navigation banner. This navigation banner is available throughout MSNBC and enables you to go quickly to any of the MSNBC main sections. In addition, the navigation banner contains an Index link that takes you to a subject index. The index lists all of the stories available in MSNBC.

Figure 6-2:
The
MSNBC
Front Page.

Reading a story

To read a story, click on the headline for the story you want to read. MSNBC spins and whirls for a moment, and then displays the story, complete with photographs. Figure 6-3 shows a story that appeared on April 15, which also happens to be National Gripe Day.

Most of the stories appearing on MSNBC contain links to other Internet sites that relate in some way to the main story. For example, the tax story pictured in Figure 6-3 included links to various tax sites, including a complete Tax Guide prepared by CNBC, the Clintons' 1996 tax return (so you can compare your own finances with the First Family's), past presidents' tax returns (including FDR and Nixon), and a site listing excerpts from Hillary Clinton's book, *It Takes a Village* (as if that will soften the blow on April 15).

At the bottom of each story on MSNBC, you find a request for feedback.

When you finish reading the story, just click on the gauge from 1 to 10 to indicate whether you recommend this story to other readers. When you click on your choice, MSNBC thanks you by displaying a list of the top ten recommended stories, as shown in Figure 6-4.

This list gives you an idea of what interests other MSNBC viewers.

Figure 6-3:
A typical
MSNBC
story.

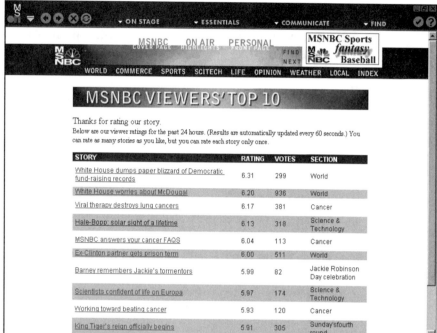

Figure 6-4:
MSNBC
Viewers'
Top 10
stories of
the day.

Inside the figure:

MSNBC VIEWERS' TOP 10

Thanks for rating our story.
Below are our viewer ratings for the past 24 hours. (Results are automatically updated every 60 seconds.) You can rate as many stories as you like, but you can rate each story only once.

STORY	RATING	VOTES	SECTION
White House dumps paper blizzard of Democratic fund-raising records	6.31	299	World
White House worries about McDougal	6.20	936	World
Viral therapy destroys lung cancers	6.17	381	Cancer
Hale-Bopp: solar sight of a lifetime	6.13	318	Science & Technology
MSNBC answers your cancer FAQS	6.04	113	Cancer
Ex-Clinton partner gets prison term	6.00	511	World
Barney remembers Jackie's tormentors	5.99	82	Jackie Robinson Day celebration
Scientists confident of life on Europa	5.97	174	Science & Technology
Working toward beating cancer	5.93	120	Cancer
King Tiger's reign officially begins	5.91	305	Sunday'sfourth round

Creating a Personal Front Page

One of the most popular features of MSN is its ability to let you create a custom Personal Front Page, which focuses its news stories on the subjects that interest you most. For example, if you're interested in UFOs, crop circles, and alien abduction, you can create a Personal Front Page that shows the stories just about those subjects.

To create your own personal front page, follow these steps:

1. **Go to the MSNBC Front Page.**

2. **Click Personal Front Page, found near the top of the MSN Front Page.**

   This takes you to your Personal Front Page. However, because you haven't yet told MSNBC what subjects interest you, your Personal Front Page looks almost the same as the impersonal Front Page. The most noticeable difference is that you see an icon labeled Modify your Personal Front Page near the top of the page.

3. **Click the Modify your Personal Front Page icon.**

   The Create Your Own Personal Front Page page appears. Now you're getting somewhere.

Figures 6-5 and 6-6 show the Create Your Own Personal Front Page page. Because this page is too large to appear in the screen all at once, I had to break it into two figures. Figure 6-5 shows the top half of the page.

Figure 6-6 shows the bottom half, which you can access by scrolling down the MSN Program Viewer window.

4. **Check the Cover Page headline categories that you want to appear on your Personal Front Page.**

   Initially, all of the headline categories have checks. However, if World, Sports, Commerce, Chat schedules, SciTech, Life, and Opinion stories bore you, uncheck them.

5. **Enter up to five keywords for topics that interest you in the Personal Topics text boxes.**

   For example, **UFOs, crop circles,** and **alien abduction**.

6. **If you want a daily update of your investments, type the ticker symbols for up to ten stocks or mutual funds in the Stock Quotes text fields.**

7. **For up-to-the-minute professional sports scores, check the Baseball, Football, Hockey, or Basketball check boxes.**

   Unfortunately, no check boxes are available for the truly great sports, such as cricket, rounders, or Heavyweight Ear Biting.

Figure 6-5:
The top half
of the
Create
Your Own
Personal
Front Page!
page.

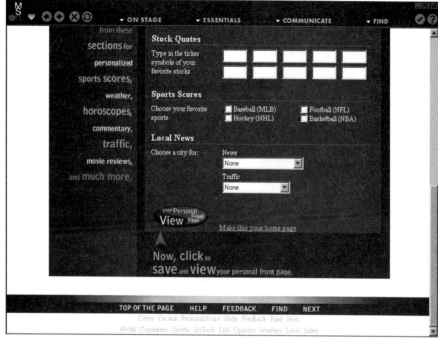

Figure 6-6:
The bottom
half of the
Create
Your Own
Personal
Front Page!
page.

8. **If you want local news, select the city from the Local News drop-down list.**

   Unfortunately, only the largest U.S. cities are available. You can get news for cities such as Los Angeles or Dallas, but if you live in Pixley or Happy Valley, you're out of luck.

   You can also select traffic news for a dozen or so major U.S. cities.

9. **Click the View Your Personal Front Page icon near the bottom of the page to save your Personal Front Page settings.**

   Alternatively, you can click the Make this your home page link to set your Personal Front Page as your MSN home page so that it automatically displays whenever you start MSN.

After you set up a Personal Front Page, you can view it at any time. To view your page, click the Channel 1 icon in On Stage, choose MSNBC Front Page, and then click the Personal Front Page icon at the top of the screen.

To get to your Personal Front Page faster, add it to your Favorite Places. (See Chapter 4 for information about how to do that.)

You can personalize your Personal Front Page even more by clicking the links that appear down the left side of the Create a Personal Front Page page (shown back in Figure 6-6). The following paragraphs summarize the settings that are available from these links:

- **Delivery Options:** Lets you tell MSNBC your e-mail address and city, state, zip code, and country so that MSNBC can better customize local news. This page also lets you access two features that enable you to have MSNBC news delivered to you automatically: News Alert and News Offline. I show you how to use those features later in this chapter.

- **Personal Topics:** Lets you enter keywords for up to five personal topics and lets you select any of 22 specialized news topics. The best of these 22 topics by far is WeirdNuz, which gives you a daily selection of oddball news stories to remind you how strange real life can be.

- **World:** Lets you choose to display world news headlines, news stories from Australia, and two international news columnists.

- **Commerce:** Lets you choose to display business news stories; view commentary by several columnists; select stock quotes using ticker symbols; and see market summaries for the Dow Industrials, S&P 500, NASDAQ, and several other international markets.

- **Sports:** Displays sports stories and lets you select specific pro football, baseball, hockey, and basketball teams to follow.

- **SciTech:** Displays cover stories about science and technology and offers several SciTech columnists.

- **Life:** Lets you choose to display lifestyle stories, movie reviews, and horoscopes.

- **Opinion:** Offers various columnists and political cartoonists.

- **Weather:** Lets you customize your weather news. You can select the region for your weather news, and you can elect to display a weather map and a four-day forecast.

- **Local:** Lets you select local news and traffic information.

News Alert

If you're a news junkie, you can set up MSNBC so that it alerts you to breaking news throughout the day. You can choose up to five keywords to select the news subjects you're interested in. You can also specify how often the news alert service should notify you with breaking news — for example, every 10 minutes if you are obsessed with news, or every hour if you're just moderately concerned.

Whenever news breaks, a pop-up window appears, displaying the headlines for the stories that interest you. From this window, you can click the headline to display the complete story, or you can click Next to see the next headline. To dismiss the News Alert window, click Close.

Setting up News Alert

To set up News Alert, follow these steps:

1. **Click the Personal Front Page icon in the MSNBC navigation banner.**

   Your Personal Front Page page appears.

2. **Click the Modify Your Personal Front Page icon that now appears in the navigation banner.**

   You jump to the Create Your Own Personal Front Page page.

3. **Click Delivery Options from the list of links at the left of the page.**

   The Delivery Options page appears.

4. **Scroll down until the News Alert section is visible, then click the Download Here link.**

   This takes you to the News Alert download page, shown in Figure 6-7.

Figure 6-7: The News Alert download page.

5. Read everything on the News Alert download page.

You find out everything there is to know about News Alert.

6. Find and click the bull's-eye icon labeled Download News Alert.

The dialog box shown in Figure 6-8 appears.

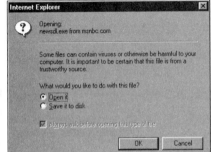

Figure 6-8:
Downloading
News Alert.

7. Check the Open It option and then click OK.

News Alert downloads itself to your computer. Downloading takes a couple of minutes, so stand up and do some stretching exercises while you wait.

8. When asked if you want to install News Alert, click Yes.

News Alert installs itself, which should take only a moment. When the installation is complete, News Alert displays its Options screen, shown in Figure 6-9.

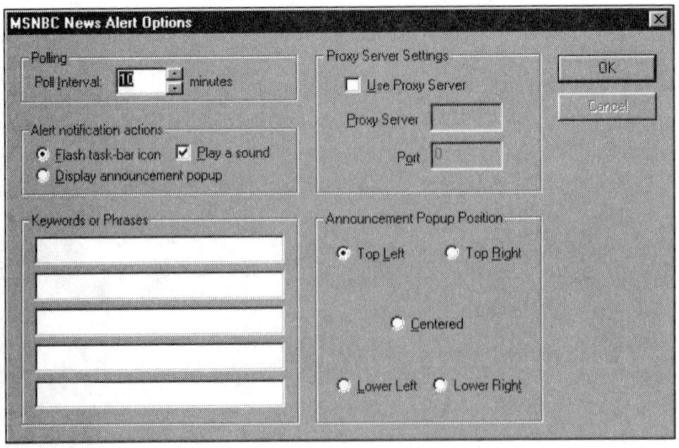

Figure 6-9:
The News
Alert
options
screen.

9. Set the Poll Interval.

The Poll Interval governs how often News Alert lets you know about breaking news. Every 10 minutes is too often for all but the most obsessed news junkies. Every 120 minutes (two hours) is probably more reasonable.

10. Set the options on the Alert notification actions option box.

You can have News Alert cause its taskbar icon to flash whenever there is new news, or you can have the News Alert window actually pop up when new news arrives. In addition, you can tell News Alert to play a sound when there is news.

11. Type the keywords for the news topics that interest you.

Use words that are likely to appear in the headlines or abstracts for the stories that interest you. (An *abstract* is a brief summary of a story — just one or two sentences.) For example, if you are interested in news about President Clinton, type **Clinton** as a keyword. (Ignore the Proxy Server Settings and Announcement Popup Position parts of the screen.)

12. Click OK.

You're done.

 That's all there is to it. If you chose the Flash Taskbar Icon option for News Alert's notification, the News Alert icon (shown in the margin) flashes red whenever there is news. You can then click on this icon to display the News Alert window. If you chose the Display Announcement Popup option instead, the News Alert window automatically pops up when there is news.

If you want to change News Alert's options (for example, to change the polling interval or keywords), right-click the News Alert icon in the taskbar and choose the Options command from the pop-up menu that appears.

Turning off News Alert

To turn off News Alert, right-click the News Alert taskbar icon and choose Exit. This deactivates News Alert until the next time you restart your computer. If you want News Alert to be deactivated even after you restart your computer, follow these steps:

1. Click the Start button⇨Settings⇨Taskbar.

The Taskbar Properties dialog box appears.

2. Click the Start Menu Programs tab.

The Start Menu Programs settings appear in the Taskbar Properties dialog box.

3. **Click the Remove button.**

   The Remove Shortcuts/Folders dialog box appears.

4. **Double-click the Start Up folder icon.**

   You may have to scroll down the list of programs and folders to find the Start Up folder.

5. **Click the MSNBC News Alert icon.**

6. **Click Remove.**

   Windows 95 removes MSNBC News Alert from your computer.

7. **Click Close to dismiss the Remove Shortcuts/Folders dialog box.**

8. **Click OK to dismiss the Taskbar Properties dialog box.**

News Offline: News in Your Inbox

MSNBC has yet another news delivery service, News Offline, which can deliver customized news stories automatically to your hard disk at regular intervals. (The default is every six hours.) You can then read the news articles offline — that is, while you are not connected to MSN. This is especially useful if you have signed up with MSN or if your local Internet Service Provider is on a plan that levies hourly connect-time charges.

Downloading and installing News Offline

Before you can begin to use News Offline, you must download and install the News Offline program files. This takes about 20 minutes (longer, if you have a slow Internet connection). To download and install News Offline, follow these steps:

1. **Click the Personal Front Page icon in the MSNBC navigation banner.**

   The Personal Front Page appears.

2. **Click the Modify Your Personal Front Page icon.**

   The Create Your Own Personal Front Page page appears.

3. **Click Delivery Options from the list of links at the left of the page.**

   The Delivery Options page appears.

4. **Scroll down until the News Offline section is visible, then click the Download Here link.**

   The News Offline download page appears, as shown in Figure 6-10.

Figure 6-10:
The News
Offline
download
page.

5. Read all of the information on the News Offline page.

This page contains everything you need to know to set up and use News Offline.

6. Find and click the "Download News Offline" icon.

A File Download dialog box appears, asking if you want to Open the News Offline setup program or just save it to disk.

7. Check the Open It option and then click OK.

News Offline downloads to your computer. This takes about 20 minutes if you have a 28.8 Kbps modem.

8. Click Yes when News Offline says it is ready to install.

News Offline installs, which should take but a moment. If News Offline asks for the name of the folder you want the program installed into, click OK to accept the default setting.

9. You're done.
You can now move on to the next job, which is personalizing your offline news.

Personalizing News Offline

Before you begin reading offline news, you need to personalize the MSNBC News Offline reader by following these steps:

1. **Click the Start button, then click Programs, MSNBC News Offline, and finally MSNBC News Offline 2.0.**

   The MSNBC News Offline program comes to life in its own window.

2. **Click the Options button at the top of the screen to reveal the Options menu and then click the Personalize button.**

   The Personal Profile dialog box appears, as shown in Figure 6-11.

3. **Adjust the settings for each category.**

   For each category listed in the Personal Profile dialog box, adjust the slider bar to indicate how many stories you want for the category. (The settings on the slider bars are admittedly vague. The exact number of articles you will get if you choose Some Articles, All Articles, or anything in between depends on how many articles in the category are available at the time you download them.)

   When you select a category, one or more check boxes appear on the right side of the Personal Profile dialog box for options that are specific to that category. For example, when you select the World category, you see options such as Top Stories, World Briefs, Middle East Crisis, and other current topics. If stories on these specific topics don't interest you, then uncheck the corresponding option.

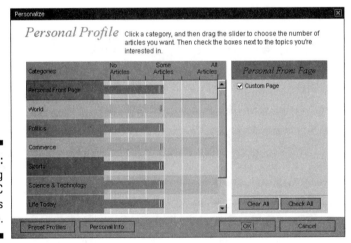

Figure 6-11:
Personalizing
MSNBC
News
Offline.

4. Click the Personal Info button.

The Personal Information dialog box appears, as shown in Figure 6-12.

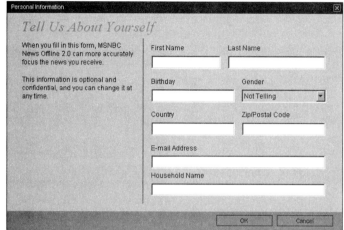

5. Type your name, birthday, zip code, and other information into the appropriate fields.

MSNBC News Offline uses this information to further personalize the news it delivers. (You can leave any or all of this information blank if you wish.)

6. Click OK.

Back you go to the Personal Profile dialog box.

7. Click OK again.

Now you're done.

Reading the news

You can read the news at any time by choosing MSNBC News Offline from the Start menu. (Choose Start⇨Programs⇨MSNBC News Offline.)

By default, your offline news updates every six hours. But you can obtain an immediate update at any time by clicking the Update Now button. When you do, News Offline begins downloading the latest news headlines and stories. This takes a few minutes, but you don't have to wait until all of the stories finish downloading to begin reading the news. When the first story downloads, it appears in the News Offline window. Additional stories get added one by one as they download.

Figure 6-3 shows how the News Offline window appears after several stories have been downloaded. A list of the various categories appears in the upper left portion of the News Offline window. To see the stories for a category, click on the category heading. News Offline then lists one or more subcategories. For example, the World category in Figure 6-13 lists three subcategories: JonBenet Ramsey Murder, The Money Trail, and Decency Debate. Click the subcategory you want to display a list of stories for that subcategory. Next, click the story you want to read to display the story in the story pane that makes up the bottom two-thirds or so of the News Offline window.

If you've had enough news for one day and you want to break off a long download, click the Stop Updating button.

Changing the update frequency

If a news update every six hours is too often (or not often enough) for your taste, you can change the frequency of automatic news updates. Here's how:

1. Start News Offline.

You can find News Offline on the Start menu, under Start⇨Programs⇨ MSNBC News Offline.

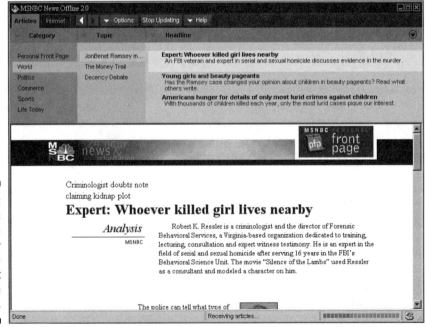

Figure 6-13:
The News Offline window lists the articles that have been downloaded.

2. Click the Options button and then choose Settings from the menu.

The Settings dialog box appears. It has three tabs: Connection, Update, and Screen Saver.

3. Click the Update tab.

The Update frequency options appears, as shown in Figure 6-14.

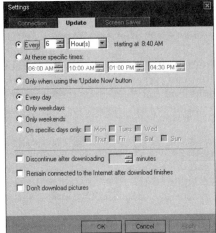

Figure 6-14:
Changing
the update
frequency.

4. Set whatever update frequency options you want.

You can set News Offline to update after a certain amount of time has elapsed (the default is every six hours).

Or, you can set up to four specific update times per day. For example, you could set News Offline to update your news at 6:00 a.m., 10:00 a.m., 1:00 p.m., and 4:30 p.m.

You can disable automatic updates altogether by deselecting the option that says Only when using the 'Update Now' button. Then, news becomes updated only when you click the Update Now button.

Notice that you can also specify which days you want the news up-dated: every day, only on weekends, only on weekdays, or on specific days of the week.

Finally, you can provide a time limit for the update, tell News Offline to remain connected to the Internet after the update, and tell News Offline to skip downloading pictures. (This makes the update faster, and besides, you've already seen O.J.'s face a million times.)

5. Click OK.

You're done!

Using the screen saver

One of the most interesting features of News Offline is that it lets you display the news as a screen saver. Whenever your computer sits idle for a few minutes, the news automatically displays to act as a further distraction in addition to whatever distraction called you away from your computer in the first place. See Figure 6-15.

Now, I'm not entirely convinced that this screen saver thing is a good idea. Suppose you are hard at work on an important project (say, just hypothetically, of course, writing Chapter 6 of *The Microsoft Network For Dummies*) when the phone rings. It's your old friend Johnny K., whom you don't really like, but you talk to for 15 minutes anyway to be polite. When you finally get off the phone, you discover that the screen saver has taken over, and now you see that new news is available about the O.J. civil trial. So instead of getting back to Chapter 6, you decide to read the story, turning your 15-minute distraction into 30 minutes.

If you think you have the willpower to avoid such distraction, call up the Options⇨Settings command and click the Screen Saver tab. This reveals the screen saver options shown in Figure 6-16.

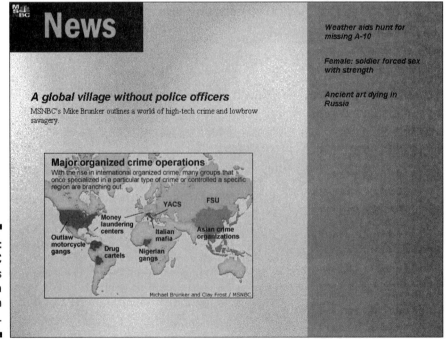

Figure 6-15: MSNBC News Offline as a screen saver.

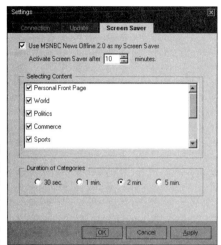

To set up the screen saver, check the "Use MSNBC News Offline as my screen saver" option. Then click OK. From now on, your screen saver is MSNBC News Offline.

After the News Offline screen saver appears, the display changes every two minutes so that it eventually lists stories from every category. To read a story, just click on the story's headline. To dismiss the screen saver, click anywhere on the screen other than one of the story headlines.

MSNBC News Offline has a minor boo-boo: You can turn on the News Offline screen saver, but you can't turn it off! What if you don't like the News Offline screen saver? You have to deactivate it by following these steps:

1. **Call up Start⇨Settings⇨Control Panel.**

2. **Double-click the Display icon.**

   The Display Properties dialog box appears.

3. **Click the Screen Saver tab.**

   This displays Screen Saver settings.

4. **Change the Screen Saver drop-down list to anything but Newsview.**

5. **Click OK.**

Now the News screen saver will be disabled. To activate it, repeat the procedure but choose Newsview as the screen saver in Step 4.

Chapter 7

Other Great Shows On Stage at MSN

. . . .

In This Chapter

▶ Channel 2, where you find programs about entertainment and pop culture, plus an oddball online game show

▶ Channel 3, the adventure channel

▶ Channel 4, which is filled with practical publications about home and lifestyle

▶ Channel 5, which offers offbeat programming about music, media, and society

▶ Channel 6, a place for kids

. . . .

A single show, MSNBC, dominates On Stage's Channel 1; however, the remaining channels offer a mix of various programs. This chapter is an MSN channel-surfer's guide to the shows on MSN Channels 2 through 6. Like TV, the programming on MSN varies from time to time. So, by the time you read this, you may find that new shows are being offered while older, less popular shows have been canceled. Also, MSN sometimes adds programs devoted to current events, such as a concert tour of a famous band or an upcoming election.

In each channel, you will also find a page called LinkStation. The LinkStation is simply a collection of links to popular Internet sites that relate to the channel's theme.

Channel 2: Entertainment, Pop Culture, and Games

Channel 2 is the place to go to get the latest news about your favorite movie star, to see a review of the new Schwarzenegger movie, or to find out what the hottest computer game is this month.

Hard Rock Live

Hard Rock Live, pictured in Figure 7-1, is an online magazine devoted to fans of the rock music scene. It's the online equivalent of the Hard Rock Café. Each week, Hard Rock Live offers an in-depth look at a different rock music performer. In addition to online shows about performers, Hard Rock Live also offers a bulletin board and chat area for online discussions.

Figure 7-1:
Hard Rock
Live.

Star Trek: Continuum

If you're a Star Trek fan, this is the ultimate Trek site. Here, you find all sorts of information about the Trek world, with sections devoted to each of the TV series *(Star Trek, Star Trek: The Next Generation, Star Trek: Deep Space Nine,* and *Star Trek: Voyager.)* You can find out about upcoming episodes of *Deep Space Nine* or *Voyager,* consult an extensive database of *Star Trek* information to find out important stuff like who played Edith Keeler in *The City on the Edge of Forever* (Joan Collins, of course), or learn the Klingon word for *nostril (tlhon).* Figure 7-2 shows the *Star Trek: Continuum* opening page.

Figure 7-2:
Beam me
up, Scotty.

Entertainment Tonight

The popular television program *Entertainment Tonight* sponsors this online look at the entertainment world. You find a preview of the stories that will air each night on the television version of *Entertainment Tonight,* additional coverage of stories mentioned in the TV show, Leonard Maltin's video and movie reviews, information about upcoming movies, and much more.

Spike's World

Spike's World is an online magazine devoted to electronic games. At Spike's World, you find everything you need to know to beat the most popular Nintendo 64, Sega Saturn, Sony Playstation, or personal-computer games. Spike's World also features a respectable library of games you can download and play on your computer.

NetWits

NetWits is an online game show that runs (Monday through Friday) on MSN at 7:00 p.m. Pacific Standard Time. You play a different game each night:

- ✔ **Monday:** Crosswords, a word hunt game similar to Boggle
- ✔ **Tuesday:** Push Your Luck, a real-time maze game
- ✔ **Wednesday:** Top o' The Mark, a strategy game resembling checkers
- ✔ **Thursday:** Switcheroo, a puzzle solving game
- ✔ **Friday:** I Challenge That, a more complicated (and interesting) version of Rock-Scissors-Paper

NetWits also runs practice games throughout the day. Check the NetWits page for game and tournament schedules.

Internet Gaming Zone

Internet Gaming Zone (also known as IGZ) is an online game room where you can play any of several different games against other Internet users. The games include classic card and board games such as Hearts, Bridge, Spades, Checkers, Chess, Go, and Reversi. In addition, several Microsoft games (which you have to purchase separately) can work in IGZ, including Close Combat, Hellbender, Monster Truck Madness, and Golf.

Before you can use IGZ, you must download the software, which takes about 15 minutes. IGZ prompts you through the steps needed to download the software. After you set up the software, you can enter IGZ game rooms, where you can join others in various games. You can also play against computer opponents. Figure 7-3 shows a lively round of Hearts in progress.

Nelson's World

Nelson's World is an online party where you and other MSN users simultaneously watch popular television shows (on your own TV) and chat about the shows online. The chat is moderated, so only the most witty, interesting, or strange comments are broadcast to the online audience. It's quirky, but fun. From Nelson's home page, you can find a schedule of upcoming events so you know when to tune in to enjoy the party.

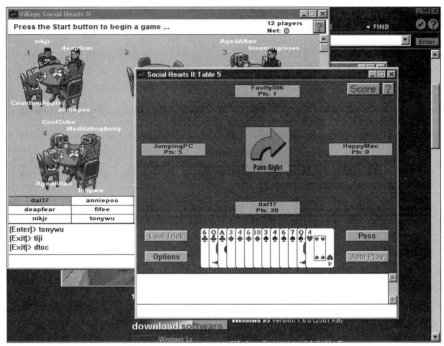

Figure 7-3:
Playing
Hearts on
the Internet
Gaming
Zone.

Pen Pals

Pen Pals is a place where teenagers can exchange e-mail with other teenagers around the world. When you sign up with Pen Pals, you can supply a bunch of information about yourself — your interests, hobbies, what kind of music you like, and so on. Then, other teenagers with similar interests can send you e-mail. You can also search for other Pen Pals who share your interests.

Figure 7-4 shows the Pen Pals home page.

Figure 7-4:
Pen Pals.

Channel 3: Adventure, Knowledge, and Discovery

Channel 3 is your source for information about the worlds of adventure and exploration. If you want to follow Jean-Michel Cousteau on a dive, research a science fair project, or tune in to history, check out Channel 3. The following sections describe some of the programs available on Channel 3.

Project: Watchfire

If you have been abducted by aliens, or think you may be some day, check out Project: Watchfire. This site is devoted to the whole UFO phenomenon. According to the site's main writer, journalist A.J.S. Rayl, UFOs are one of the most interesting subjects whether real or imagined.

Rifff

Rifff is an interactive music site that features a different artist every week. The best part about this site is its interactive, online music videos. The videos take forever to download, but most are worth the wait. Figure 7-5 shows a glimpse of Rifff.

The Rifff site is cool, but I have two unanswered questions:

- ✔ What is Rifff doing on Channel 2 instead of Channel 5?
- ✔ Why are there so many f's?

Mungo Park

The real Mungo Park was one of Britain's first African explorers. He died in an attempt to navigate the great Niger river in 1805. Mungo Park is an online adventure magazine devoted especially to underwater exploration. If wet stuff interests you, this is the place to come. The most interesting fea-tures are of the so-called "Live Ex" variety: live coverage of ongoing expeditions, such as exploring the coral reefs of Fiji, kayaking with Orcas on the Inside Passage, or floating the croc-infested waters of Ethiopia's Tekeze River. Figure 7-6 shows a page from one of the Mungo Park Live Ex pages.

Figure 7-5:
A music
video
on Rifff.

Figure 7-6:
A Live Ex
on Mungo
Park.

Mama Planet

If saving the planet is your favorite pastime, Mama Planet is a place you want to check out. The site is an ecological journal that gets updated every other week with features about environmental issues. You also find activities, celebrity interviews, online chats, experiments, and links to other ecology sites on the Internet.

Retrospect 360

Retrospect 360 describes itself as "an interactive exploration of the 20th century." It offers glitzy multimedia presentations on various topics. Topics change periodically, so be sure to check out Retrospect 360 on a regular basis.

Slate

Slate is a daily online magazine devoted to politics, culture, and current events. Insightful analysis highlights the site. Think of it as an online replacement for *Time* or *Newsweek* magazine. Figure 7-7 shows a recent contents page from Slate.

In addition to browsing the contents of Slate online, there are three more ways you can read Slate:

- ✔ **Slate on Paper:** A printable version of Slate publishes every Friday. You can download the print version in either Microsoft Word or Adobe Acrobat format, then print the magazine on your own printer. The file takes less than 3 minutes to download at 28.8 Kbps and prints about 35 pages.

- ✔ **Slate on Paper by E-Mail:** You can have the paper version of Slate e-mailed to you automatically once a week.

Figure 7-7:
Slate.

> ✔ **Slate Offline:** Slate works with a free program called FreeLoader, which enables you to download the entire contents of the Slate magazine to your computer's hard drive. You can then read Slate later when you are not connected to MSN. The FreeLoader version of Slate is similar to the offline version of MSNBC, which I describe in detail in Chapter 6.

To enable any of these options, click the Slate Help link from the Slate contents page and follow the instructions.

Channel 4: Home, Self, and Wealth

The programs on MSNBC Channel 4 spotlight the world of home, self, and wealth. The following sections describe some of the more interesting programs to be found on Channel 4.

Forever Cool

Facing midlife? Check out Forever Cool, an MSN program devoted to people in their 40s and 50s who are thinking about making changes in their lives. These folks are the '60s generation come of age. They invented Cool, and they still know about Cool.

Forever Cool features real-life stories about people who have made major life changes, such as moving from Arkansas to New York or leaving the comfort of a 9 to 5 job to open a bed and breakfast.

Great Stuff

Great Stuff is an unusual type of online magazine. It allows you to actually participate in the creation of a work of art or literature. You can collaborate with a group of authors or artists, make suggestions, and offer criticism (constructive or not).

UnderWire

UnderWire is an online magazine devoted to women on the Internet. Three of UnderWire's regular features are: BodyWorks, which helps you set and reach individual fitness goals; It's Personal, which dives into intimate relationships; and Social Studies, which tackles such diverse subjects as politics, etiquette, and life with dogs.

@WaterCooler

@WaterCooler, shown in Figure 7-8, is an online magazine devoted to career issues. Here, you find advice about getting that promotion, staying focused, making connections, and getting what you want.

Money Insider

Money Insider is an online magazine published by Microsoft to offer information and advice about financial matters. It helps you take charge of your finances, plan for the future, and enjoy the present. You find helpful articles about subjects such as straightening out your credit report and investing in mutual funds.

MotorSite

MotorSite features everybody's favorite automotive duo, Click and Clack from National Public Radio's CarTalk segment. MotorSite includes a really cool comic-strip feature called As The Wrench Turns. The feature presents a comic-strip dialogue with a caller in which Click and Clack dispense a little bit of car advice and a ton of their peculiar brand of wit, as shown in Figure 7-9.

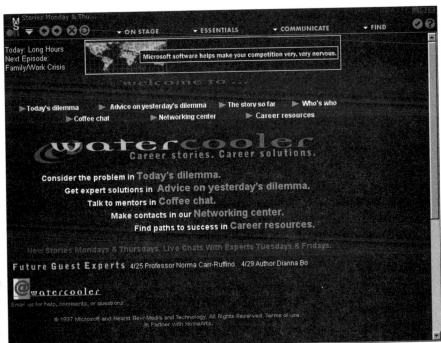

Figure 7-8: @Water-Cooler.

Figure 7-9:
Click and
Clack at
work on
MotorSite.

OnParenting

If you are a parent — or will be one soon — this online magazine is devoted to you. Each weekly issue offers news and advice on pregnancy and parenting. You find information about schools, traveling with kids, recipes, health issues, and more.

Disney's Family.Com

Family.Com is an online magazine devoted to parenting, from the good folks at Disney. In addition to helpful articles and information on all sorts of parenting topics, Family.Com offers bulletin boards and chat rooms where you can exchange ideas with other parents.

One of my favorite resources on Family.Com is its large collection of activities suitable for various age groups. For example, a search for Craft projects suitable for ages 12 and above yields a list of more than 80 projects, such as "Use Produce to Decorate T-Shirts" and "Make a Box for Summer Memories."

V-Style

V-Style is a biweekly magazine that explores the elusive topic of style. V-Style focuses on interesting people, unique objects, and the trends that create and define style. Figure 7-10 shows the V-Style contents page. Each issue of V-Style includes a StyleMaker section that features a stylish celebrity such as Bette Midler or Madonna; an IceBreakers section, which looks at current news and issues; and Selections, an online gallery of images of objects all related to a stylish theme.

Figure 7-10:
V-Style.

Channel 5: Music, Media, and Attitude

Channel 5 is where you will find online magazines devoted to music, culture, and the arts.

MINT

MINT is an on-the-edge online magazine that focuses on the cutting edge of out-there culture. Recent articles have included Andre the Giant, The Notorious Bigfoot, Reincarnation, and Pet Psychic.

One Click Away

One Click Away is a guide to Internet culture, filled with links to the most interesting Internet sites. Figure 7-11 shows the One Click Away main page. You can reach a different Web site every day by clicking Hit, or you access an entire week's worth of cool Web sites by clicking Picks.

Figure 7-11:
One Click
Away.

This is Not a Test

This is Not a Test is a live "cybercast" — a live broadcast every Wednesday featuring biting analysis of current events and politics, strange interviews, and other off-the-wall — but often humorous — stuff. If you're into social satire, you'll want to check this site out.

On Air

On Air brings you live multimedia concerts featuring popular bands. The music portion of the concert broadcasts over local college-run FM radio stations, so you must set up a radio near your computer. Then, at the time of the concert, you listen to the music through your radio and participate in an online chat with the band during the concert. Very cool.

Duckman Presents

Duckman Presents is a strange electronic show featuring an annoying animated duck, shown in Figure 7-12. If you don't click on something right away when the page in Figure 7-12 appears, Duckman starts nagging. "Hurry up and click on something, will you? I'm missing Baywatch!" he'll shout. Or, "Move to another area! We have a tour coming through." You'd better oblige Duckman and click on something soon.

Spoken World

Spoken World is an online presentation of interactive spoken fiction. You can weave your way through the story in any sequence you wish, following events from various perspectives as spoken by characters in the story. Figure 7-13 shows a segment of a Spoken World story called Dream Sheets. New installments get added periodically to the story, so you need to check back with Spoken World once in a while to keep up with the story.

Figure 7-12:
Duckman
Presents.

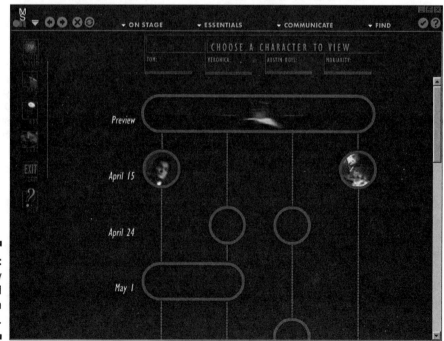

Figure 7-13:
A story
presented
in Spoken
World.

Almost TV

Almost TV is a live chat program in which participants watch TV and chat about it online. The Almost TV host picks which program to watch and moderates the discussion. In many cases, a celebrity guest appears during the chat to liven up the conversation. The schedule varies, so be sure to check ahead of time to determine programs and times.

Channel 6: Kids, Friends, and Fun

Channel 6 is the home a special MSN program designed just for kids, by the world's best provider of entertainment for kids: Disney. Here you'll find Disney's Daily Blast. You'll also find a special chat area just for kids, called the Chat Box.

Disney's Daily Blast

Disney's Daily Blast is one of the best sites for kids on the Internet. It features an almost limitless array of fun things to do online, including a collection of nifty games you can play (new games are added frequently, so you won't get bored), news stories presented in a kid-friendly way, Disney comics, and more — a lot more.

The Chat Box

The Chat Box is an area where kids can gather to chat online. The Chat Box runs several chat rooms that are similar to Internet Relay Chat (aka IRC). However, the Chat Box chat rooms are chaperoned (and one of them is fully moderated) so that everyone can be sure to have a safe and enjoyable chatting experience. Figure 7-14 shows The Chat Box.

Here are the Official Rules for chatting at The Chat Box:

- No Swearing!
- No Insults!
- No Confidential Information!
- No Useless Screen Junk!
- No False Complaints!
- No Gum Chewing!

Microsoft rigidly enforces all of these rules except the last one. Break one of the rules and you get banned from chatting.

Figure 7-14:
The Chat
Box.

Chapter 8

The Bare Essentials

*M*SN's Essentials area offers a collection of useful services which are available only on MSN, such as Microsoft Cinemania, which provides detailed reviews of the latest theatrical and video releases, or Microsoft Expedia, an online travel service through which you can book airline flights, hotel reservations, and rental cars.

This chapter gives you an overview of the services that are available from the Essentials page. Keep in mind that Microsoft may add additional services to the Essentials page in the future. By the time you read this, the Essentials page will probably include other services.

Accessing Essentials

To access the services that are available from Essentials, click Essentials in the Navigation bar at the top of the MSN window and then choose Essentials Home Page from the menu that appears. The screen shown in Figure 8-1 is displayed. At the left edge of this screen, you'll find a list of categories: Local Info, Personal Finance, Computers & Software, and so on. Click one of these categories to see a list of services that are available for that category. When you decide what service you want to use, click the link to that service.

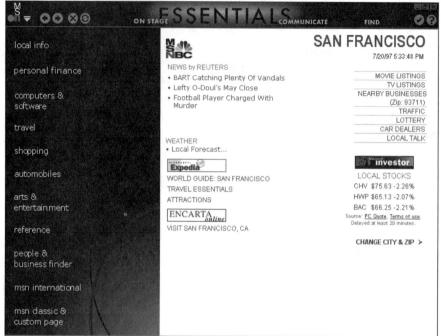

You can bypass the Essentials page and go directly to an Essentials service by clicking Essentials in the Navigation bar and choosing the service you want to go to directly from the menu that appears. The menu includes the same categories as the Essentials page. To select a service, just point to the category that contains the service, and then click the service you want to go to.

What Are the Essentials?

The following sections briefly describe the services that are available in each Essentials category. I describe several of the more useful services in more detail in Chapters 13 through 16.

Local Info

The Local Info service gives you up-to-date information about any of more than 100 cities in the United States, including movie and TV listings, traffic information, lottery winners, weather reports, local stock reports, and a directory of local businesses. Local Info was shown back in Figure 8-1 and is displayed by default when you go to Essentials. To get to Local Info from anywhere in MSN, just point to the Essentials menu in the Navigation bar at the top of the MSN window, point to on Local Info to display the Local Info menu, then choose Home.

Local Info has three menu choices: Home, Other Cities, and Sidewalk. Home lets you tell MSN your home city so that it can automatically display information for your locality. To change your home city, click the City & Zip link near the bottom right of the page. Other Cities enables you to display the local information for any of 64 cities. Select the city you want to display from the drop-down list and then click Visit This City.

If you want to change your home town, click Change City & Zip on the Essentials home page. Then select your city (or the city nearest you) from the drop-down list.

Sidewalk provides an additional listing for cool happenings in selected cities: New York, Boston, Seattle, San Francisco, and Twin Cities.

Personal Finance

The Personal Finance service is the home of an online investment service known as Microsoft Investor, shown in Figure 8-2. Investor enables you to track your investments, get up-to-date stock information, research companies, show historical information, and purchase stocks and mutual funds online. Investor is described in more detail in Chapter 13.

Computers & Software

The Computers & Software service is where you will find Computing on MSN, a collection of forums and online magazines designed to help you with your computer troubles. To get to Computing on MSN, click Essentials, and choose Computers & Software⇨Computing on MSN from the menu. You'll see a page that says *Do you have a question?* and includes a blinking button titled *Click here.* Click the blinking button to go to another page that describes what Computing on MSN is. On this page are several links. Click the link that says *ENTER COMPUTING ON MSN*. You'll head to the Computing on MSN page, shown in Figure 8-3. From this page, you can access any of the various Computing on MSN features.

Figure 8-2:
Investor is
available
from the
Personal
Finance
section
of MSN
Essentials.

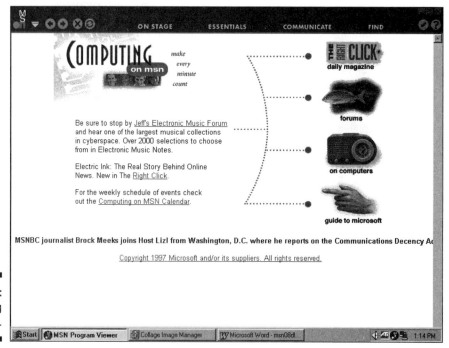

Figure 8-3:
Computing
on MSN.

Travel

The Travel category is the home of Expedia, an online travel agency. With Expedia, you can purchase airline tickets, make hotel reservations, and book car rentals. Expedia is big enough that I've devoted an entire chapter to the service. See Chapter 14 when you're ready to get away from it all.

Shopping

The Shopping service sports The Plaza on MSN, an online shopping mall. The Plaza on MSN currently has seven online stores: American Greetings, At Once Software, Avon, 1-800-Flowers, iQVC, Scandinavian Pavilion, and Tower Records. Microsoft promises that more stores will be added soon. Online shopping is too much fun to cover in this chapter. See Chapter 15 for more information.

Automobiles

The Automobiles service has a single entry: CarPoint, an online service which can help you purchase or lease your next car. You can read reviews of current car models, take an online test drive, get helpful hints about buying or leasing a car, and — best of all — learn the dealer cost for the model and options you want so you can bargain wisely.

Arts & Entertainment

The Arts & Entertainment category includes three services. The first service, called Music Central, is the place to go if you are a music buff. It includes news and stories about the music industry, interviews with popular artists, and an online store from which you can purchase CDs. Music Central is shown in Figure 8-4.

The second Arts & Entertainment service is Cinemania, an online version of the popular computerized film & video catalog from Microsoft, shown in Figure 8-5.

The third Arts & Entertainment selection is the Internet Gaming Zone, which features a collection of games you can play online against other Internet users. Some of the games in Zone are classic board and card games such as backgammon, bridge, spades, chess, and checkers. But the Zone also lets you play several Microsoft games — including Hellbender, Golf, and Monster Truck Madness — with other Internet opponents. To play these games, you must purchase your own copy of the game you want to play from your local software store.

Figure 8-4:
Music
Central
from
Essentials
Arts and
Entertain-
ment.

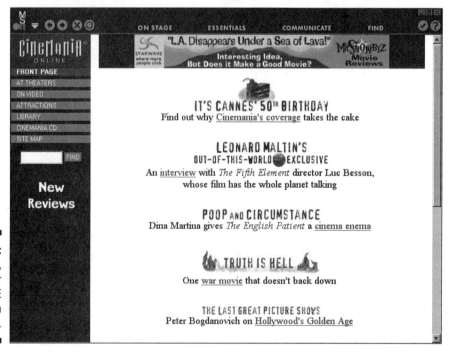

Figure 8-5:
Cinemania,
another
A&E
offering on
Essentials.

Reference

The Reference service includes three online references: Encarta, Parent Handbook, and Wine Guide.

Encarta is a scaled back version of the Microsoft multimedia encyclopedia. With the online version of Encarta, you can search for articles by typing in one or more keywords. For example, a search for *Neil Armstrong* will turn up the article shown in Figure 8-6.

The Parent Handbook is a part of the online magazine *OnParenting*, which can also be accessed from OnStage Channel 4. The handbook is a collection of more than 600 articles on family health and parenting. Figure 8-7 shows an example of an article from the Parent Handbook.

The Wine Guide offers expert advice about — what else? — wine. Looking for a wine that will go well with Saltimbocca alla Romana? Try a 1992 Babcock Reserve Chardonnay. Need a 3-star California white wine? The Wine Guide lists 12.

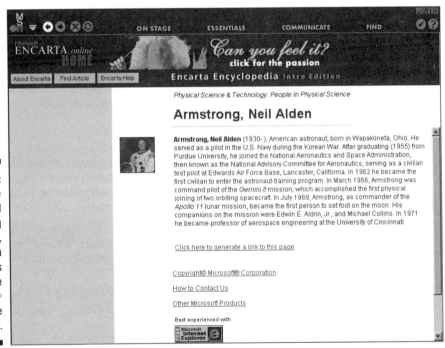

Figure 8-6: An article about Neil Armstrong in Encarta, which you can access from the Essentials⇨ Reference menu.

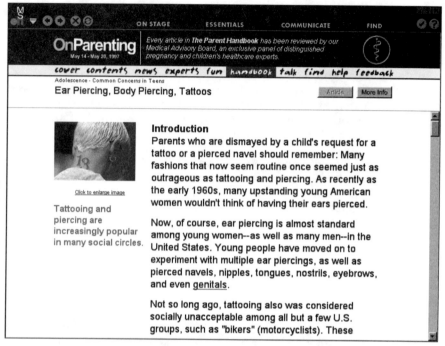

Figure 8-7:
An article
from the
Parent
Handbook,
part of the
OnParenting
online
magazine.

People and Business Finder

The People Finder service consists of four services that help you find people and businesses online:

✔ **People Finder:** Shown in Figure 8-8, the People Finder service helps you find addresses and phone numbers for individuals. To use People Finder, just type in the first and last name of the person you are looking for, and then click the Search button (shaped like a key). Narrow the search by typing in the city and selecting the state from the drop-down list.

If People Finder finds a listing for the name you entered, it will display the person's name, address, and phone number. If more than one listing matches the name you entered, all of the matching names will be displayed.

✔ **Email Finder:** Similar to People Finder, but instead of displaying a person's address and phone number, Email Finder shows the person's e-mail address. If you want to send e-mail to a friend or colleague but you don't know the e-mail address, Email Finder is the way to find it.

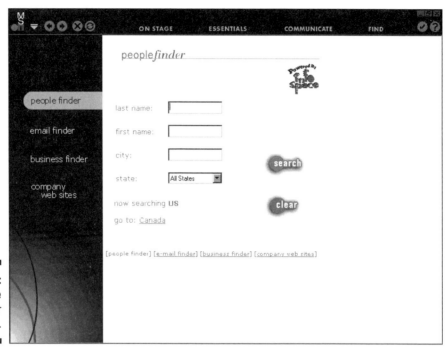

Figure 8-8:
The People
Finder
service.

✔ **Business Finder:** You can search for up to 75 categories of businesses in a particular city using the Business Finder service. If you want, you can narrow the search by supplying all or part of the business name. Or, you can just select the category, type and city, and then click Search to show a listing of all businesses of that category in the city you typed. For example, Figure 8-9 shows a listing of Chinese restaurants in Fresno, CA.

✔ **Company Web sites:** A directory of companies that maintain home pages on the World Wide Web. To find a company Web site, type in the name of the company and, if you know it, the city. Then click Search. MSN will display a list showing all the Web sites that match the business name and city you entered. For example, Figure 8-10 shows the results for a search on "IDG Books." To go to one of these Web sites, just click one of the Web addresses listed for the company.

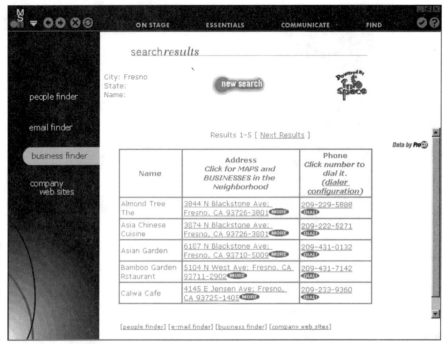

Figure 8-9:
The
Business
Finder
service.

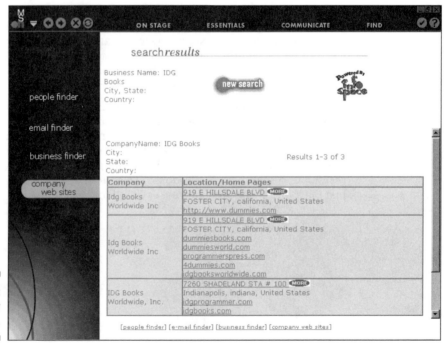

Figure 8-10:
Company
Web sites.

MSN International

The MSN International service in the Essentials menu enables you to access international versions of MSN. MSN is currently available in seven international flavors:

- ✔ Australia
- ✔ Canada
- ✔ France
- ✔ Germany
- ✔ Japan
- ✔ UK & Ireland
- ✔ United States

Normally, the MSN setup program automatically configures the correct international version of MSN for you, so you'll only need to use this option if you want to switch to another version.

MSN Classic & Custom Page

If you were one of the early users of MSN, you may long to occasionally drop back to the original version of MSN, now called MSN Classic. You can do that by choosing Classic Categories from the MSN Classic & Custom Page option. The old, familiar MSN Classic Categories window appears, as shown in Figure 8-11.

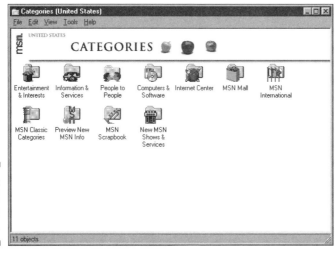

Figure 8-11:
MSN
Classic
Categories.

As I write this, there are still a few (very few) MSN areas that you can access only via MSN Classic Categories. But by the time you read this, those few remaining Classic services will probably have migrated to the new Web-based format, which is accessed by the MSN Program Viewer.

Also available from the MSN Classic & Custom Page menu is MSN.com, a service that enables you to create a personalized Web start page for use with Internet Explorer. For more information about MSN.com, see Chapter 25.

Chapter 9

Finding Stuff on The Microsoft Network

● ●

In This Chapter

▶ Using The Microsoft Network (MSN) search service to locate interesting sites on MSN and the Internet

▶ Browsing the MSN subject categories

▶ Finding out about upcoming online events such as chats and live news coverage.

● ●

*T*he Microsoft Network is a big place — huge, in fact. Finding just the information you need is not always as easy as it could be. You can point and click your way around MSN for hours without finding the information you want.

Fortunately, MSN includes a special Find command that can eliminate those hours of pointless pointing and clicking. The Find command helps you find just the topics you want. Read on to find out more.

Searching by Keyword

The easiest way to find information on MSN is to search for the information you want using a *keyword*. Here is the procedure:

1. **Point to the word Find in the Navigation bar, and then choose Search MSN and the Web from the menu that appears.**

   The Find page appears, as shown in Figure 9-1.

2. **Type the word or phrase you want to look for (the keyword) in the Enter a word or phrase box.**

   For example, to look for MSN areas that have to do with space, type **space**.

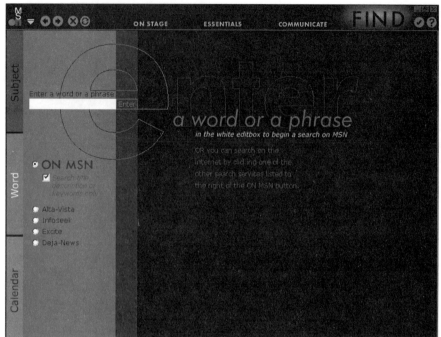

Figure 9-1:
Searching
MSN.

3. Click Enter.

You can also press the Enter key. MSN spins its wheels for a moment, and then displays your search results. Figure 9-2 shows the results of a search on the word *space*.

4. Click the page you want to go to.

In Figure 9-2, six MSN pages are listed for *space*. Click the link that interests you and you are instantly teleported to the MSN service you select.

5. To see additional listings for the word or phrase you typed, click the Next button at the bottom of the page.

A list of additional MSN pages to Web sites containing the word or phrase you entered appears. In addition to MSN pages, Find may also list Web pages that are outside of MSN. Note that the Microsoft Network can't be held accountable for the content that appears on sites that are outside of MSN. MSN lists these sites for your convenience only.

Note: The number of pages of search results is shown at the bottom of the search results page. For example, in Figure 9-2, 15 pages of search results exist.

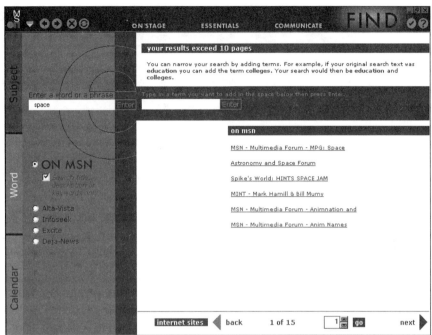

Figure 9-2:
There's a
lot of stuff
on MSN
about
space.

Here are important tidbits to keep in mind when searching MSN:

✔ You're better off to search for more general words than for very specific ones. For example, a search for *Gilligan's Island* will probably return no matches, but a search for *TV* will get you going in the right direction.

✔ Unfortunately, the MSN search facility doesn't really search all of MSN. For example, a search for *Abraham Lincoln* doesn't list any MSN pages even though there is plenty of information about Abraham Lincoln to be found in Encarta. Similarly, a search for *Honda Accord* returns no pages, even though there is information about this popular car in CarPoint.

✔ To begin a new search, type a new word or phrase in the text box and then click Enter or press the Enter key.

✔ If you receive a message indicating that no matches can be found, try again, but use a more general word or phrase.

✔ If you didn't find information you're looking for, try thinking of another word or phrase that means the same thing. Also, double-check your spelling to make sure you didn't make a silly misteak.

You can search the Internet for information about a particular subject by typing the word you want to search for, clicking one of the Internet search services listed (AltaVista, Infoseek, Excite, or Deja-News), and clicking Enter. This will send you to the Internet search service you selected. For example, Figure 9-3 shows the results of an AltaVista search for *Manhattan Project*.

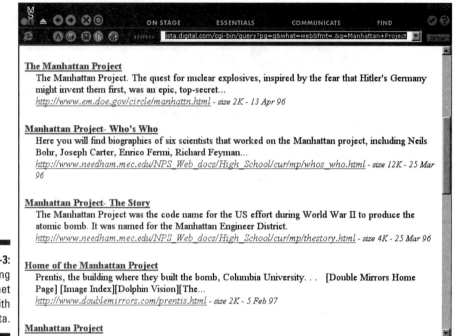

The Manhattan Project

The Manhattan Project. The quest for nuclear explosives, inspired by the fear that Hitler's Germany might invent them first, was an epic, top-secret...

http://www.em.doe.gov/circle/manhattn.html - *size 2K - 13 Apr 96*

Manhattan Project- Who's Who

Here you will find biographies of six scientists that worked on the Manhattan project, including Neils Bohr, Joseph Carter, Enrico Fermi, Richard Feyman...

http://www.needham.mec.edu/NPS_Web_docs/High_School/cur/mp/whos_who.html - *size 12K - 25 Mar 96*

Manhattan Project- The Story

The Manhattan Project was the code name for the US effort during World War II to produce the atomic bomb. It was named for the Manhattan Engineer District.

http://www.needham.mec.edu/NPS_Web_docs/High_School/cur/mp/thestory.html - *size 4K - 25 Mar 96*

Home of the Manhattan Project

Prentis, the building where they built the bomb, Columbia University. . . [Double Mirrors Home Page] [Image Index][Dolphin Vision][The...

http://www.doublemirrors.com/prentis.html - *size 2K - 5 Feb 97*

Manhattan Project

Figure 9-3:
Searching
the Internet
with
AltaVista.

Browsing MSN Categories

If keyword searches aren't your thing, you can sift through the MSN pre-defined subject categories to find interesting sites. You access MSN subject categories by pointing to Find on the Navigation bar and choosing Browse All of MSN from the menu that appears. Or, you can choose Search MSN and the Web from the Find menu, then click the word Subject that appears at the left side of the page. Either way, the MSN subject category listing will appear.

The MSN subject index organizes MSN features into the following categories:

- ✔ **Arts & Entertainment:** Art, E-Zines, Fun & Funny, Games, Kids, Literature, Movies, Music, Photography, Television

- ✔ **Computers:** Computer Companies, Graphics, Help Desks, Interactive, Internet, Shareware

- ✔ **Microsoft Products:** Internet Products, Games, Hardware, Personal Finance, MS Press, Windows 95, Microsoft Office, Developer Products, Microsoft BackOffice, Windows NT Workstation, Windows NT Server

✔ **Lifestyles:** Politics, Religion, Society & Culture, Advice, News, Shopping, Home & Gardening, Cars, Food & Dining

✔ **Personal Finance:** Stock Quotes, Investment Information, Home Banking, Mutual Funds, Mortgage & Home Equity

✔ **Education:** K-12, College, For Teachers

✔ **Reference:** Dictionary, Encyclopedia, Thesaurus, Science, History

✔ **Sports & Leisure:** Outdoors, Baseball, Basketball, Football, Soccer, Hockey, Golf, Tennis

✔ **Health & Medicine:** Physical Fitness, Nutrition, Disease, Family Health

✔ **Travel:** Tickets Online, North American, European, Asian & Australian, Latin American, African, Weather Reports, Hotels, Car Rental, Adventure

You can click any of the categories to reveal a list of subcategories. You can then click one of the subcategories to display a list of MSN pages, as shown in Figure 9-4.

Figure 9-4:
Fun and
Funny
places on
MSN.

Checking the Calendar

The MSN Calendar enables you to find out about upcoming online events, such as online coverage of news events, chats with celebrities, or scheduled online games. To access the MSN Calendar, point at Find in the Navigation bar, then choose View MSN Calendar from the menu that appears. Or, choose Search MSN and the Web, and then click the Calendar button at the left side of the screen. Either way, the MSN Calendar will appear as shown in Figure 9-5.

Events on the MSN Calendar are color coded according to their type, as shown in the legend. For example, special events are blue, chats are pale green, and contests are orange. You can go directly to any of the events listed by clicking on the event in MSN Calendar.

When you first open MSN Calendar, it shows the current day's scheduled events. You can move forward or backward through the calendar one day at a time by clicking Previous or Next near the top right of the page. Or, you can switch to Week view by clicking the Week button at the top left corner of the Calendar. This displays an entire week's online events, in less detail than Day view. You can switch quickly to Day view of a particular day by clicking on the date.

You can also switch to Month view by clicking Month in the top left corner. As you can see, only the most important activities of each week are listed in Month view.

Figure 9-5:
The MSN Calendar shows all of the day's scheduled online activities.

Part III

Reach Out and Electronically Touch Someone

The 5th Wave By Rich Tennant

"OOPS, I FORGOT TO LOG OFF AGAIN."

In this part . . .

Staying in touch is one of the main reasons most people sign up to use an online service such as The Microsoft Network. In the three chapters in this part, you find out how to use MSN's three main communication services: e-mail, chat, and forum bulletin boards.

Chapter 10

Using MSN Electronic Mail

*O*ne of the main reasons many people use online services such as The Microsoft Network (MSN) is for electronic mail, or *e-mail,* as it is called. You can think of e-mail as the high-tech equivalent of Mr. McFeeley, the friendly, bespectacled mailman we all grew to love on *Mr. Rogers' Neighborhood.*

Sending an e-mail message is much like sending a letter through regular mail. In both cases, you write your message, put an address on it, and send it off through an established mail system. Eventually, the recipient of the message receives your note, opens it, reads it, and — if you're lucky — answers by sending a message back.

E-mail offers certain advantages over regular mail. For example, e-mail arrives at its destination in a matter of minutes, not days. E-mail can be delivered any day of the week, including Sundays and holidays. And, as a special advantage, your great-aunt can't send you a fruitcake through e-mail.

About the only thing that keeps the post office in business anymore, other than transporting fruitcake, is that e-mail only works when both the sender and the receiver have computers that are connected to an online service or the Internet — you can't send e-mail to someone who isn't online.

Electronic mail in MSN is handled through a nifty little program called Microsoft Internet Mail. Internet Mail is one of the best improvements in the new version of MSN. The old version of MSN used the clunky e-mail program that came free with Windows 95, called Exchange. Exchange was s-l-o-w. Internet Mail is much faster.

Starting Microsoft Internet Mail

When you log on to MSN, the On Stage start page indicates if you have e-mail waiting by displaying a message such as `You have 3 new e-mail message(s)`. Clicking on this message is the easiest way to start Internet Mail so that you can read your new e-mail, or compose new e-mail.

You can start Internet Mail several other ways:

- ✔ Point to Communicate in the Navigation bar, and then choose the Send or Receive E-mail command from the menu that appears.
- ✔ Point to Communicate in the Navigation bar, choose All Communication Services, and then click Start E-mail on the Communication page.
- ✔ Click the Windows 95 Start button and choose Programs⇨Internet Mail.

However you open it, Internet Mail springs to life, displaying the window shown in Figure 10-1.

Notice that the Internet Mail window is divided into two major sections, called *panes*. The top pane, called the Inbox, is a list of all the e-mail you have received. The bottom pane shows the text of the currently selected message.

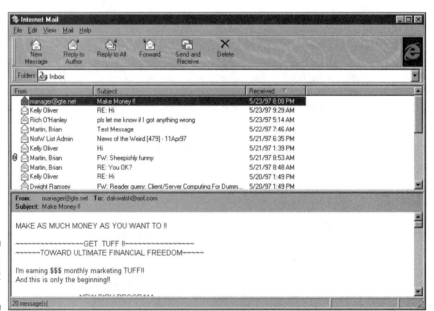

Figure 10-1:
Internet
Mail.

Each time you start Internet Mail, the program automatically checks to see if you have new mail. Provided that you leave Internet Mail open (you can minimized it if you wish), Internet Mail periodically checks to see if new mail has arrived. The subject title of any new messages that you haven't yet read appears in boldface in the Inbox pane. (If you want, you can change how often Internet Mail checks for new mail by choosing the Mail⇨Options command, clicking the Read tab, and setting the time interval you want to use.)

Sending Electronic Mail

To send electronic mail, all you have to do is follow these steps:

New Message

1. **In the Internet Mail window, click the New Message button on the left side of the toolbar.**

   You can also choose Mail⇨New Message, or use the keyboard shortcut Ctrl+N. The New Message dialog box, shown in Figure 10-2, appears.

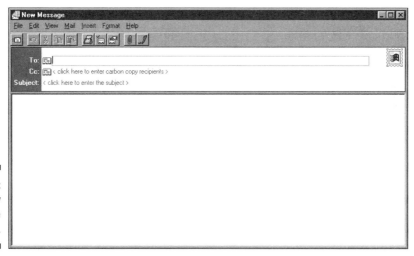

Figure 10-2:
The New Message dialog box.

2. **Type the e-mail address of the person to whom you want to send the message.**

   When the New Message dialog box appears, the cursor is in the To: text box, where you type the e-mail address for the mail recipient. You can send mail to more than one recipient by typing more than one name or address in the To: field. Type a semicolon between each name.

You can send e-mail to other MSN members, or to anyone who has an Internet e-mail address. For examples of different kinds of e-mail addresses, check out the nearby sidebar, "Addressing your e-mail."

If the e-mail address of the person you want to send the message to is in your address book, you can click the little Rolodex-card icon that appears next to the To field to summon your address book. See the section "Using the Address Book," later in this chapter, for more information.

3. **If you want to send a copy of the message to another e-mail user, type that person's e-mail address in the Cc: field.**

   Click where you see the words ⟨click here to enter carbon copy recipients⟩ and then type the e-mail address of anyone to whom you want to send a copy of the message. To cc: the message to more than one person, type each person's e-mail address, using semicolons to separate the addresses.

4. **Type a succinct but clear title for the message in the Subject field.**

   Click where you see the words ⟨click here to enter the subject⟩ and then type the subject of your message. For example, type **Let's Do Lunch** or **Jetson, You're Fired!**

5. **Type your message in the message area of the New Message dialog box.**

   Figure 10-3 shows what your message looks like with all of the information typed in and ready to go.

Figure 10-3:
A message ready to be sent.

Addressing your e-mail

Just as with paper mail, before you send e-mail, you have to know the address of the person to whom you're sending the mail. The easiest way to find out someone's e-mail address is simply to ask for it. However, you can also find e-mail addresses by using the MSN Email finder, which is located on the Essentials menu. Refer to Chapter 8 for more information.

To send mail to an MSN user, all you have to type in the e-mail address text box is the user's member ID. For example, to send mail to user CharlieX, address the mail to simply *CharlieX*.

To send mail to a user of one of the major online services, compose the user's e-mail address as follows:

✔ For America Online users, type the user name followed by `@aol.com`; for example, `Lurch@aol.com`.

✔ For CompuServe users, type the numeric user ID followed by `@compuserve.com`. Be sure to use a period rather than a comma to separate the two parts of the numeric user ID; for example `12345.6789@compuserve.com`.

To send mail to an Internet user, you'll need the user's full e-mail address; for example, `jetson@spacely.com`.

6. When you finish typing your message, click the Send button.

Internet Mail dismisses the New Message dialog box and places the message in your Outbox — a folder that contains messages you have created but that have not yet been delivered to their intended recipients.

7. To send the message, click the Send and Receive button.

You can also press Ctrl+M or choose Mail⇨Send and Receive.

Note: You can skip this step if you first configure Internet Mail to send all mail messages immediately. To do so, choose Mail⇨Options, check the Send messages immediately option (found under the Send tab), and then click OK.

If you create an entry for a person in your address book, you can simply type that person's name instead of typing the full Internet address. For more information, see "Using the Address Book," later in this chapter.

If you're not sure whether you've typed a name correctly, click the Check Names button. This feature checks the names you've typed against the Address Book to reveal any errors.

Internet Mail assumes that any Internet address you type is correct. Check Names checks to make sure the address is in the correct format, but does not check to make sure that the Internet address actually exists.

Using the Address Book

You may have a relatively small number of people with whom you will exchange e-mail on a regular basis. Rather than retype their Internet addresses every time you send e-mail to these people, you can store your most commonly used addresses in the Internet Mail Address Book. As an added benefit, the Address Book enables you to refer to your e-mail friends by name (for example, George Jetson) rather than by Internet address (george@spacely.com).

Adding a name to the Address Book

Before you can use the Address Book, you need to add the names of your e-mail correspondents to it. The best time to add someone to the Address Book is after you receive e-mail from that person. Here's the procedure:

1. **Open an e-mail message from someone you want to add to the Address Book.**

   The message is displayed. For more information about reading e-mail, see the section "Receiving Electronic Mail," later in this chapter.

2. **Right-click the user's name, and then choose Add to Address Book.**

   The address is added to the Address Book.

3. **Close the message.**

   Thereafter, you can access the person's Internet address in the Address Book whenever you are creating an e-mail message. (See the section "Using an address from the Address Book," later in this chapter.)

To add someone to your Address Book from whom you have not yet received mail, follow these steps:

1. **In Internet Mail, choose the File⇨Address Book command.**

   The Windows Address Book appears, as shown in Figure 10-4.

2. **Click the New Contact button.**

   The Properties dialog box appears, as shown in Figure 10-5.

3. **Type the person's name.**

   You can type separate first, middle, and last names, and you can type a separate display name which appears in the Address Book if you wish.

4. **Type the e-mail address in the E-mail Addresses field, and then click Add.**

   If the person has more than one e-mail address, repeat this step for each address.

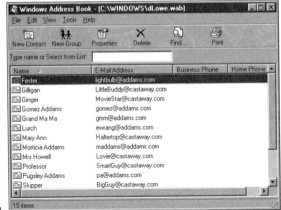

Figure 10-4: The Address Book in all its glory.

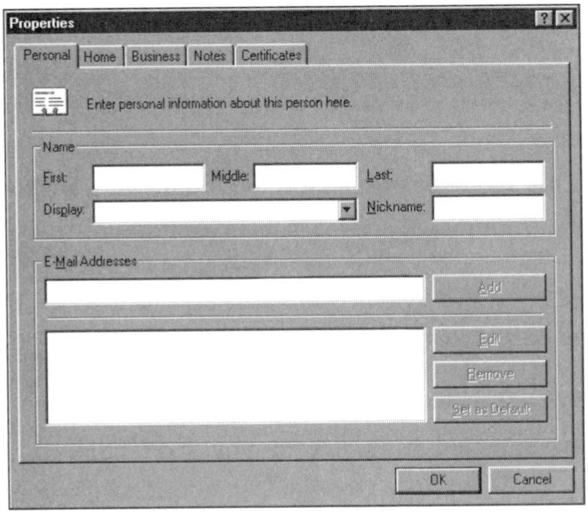

Figure 10-5: The Properties dialog box for an Address Book entry.

5. **If you want to, you can include additional information, such as phone numbers and addresses, under the Home Phone, Business Phone, and Notes tabs.**

6. **Click OK.**

   The Address Book entry is created.

Using an address from the Address Book

To send a message to a user who is already in the Address Book, follow these steps:

1. In the New Message window, click the little Rolodex-card icon next to the To: field.

The Select Recipients dialog box appears, as shown in Figure 10-6.

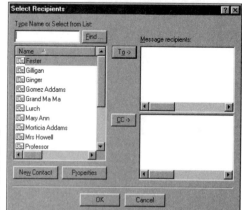

Figure 10-6:
The Select
Recipients
dialog box.

2. Double-click the name of the person to whom you want to send mail.

The person's name is added to the To: list on the right side of the dialog box. If double-clicking is against your religion, just click once on the person's name and then click the To button.

Note: You can add more than one name to the To: list, and you can add names to the CC: list by selecting the name and clicking the rolodex card icon next to the CC: field.

3. After you have selected all the names you want, click OK.

Poof! You're back at the New Message dialog box, and the names you selected appear in the To: and CC: fields.

Changing and deleting Address Book entries

On occasion, one of your e-mail buddies switches Internet providers and gives you a new Internet address. Or you may lose touch with someone and decide to remove his or her name from your Address Book. Either way, the following steps guide you through the process of keeping your Address Book up to date:

1. **From Internet Mail, choose File⇨Address Book.**

   The Address Book dialog box appears (refer to Figure 10-4 for a look at the Address Book).

2. **Click the address you want to change or delete.**

3. **To delete the address, click the Delete button.**

4. **To change the address, click the Properties button.**

   When the Properties dialog box appears, make any necessary changes, and then click OK.

5. **Click OK when you're finished.**

Checking your message for spelling errors

If you have Microsoft Office or any of its programs (Word, Excel, or PowerPoint), Internet Mail includes a bonus feature: a spell checker that is capable of catching those embarrassing spelling errors before they go out to the Internet. The spell checker checks the spelling of every word in your message, looking the words up in its massive dictionary of correctly spelled words. Any misspelling is brought to your attention. The spell checker is under strict orders from Bill Gates himself not to giggle or snicker at any of your misspellings, even if you insist on putting an *e* at the end of *potato*. The spell checker even gives you the opportunity to tell it that you are right and it is wrong — that it should learn how to spell the way you do.

To spell check your messages, follow these steps:

1. **Choose Mail⇨Check Spelling to spell check your message.**

   The spell checker comes to life, looking up your words in hopes of finding a mistake.

2. **Try not to be annoyed if the spell checker finds a spelling error.**

   Hey, you're the one who told it to look for spelling mistakes; don't get mad if it finds some. When the spell checker finds an error, it highlights the offending word and displays the misspelled word, along with a suggested correction, in the Spelling dialog box. The dialog box is shown in Figure 10-7.

3. **Choose the correct spelling and then click Change, or click Ignore to skip to the next word spell checker doesn't recognize.**

   If you agree that the word is misspelled, scan the list of suggested corrections and click the spelling that you like. Then click the Change button.

   If, on the other hand, you prefer your own spelling, click Ignore. To prevent the spell checker from asking you over and over again about a particular word that it doesn't recognize, such as someone's name, click Ignore All.

Figure 10-7:
The spell
checker
points out
an embar-
rassing
spelling
error.

4. Repeat Steps 2 and 3 until the spell checker gives up.

When you see the message `The spelling check is complete,` your
work is done.

Sending Attachments

An attachment is a file that you send along with your message. Sending an
attachment is kind of like paper-clipping a separate document to a letter. In
fact, Internet Mail uses a paper-clip icon to indicate that a message has an
attachment, and the button you click to add an attachment sports a paper-
clip design.

Adding an attachment

Note: Sending large attachments can sometimes cause e-mail troubles,
especially for attachments that approach a megabyte or more in size.
There's no predicting when and where such trouble will occur, and no one in
the Internet business likes to admit that it happens, but it does. If you send a
large attachment to someone but your e-mail message doesn't make it to the
recipient, try sending the message and attachment again.

Here is the procedure for adding an attachment to an outgoing message:

1. Click the Insert File button.

The Insert Attachment dialog box appears, as shown in Figure 10-8
appears.

**2. Rummage through the folders on your computer's disk until you find
the file you want to insert.**

When you find the file you want to attach, click the filename to select it.

Figure 10-8:
Inserting an
attachment.

3. Click Attach.

The file is inserted into the message as an attachment. An icon appears
in a separate pane in the New Message dialog box, as you see in Figure
10-9. Which icon appears depends on the program with which the
attachment is associated.

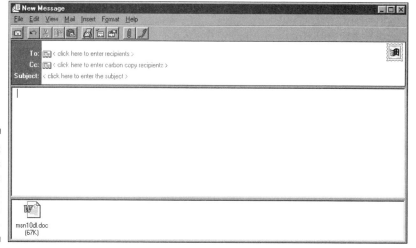

Figure 10-9:
Attachments
appear as
icons in
e-mail
messages.

4. Finish the message, and then click the Send button.

Complete the rest of the fields in the New Message dialog box, and type
a message to go along with the attachment. When your message is
complete, send it on its way.

Changing the encoding scheme

Internet e-mail was designed to send text-based messages, not messages that include binary data such as program files or graphics. To get around this limitation, e-mail programs convert attachments to a special encoded format. In this format, binary information is converted into a form that can be sent over normal Internet e-mail. When the mail arrives at its destination, the encoded data is decoded so that the recipient can access the binary file in its original form.

Two popular methods are used to send encoded data. By default, Internet Mail uses an encoding scheme called *MIME*. If the recipient of your message complains that he or she cannot read the attachment, you can change the encoding scheme to an alternate scheme called *Uuencode* (pronounced "you-you-encode"). Neither scheme appears to have an inherent advantage over the other, except that your recipient may be able to deal with Uuencode, but not MIME — or vice versa.

To change encoding schemes, follow these steps:

1. **Attach a file according to the procedure described in "Adding an Attachment."**

   Stop before completing the last step — sending your message.

2. **In the New Message dialog box, choose Format⇨Settings.**

   The Plain Text Settings dialog box appears, as shown in Figure 10-10.

Figure 10-10: The Plain Text Settings dialog box.

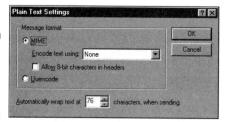

3. **Change the Message format setting from MIME to Uuencode.**

4. **Click OK.**

The preceding steps change the format to Uuencode for the current message only. To change the default message format for all messages, choose Mail⇨Options from the Internet Mail main window. Change the Mail Sending Format option in the Send tab of the Options dialog box.

Adding a signature

As you use the Internet, you discover that many Internet users conclude all of their e-mail and newsgroup messages with special signatures: a line or two of text that includes their names, contact information — such as their e-mail addresses — sometimes their phone or fax numbers, and often witty sayings. Special e-mail software automatically adds these signatures to the end of every message, so they don't have to type their signatures each time.

Internet Mail enables you to tag your own signature onto the end of your e-mail messages. Follow these simple steps to set up your own signature:

1. **Choose Mail⇨Options.**

   The Options dialog box appears.

2. **Click the Signature tab.**

   The signature options appear.

3. **Click the Text button.**

4. **Type the text you want to use for your signature into the box.**

   Figure 10-11 shows an example.

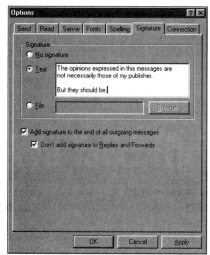

Figure 10-11:
A typical
signature.

5. **Check the Add Signature options to make sure they are to your liking.**

   The default settings are probably what you want to use. The signature will be automatically added to all new messages, but won't be added to message replies or forwarded messages.

6. **Click OK.**

If your signature is lengthy, you may want to create it in a separate file and choose the File option for the signature. This option is commonly used along with a program that automatically changes the signature file in some way each day — perhaps to add the date or to insert a random quotation. Such tricks are clearly in the realm of nerddom and best avoided by ordinary folk.

Receiving Electronic Mail

E-mail wouldn't be much good if it worked like a send-only set, sending out messages but not receiving them (I once had an aunt who worked that way). Fortunately, you can receive e-mail as well as send it — assuming, of course, that you have friends who write.

To read electronic mail that has been sent to you by other users, follow these steps:

1. **Start Internet Mail.**

   Refer back to the section "Starting Internet Mail," at the beginning of this chapter, if you're not sure how to do this.

   After Internet Mail starts, it immediately checks to see whether you have any new messages. If you do, your computer beeps and the subject line and sender name for the new messages are displayed in boldface in the Internet Mail window.

2. **Double-click on a new message to read it.**

   The message is displayed in its own window.

3. **Read the message.**

4. **After you read the message, dispense with it in one of the following ways:**

   - If the message is worthy of a reply, click the Reply to Sender button. A new message window appears, where you compose a reply message. The To: field is automatically set to the user who sent you the message, the subject is automatically set to RE: (whatever the original subject was), and the complete text of the original message is inserted at the bottom of the new message. Compose your reply and then click the Send button.

   - If the message was originally sent to several people, you can click the Reply to All button and compose your reply to send a reply to all of the original recipients.

   - If the message was intended for someone else, or if you think someone else should see it (maybe it contains a juicy bit of gossip!), click the Forward button. A new message window appears, allowing you to select the user or users to whom the message should be forwarded. The original message is inserted at the bottom of the new message, with space left at the top for you to type an explanation of why you are forwarding the message. (Hey, Mr. Spacely, get a load of this!)

- To print the message, click the Print button.

- To save the message, click the Save button.

- If the message is unworthy of filing, click the Delete button. Poof! (Actually, the deleted message is sent to the "Deleted Items" folder, from which you can later retrieve it in an emergency. See the section "Using Mail Folders," later in this chapter, for more information.)

5. **If you have additional messages to read, click the Next or Previous buttons to continue reading messages.**

- Click the Next button to read the next message in sequence.

- Click the Previous button to read the previous message.

If you prefer, you can instead close the message you are reading and then double-click the next message you want to read from your Inbox folder.

6. **You're finished!**

Saving an Attachment as a File

If someone is kind enough to send you a message that includes an attached file, you can save the attachment as a separate file by following these steps:

1. **Open the message that has the attachment.**

   You can tell which messages have attachments by looking for the paper-clip icon next to the message title in your Inbox.

2. **Right-click the attachment icon and then choose the Save As command from the pop-up menu.**

   A Save As dialog box appears.

3. **Choose the location where you want to save the file.**

   You can use the controls on the standard Save As dialog box to navigate to a different drive or folder.

4. **Type a file name.**

   Internet Mail, always trying to help you out, proposes a file name. You need to type a new file name only if you don't like the file name that Internet Mail proposes.

5. Click Save.

The attachment is saved as a file.

You can immediately view an attachment by double-clicking on it. If the attachment is a document, Windows 95 launches the appropriate application to open the document. If the attachment is a sound file, Windows 95 plays the sound — provided your computer is equipped with a sound card.

Beware of attachments from unfamiliar sources: they may contain a virus which may infect your computer. Unfortunately, Internet Mail doesn't have any built-in virus protection. If you are concerned about viruses — and you should be — purchase and install separate virus protection software.

Using HTML Formatting

Internet Mail has a nifty feature that enables you to add formatting to your e-mail messages. To accomplish this feat, Internet Mail uses the same HTML formatting codes used to create pages on the Web. Of course, when you send an HTML-formatted message to another Internet user, that user must have a mail program that is capable of reading HTML-formatted messages. Otherwise, your beautiful formats are for naught.

To use HTML formatting, call up the New Message window to compose a new message, and then choose Format➪HTML. A new toolbar appears in the New Message window, as shown in Figure 10-12.

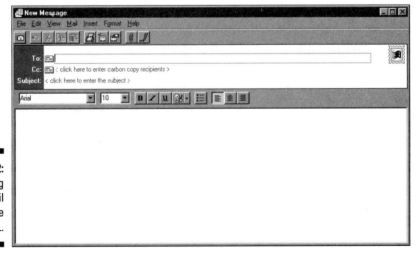

Figure 10-12:
Formatting
an e-mail
message
with HTML.

Table 10-1 shows how you can use the options on the Formatting toolbar to enhance the text in your e-mail messages.

Table 10-1   Options on the New Message Formatting Toolbar

Button	Format
Arial	Changes the font
10	Sets the size of the text font
	Changes the text color
B	Makes the text bold
I	Makes the text italic
U	Underlines the text
	Creates a list formatted with bullets (little dots)
	Left-aligns the text
	Centers the text
	Right-aligns the text

Internet Mail Keyboard Shortcuts

Several keyboard shortcuts are available to you as you compose an e-mail message. Most of these shortcuts, summarized in Table 10-2, are fairly standard throughout Windows, so they should come as no surprise to you.

Table 10-2   Keyboard Shortcuts for Editing E-Mail Messages

Keyboard Shortcut	What the Shortcut Does
Moving and Selecting	
Ctrl+Left arrow	Moves cursor left one word
Ctrl+Right arrow	Moves cursor right one word
Home	Moves cursor to the beginning of the line

(continued)

Table 10-2 *(continued)*

Keyboard Shortcut	*What the Shortcut Does*
End	Moves cursor to the end of the line
Ctrl+Home	Moves cursor to the beginning of the message
Ctrl+End	Moves cursor to the end of the message
Ctrl+A	Selects the entire message
Editing	
Ctrl+X	Cuts the selection to the clipboard so you can paste it in another location
Ctrl+C	Copies the selection to the clipboard
Ctrl+V	Pastes the contents of the clipboard to the location of the insertion point
Ctrl+Delete	Deletes to the end of the word
Ctrl+Z	Undoes the last action you did (unavailable for some actions, such as sending a message)
Shortcuts for reading mail	
Ctrl+F	Forwards the message to another user
Ctrl+R	Replies to the sender of a message
Ctrl+Shift+R	Replies to the sender of a message and all the message's recipients
Ctrl+>	Skips to the next message
Ctrl+<	Returns to the previous message
Other Shortcuts	
Alt+S	Sends the message
F7	Checks the spelling of the message
Ctrl+N	Composes yet another message
Ctrl+K	Checks the names listed in the To: and CC: fields against the Address Book

Using Internet Mail Folders

Internet Mail includes a separate toolbar, called Folders, which enables you to access any of four message folders that are available in Internet Mail. Normally, only the Inbox folder is displayed. You can display other folders by clicking the down-arrow at the right side of the Folders drop-down list. You then select the folder you want to display.

The four message folders are as follows:

- ✔ **Inbox:** Where your incoming messages are stored

- ✔ **Outbox:** Where messages you have written are stored until they are sent to their intended recipients

- ✔ **Sent items:** Where messages are placed after they have been sent

- ✔ **Deleted items:** Where deleted messages are stored (this folder enables you to retrieve a deleted message)

Internet Mail also enables you to create your own message folders. For example, you may want to create separate folders for different categories of messages, such as *work related, friends and family,* and so on. You may also want to create date-related folders for storing older messages. For example, you can create a 1997 folder to save all of the messages you received in 1997. The following sections explain how to work with message folders.

Creating a new folder

Before you start saving important messages, you should first create one or more folders in which to save the messages. You may want to use just a single folder, with a name such as *Saved Items,* or you may want to create several folders for saving messages according to their content. For example, you may create a *Personal Items* folder for personal messages, and a *Business Items* folder for business messages. You have to come up with a good scheme for organizing saved messages, but my advice is to keep your method simple. If you create 40 folders for storing saved messages, you'll never remember which message is in which folder.

To create a new folder, follow these steps:

1. From the Internet Mail main window, choose File➪Folder➪Create.

The New Folder dialog box appears, as shown in Figure 10-13.

Figure 10-13:
Creating a
new folder
for saving
messages.

2. Type a name for the new folder.

For example, type *Work Related.*

3. Click OK.

The folder is created. You'll be able to see it along with the Inbox, Outbox, Sent Items, and Deleted Items folders when you use the Folders drop-down list in the Internet Mail toolbar.

Moving messages to another folder

After you create a folder for your messages, moving a message to the folder is easy. Just follow these steps:

1. From the Inbox, select the message you want to save.

2. Choose Mail⇨Move To.

A menu listing all of the available folders appears.

3. Click the folder to which you want to move the message.

The message moves to the folder you selected and is deleted from the Inbox folder.

If you prefer, you can make a copy of the message rather than move the message. Just choose Mail⇨Copy To instead of Mail⇨Move To. This leaves the original message in place, so the message now appears in both folders.

When you delete a message from your Inbox, the message isn't actually deleted. Instead, it is moved into a folder named Deleted Items. You can "undelete" a deleted message by opening the Deleted Items folder and then moving the deleted message back into your Inbox or some other folder.

Chapter 11

Can We Talk? (Or, Chatting Online)

. . . .

In This Chapter

▶ Getting in to online chats

▶ Chatting with other users using comic book style characters

▶ Using macros to improve your chat efficiency

. . . .

E-mail is an effective means of communication because it is convenient, yet timely. Still, it may take a day or more for someone to respond to your e-mail message. When you absolutely must have instant gratification from your online communications, you need to turn to chat.

A *chat* is an online conversation between two or more Microsoft Network (MSN) users who are signed on to the network at the same time. When you chat with another user, anything you type is almost instantly displayed on the other person's screen, and vice versa. While e-mail is kind of like sending a postcard or a letter, chat is more like talking on the phone.

Chatting on MSN is so simple that you'll get the hang of it right away. You find out the starting details in this chapter.

The Green Chat

If you've never chatted online before, the place to begin is with the MSN simplified chat program found at Chat Central. I call it the Green Chat because it works in a window which has a green border around it, as shown in Figure 11-1. Well, you can't really tell from the black-and-white reproduction that the window border is green, but trust me, it is.

Figure 11-1:
The Green
Chat.

To get to the Green Chat, click Communicate in the Navigation bar, and then select Chat Central from the menu that appears. As you can see, Chat Central is usually a busy place. Messages from all the good folks talking on Chat Central scroll rapidly through the green window, often so fast you can't follow the conversation.

If you want to participate in the fun on Chat Central, just type a message in the message box, and then press Enter. Your message is broadcasted to everyone else. In a matter of moments, someone is bound to reply to your message.

Chat Central is not the MSN main chatting area, however. In fact, Chat Central is meant to be merely a stepping off point for the many other chat rooms on MSN. The real chatting action is done with a special chat program called Microsoft Chat. Most serious chat users don't even bother with Chat Central. Instead, they launch straight into Microsoft Chat as described in the next section.

Starting Microsoft Chat

Although Chat Central is a fine introduction to the world of online chatting, turn to Microsoft Chat, Microsoft's dedicated online chatting program, for serious chatting. You can access Microsoft Chat from within the MSN Program Viewer. I give you the details later in this section. The easiest way to start Microsoft Chat is from the Start menu. Here is the complete procedure for starting Microsoft Chat, and entering one of the many chat rooms available on MSN:

1. Click the Start button on the Windows 95 taskbar, and then choose <u>P</u>rograms⇔Microsoft Chat.

The Connect dialog box, shown in Figure 11-2, appears.

Figure 11-2: The Connect dialog box.

2. Type the name of the chat room you want to join in the <u>G</u>o to chat room text box.

In Figure 11-2, *TheLobby* is already entered in this text box. TheLobby is the name of a Chat Central chat room. If you have just come from Chat Central, TheLobby should be the default chat room. If you've been around the block and know the name of another chat room you'd like to enter, type it instead. For now, stick with TheLobby. For information about how to find other chat rooms, see the section "Changing Rooms," later in this chapter.

3. Click OK.

Microsoft Chat connects you to the chat room, as shown in Figure 11-3.

You can also access Microsoft Chat directly from the MSN Program Viewer. Go to Chat Central, and then click the Chat Search button. This will take you to the page shown in Figure 11-4. Click Show All Chats, Show Top Chats Now, or type a keyword and then click Search to display a list of available chat rooms. Then click on the name of the chat room you want to join. MSN starts Microsoft Chat and automatically connects you to the chat room you selected.

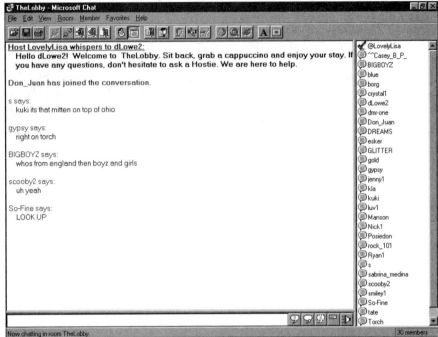

Figure 11-3:
Microsoft
Chat.

Figure 11-4:
Starting
Microsoft
Chat from
the MSN
Program
Viewer.

Understanding the Chat Window

When you first see the Microsoft Chat window, you may be bewildered — especially if you jump into a busy chat room, such as TheLobby, and messages fly by so fast you can't read them. After you become familiar with the chat window and how chatting works, you won't be so overwhelmed.

The chat window is divided into three areas:

✔ **Viewing pane:** The chat itself is in the middle portion of the screen, called the viewing pane. Here you see messages sent by you and others who are chatting. The viewing pane has scroll bars, so you can scroll up to read messages that flew off the screen.

✔ **Member list pane:** Down the right edge of the screen is a member list pane, which lists all of the participants who are currently in the chat room. Each participant is identified with one of three icons:

 A regular participant, who can listen and speak.

 A spectator, who can listen to the conversation, but cannot speak.

 A host, who moderates the chat. The host tries to keep the conversation on track and makes sure no one crosses the bounds of decorum. Cross the line and you may find yourself made a spectator.

✔ **Compose pane:** At the bottom of the screen is the compose pane, where you compose messages that you want to contribute to the chat.

Sending a Message

When you first enter a chat room, your best bet is to eavesdrop for awhile to figure out what is happening. When you get up the nerve to contribute your own messages to a chat, follow these simple steps:

1. **Compose a brilliant message in the message box.**

   The message box is at the bottom of the screen, in the compose pane.

   If you have just entered a chat room, it is customary to send a greeting before jumping into the chat. Type **Hello, Howdy Doody,** or whatever suits your fancy.

   If you are addressing a comment to a specific person, preface your comment with the person's name. For example:

   Hawkeye: Ever heard of the second amendment?

   To create a line break in a message, press Ctrl+Enter. If you press only the Enter key, your message is sent as it is.

2. **When you are ready to send your message, click one of the Send buttons that appears next to the message box.**

The four Send buttons determine how your message is conveyed to the group:

- **Say button:** Sends a normal message. Microsoft Chat prefaces your message with *so-and-so says...*

- **Think button:** Used as an aside. Microsoft Chat prefaces your message with *so-and-so thinks...*

- **Whisper button:** Used to send a private message to a single user. First, select the user from the list of chat participants on the right side of the screen. Then click the Whisper button.

- **Action button:** Used to send a descriptive message, often to suggest body language. For example, *Billy Bob shrugs and wipes his forehead.*

When you compose an action message, keep in mind that Microsoft Chat always adds your name before the message. For example, if your name is John and you send the action message "sits back and enjoys a cold one," Microsoft Chat displays the message "John sits back and enjoys a cold one."

Leaving

When you're tired of chatting, you can leave Microsoft Chat by choosing the File➪Exit command or clicking the Chat window's Close button. If you have been actively participating in the chat, proper chat etiquette is to say goodbye first. But if you haven't been participating in the chat, you can leave without saying goodbye and no one will be offended.

See You In The Funny Papers

Microsoft Chat, like most chat programs, displays the conversation in a chat room as a never ending stream of text. However, Microsoft Chat also offers a unique alternative to plain text: a comic strip version of the chat, as shown in Figure 11-5.

To switch to Comics View mode, click the Comics View button in the toolbar or choose the View➪Comic Strip command.

To return to normal text view, click the Text View button or choose the View➪Plain Text command.

Figure 11-5:
Chatting in
Comics
view.

In Comics view, each person in the chat room is represented by one of several comic strip characters that come with Microsoft Chat. You can choose the character you want to represent you, but if you don't choose, Microsoft chooses one for you free of charge.

When you switch to Comics View, the text mode viewing pane is changed to a series of comic strip panels. In addition, a portion of the member list pane is replaced by an image representing your own character and a gizmo called the Emotion Wheel, which enables you to control your character's facial expressions.

Microsoft has indicated that, in a future release of Microsoft Chat, you will be able to create your own characters. For now, you're limited to the characters that come with Microsoft Chat. Figure 11-6 shows the stock characters. Read "Having It Your Way," later in this chapter, to find out how to choose a character.

The Tom and Ray characters shown in Figure 11-6 don't actually come with Microsoft Chat. Instead, they come from the Tom and Ray chat that is available in CarTalk, which you can access from Channel 4 on the MSN Program Viewer's On Stage menu.

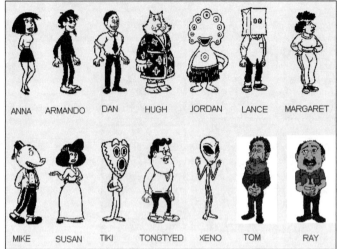

Figure 11-6:
The
characters
that come
with
Microsoft
Chat.

Each time you send a message in the chat room, Microsoft Chat adds your character to the comic strip and includes your message in a bubble. If possible, Microsoft Chat adds your character to the current comic strip frame, zooming back if necessary so that all of the characters in the frame are visible. Whenever the frame gets too crowded, Microsoft Chat creates a new frame and scrolls the entire comic strip so you can see the new frame.

Getting Emotional

Perhaps Microsoft Chat's most surprising feature is that it examines the text of each message and attempts to draw the characters accordingly. Here are some of the inferences Microsoft Chat makes about your messages:

- ✔ If you **SHOUT** something in all capital letters, Microsoft Chat draws your character with a wide open mouth.
- ✔ When your message begins with the word **You** or contains a phrase such as **are you, will you,** or **did you,** your character points to the other person.
- ✔ If you type **LOL** or **ROTFL,** your character laughs.
- ✔ If you type a smiley such as **:), :-), :(, or :-(,** Microsoft Chat draws your character smiling or frowning.
- ✔ If you type **Hi, Howdy, Hello, Welcome,** or **Bye,** your character will wave.

You can also set your own emotion when you send a message by using the Emotion Wheel. To pick an emotion, just click somewhere in the Emotion Wheel. The sample character above the Emotion Wheel changes to show how your character's expression appears when you send your message. To return to a neutral expression, click in the exact center of the Emotion Wheel.

Note that any emotion from the Emotion Wheel overrides any facial expression that would have been selected based on the text of your message.

Getting Personal

In Microsoft Chat, each user can fill out a Personal Information profile, which includes the user's real name and a description of the user. You compose your own description, which can include your interests, hobbies, home town, gender, age, or anything else that may be interesting. (Of course, you should limit the amount of personal information you give out here. Most importantly, don't list your phone number or address.) In the following sections, I show you how to set your own Personal Information profile and how to display the profile for other users.

Setting your Personal Information profile

To set your Personal Information profile, follow these steps:

1. **Choose View⇨Options.**

   The Options dialog box appears, as shown in Figure 11-7. (If the Personal Information options are not displayed, click the Personal Info tab.)

2. **Type your name in the Real Name text box.**

   Of course, there's nothing to stop you from typing **Elvis Presley** or **Jimmy Hoffa**.

3. **Type the name you want to use in the chat rooms in the Nickname text box.**

   Use your first name if you wish, or choose something more interesting, such as **Snoopy** or **Baby Cakes**.

4. **Type your e-mail address in the E-mail address text box.**

   If they have your e-mail address, people will be able to send you e-mail directly from within Chat. This is useful, for example, if someone wants to send you a file as an e-mail attachment.

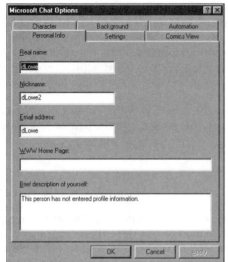

Figure 11-7:
Setting the
Personal
Information
options.

5. **If you have your own home page on the Internet's World Wide Web, type the URL in the WWW Home Page text box.**

   This enables people to visit your home page from within Chat.

6. **Type a description of yourself in the Brief description of yourself text box.**

   Type something interesting about yourself here if you want others to know something about you. You might include information such as what city you live in, what line of work you're in, and so on.

7. **Click OK.**

   Your personal information is updated so that other users can view it.

Getting a member's profile

Microsoft Chat enables you to find out information about the other users who are in a chat room with you, provided that those users have filled out the Personal Information dialog box. To display a chat user's personal information, follow one of these procedures:

✔ Right-click the user's nickname in the member list that appears at the right of the Microsoft Chat window, and then select Get profile from the quick menu that appears.

✔ Select the user's nickname in the member list, and then choose Member⇨Get Profile from the main menu.

Microsoft Chat draws a new frame showing the user's character, with the user's personal information displayed at the top, as shown in Figure 11-8.

Figure 11-8:
Displaying
a user's
profile.

Ignoring Obnoxious Users

Every once in a while, you get into a chat room with someone who insists on dominating the conversation with a constant stream of obnoxious remarks. Or, you may be pestered by a couple of chat users who go on and on about a topic that holds absolutely no interest for you.

Fortunately, Microsoft Chat gives you a way to tune these people out. Just follow these steps:

1. **Select the nickname of the person you want to ignore from the nickname list that appears at the right of the Microsoft Chat window.**

2. **Choose Member⇨Ignore.**

   This causes any messages from the user you silenced to not be displayed on your computer. The ignored user is still able to participate in the chat, and other users see the ignored user's messages as if nothing happened.

Alternatively, you can right-click the member's name in the member list and select Ignore from the pop-up menu that appears.

To reinstate someone you have ignored, repeat the procedure. Select the member in the member list and then choose the Ignore command again.

The person you tune out has no clue what you have done. He or she will keep babbling on, wondering why you never seem to answer. Of course, if no one ever seems to answer you, it could be that *you* are the one who is being ignored!

Having It Your Way

Microsoft Chat enables you to customize the appearance of the chat comic strip in several ways by using the View⇨Options command.

✔ You can select one of the twelve comic characters to represent you in Microsoft Chat.

✔ You can change the background scenery.

✔ You can change the arrangement of comic strip frames used in the Microsoft Chat window.

Changing your image

Wouldn't it be nice if you could just snap your fingers to instantly change your image? Politicians are deft at changing their images, but most of us are not. Microsoft Chat offers a welcome chance to change your image, merely by following this procedure:

1. Choose View⇨Options.

The Options dialog box appears.

2. Click the Character tab.

The Character options appears, as shown in Figure 11-9.

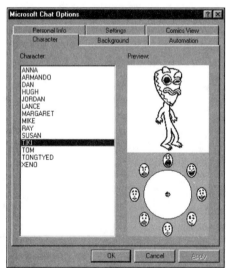

Figure 11-9:
Overhauling your image.

3. Select the character you want to represent you.

As you click on each character name, a picture of the character appears in the Preview window of the dialog box. If you want to see how the character appears with various expressions, you can click in the Emotion Wheel at the bottom right corner of the Options dialog box.

4. Click OK.

Unfortunately, you are limited to the 14 characters provided with Microsoft Chat. Microsoft has hinted that, in a future release, you will be able to create your own characters. But until then, you'll have to be content with the present stock characters.

A change of scenery

You can change the background scenery that Microsoft Chat uses. The scenery change applies only to your computer. You cannot change the background scenery that other users see on their screens. To change the comic strip background, follow these steps:

1. Choose View⇨Options.

The Options dialog box appears.

2. Click the Background tab.

The Background options appear, as shown in Figure 11-10.

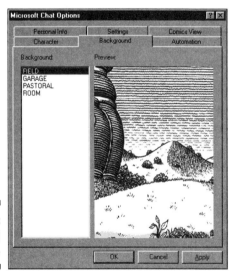

Figure 11-10:
Changing
the scenery.

3. Select the background you want to use.

Microsoft provides four backgrounds with Microsoft Chat: FIELD, GARAGE, PASTORAL, and ROOM.

Actually, the Garage background is designed to work with Bob & Ray's CarTalk chat room, found in On Stage on Channel 4, but you can use it in other chats as well. (If you don't have this background, it's because you haven't yet visited CarTalk's chat room.)

4. Click OK.

Although you can't draw your own characters, Microsoft Chat does enable you to create your own backgrounds. In fact, you can use any graphics file stored in bitmap format (.BMP) file as a background for Microsoft Chat. All you have to do is copy the file you want to use as a background to the folder `c:\Program Files\CChat\ComicArt\Backdrop`. Any bitmap files that appear in this folder are displayed when you call up the Background options.

Changing Rooms

When you get tired of chatting in a room, you can always leave and wander into another room. Just follow this procedure:

1. Say goodbye.

It's rude to leave without saying goodbye, especially if you've been active in the conversation. Send a parting message. And, if you're in a silly mood, type an action message such as **exits stage right,** or **leaves with a bang**.

2. Choose Room⇨Room List.

The Chat Room List dialog box appears, listing all of the chat rooms on your chat server. See Figure 11-11 for a look at this dialog box.

Chat Room List			? ☒

Display chat rooms that contain: [   ]   ☐ Also search in room topics

☑ Show only registered rooms   Members: Min: [0]   Max: [9999]

Room	Members	Topic
#ALTAIR_TALKSHOP	1	Computer Industry Discussion. (US #ALTAIR_TALKSHOP)
#WINDOWS95_TALKSHOP	3	Windows 95 Topics. (US #WINDOWS95_TALKSHOP)
AA_CoffeeShop	2	AA Coffee Shop. (US AA_CoffeeShop)
AchillesHeel	2	Spiritualists & Healers (US AchillesHeel)
AgelessChat	30	Come join the 30+ yrs crowd! (US AgelessChat Chatworld)
AgelessChat1	1	Come join the 30+ yrs crowd! (US AgelessChat Chatworld)
AphroditesChamber	3	A Romantic Haven (US AphroditesChamber)
Bienvenue	7	Acceuil MSN France (FR Bienvenue)
cafe_access	1	The DisAbilities Meeting Place! (US cafe_access)
CafeDuSport	4	Sport (FR CafeDuSport)
chatpoker	9	Chat Games live Poker area. (UK chatpoker)
chatquiz	17	Chat Games live quiz games area. (UK chatquiz)
ChatSpot	1	Drop in chat room--open for use all the time. (US ChatSpot)
Christianity	8	Christianity. (US Christianity)
CupidsCorner	7	Romance Seekers (US CupidsCorner)
Freizeit	8	Hier geht's rund - rund um Freizeit! (DE Freizeit)
FriendlyTap	14	Have a virtual beer with your friends here! (US FrieindlyTap Chatworld)
Herzflimmern	7	Lust auf Flirten? (DE Herzflimmern)
HospitalitySuite	15	A place to get help or offer help to other members. (US HospitalitySuite C...

[Update List] [Go To] [Create Room...] [Cancel]

58 rooms shown   Time of last search: 2:30:58 PM

Figure 11-11:
The Chat
Room List.

3. Double-click on the chat room you want to join.

You're taken to the chat room that you selected.

Unfortunately, Microsoft Chat won't let you visit two chat rooms at one time. However, you can chat in two or more rooms at one time simply by running multiple copies of Microsoft Chat. For example, suppose that you're chatting in the TheLobby chat room, and you want to also drop in to the FriendlyTap chat room. Rather than leave TheLobby, choose Start⇨Programs⇨Microsoft Chat to start up a second instance of Microsoft Chat. Then select FriendlyTap as the chat room. Arrange the windows so that they appear side by side. This way you can monitor both chats.

Using Macros

Microsoft Chat sports a handy feature for chat-a-holics called *macros.* These enable you to summon up your most common responses or messages with a single keystroke. For example, suppose you frequently find yourself typing, **What is the meaning of life?** Rather than type this entire question every time you want to ask it in a chat, you can create a macro for the question. You can then ask the question by pressing the keyboard shortcut that you assigned to the macro.

Creating a macro

Microsoft Chat enables you to create and store up to ten different macros. Each macro is assigned to a combination of the Alt key plus one of the numeric digit keys: Alt+0 through Alt+9. Here is the procedure for creating a macro:

1. Choose the View⇨Options command and then click the Automation tab.

The dialog box shown in Figure 11-12 will be displayed.

2. In the Key Combination list box, choose the key combination you want the macro assigned to.

The possible combinations are Alt+0 through Alt+9.

3. Type a name for the macro in the Name field.

Use a simple name that suggests the content of your macro. For example, type **Life.**

4. Type the text for your macro in the large text box.

For example, type **What is the meaning of life?**

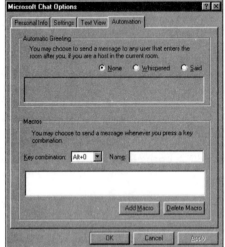

5. Click the Add Macro button.

The macro is created.

6. Repeat Steps 2 through 5 if you want to create additional macros.

Note that you can have only one macro assigned to a keyboard short-cut at a time. For example, if you create a macro for Alt+1, and then create another macro that also uses Alt+1, the original Alt+1 macro is deleted.

7. Click OK.

The Options dialog box is dismissed.

Using a macro

Here are two ways to use a macro you have created:

✔ Press the keyboard shortcut assigned to the macro.

✔ Choose the View⇨Macros command to display a list of your macros, and then select the macro from the list.

Either way, the complete text of your macro will be instantly sent to the chat for all to see.

Chapter 12

A Funny Thing Happened on the Way to the Forum

. . . .

In This Chapter

▶ Exploring the MSN forums

▶ Finding a forum that interests you

▶ Using forum bulletin boards

▶ Downloading files from a forum library

. . . .

*F*orums are the watering holes of MSN, where people with common interests gather to exchange ideas, swap stories, tell jokes, and generally shoot the breeze. At the time that I wrote this book, MSN had about 60 active forums, with topics ranging from Amazing Science to Youth Sports. Forums are constantly being added.

This chapter leads you through the basics of using the MSN forums. You'll find out how to access the MSN forums, how to use forum bulletin boards, how to download files from a forum's file library, and more.

Getting Into a Forum

To access MSN forums, all you have to do is follow these simple steps:

1. **Click Communicate in the Navigation bar, and then choose MSN Forums.**

   The Forum home page is displayed, as shown in Figure 12-1. As you can see, this page includes a list of custom forums. Initially, MSN selects a collection of popular forums to display on this page. Later in this chapter, I'll show you how to customize this page so that it lists your favorite forums.

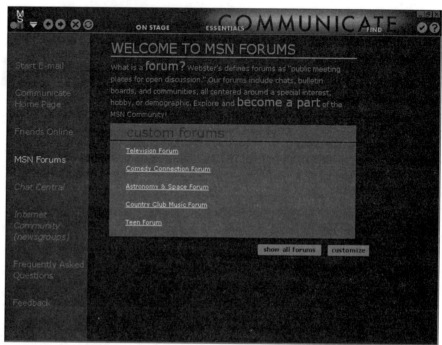

Figure 12-1:
The Forum
home page.

2. Click the Show All Forums button.

A list of all the forums available on MSN is displayed.

3. Scroll through the list until you find a forum that interests you, and then click the forum's name.

You are teleported to the forum you selected. For example, Figure 12-2 shows the opening page for one of my favorite forums, Comedy Connection.

What Are All Those Buttons?

All MSN forum pages have a similar appearance. In particular, all forums sport a row of buttons down the left edge of the page. These buttons are designed to make it easy for you to find your way through the forum's common features. Table 12-1 summarizes the function of the forum buttons.

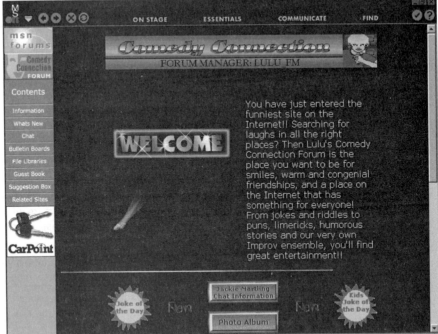

Figure 12-2:
The
opening
page of the
Comedy
Connection
forum.

Table 12-1	What All Those Buttons Do
Button	*What It Does*
msn forums	Returns you to the MSN Forums home page so you can select another forum.
Comedy Connection FORUM	Returns you to the home page for the current forum. The appearance of this button varies depending on the forum you are using.
Contents	Displays a page that lists and describes the various features available in the forum.
Information	Displays a page of information about the forum, such as who is on the forum staff and what online events are upcoming. Check here first to find out what a forum is about. The information page also lists any ground rules for participating in forum chats and bulletin boards.

(continued)

Table 12-1 *(continued)*

Button	What It Does
Whats New	Lists any new features that have been recently added to the forum.
Chat	Displays a list of the chat rooms that are available on the forum. Most forums have several chat rooms. For more information about chatting, see Chapter 11.
Bulletin Boards	Lists the bulletin boards that are available on the forum. I'll have more to say about bulletin boards later in this chapter.
File Libraries	Enables you to access the forum's file libraries, from which you can download files. For more information, see the section "Using File Libraries," later in this chapter.
Guest Book	Provides a place where you can introduce yourself so that other users of the forum will know who you are.
Suggestion Box	A place to send feedback about the forum to one of the forum managers.
Related Sites	Displays a page of MSN and Internet sites which contain similar subject matter.

Using Bulletin Boards

One of the most important features of MSN forums are their bulletin boards. A *bulletin board,* also known as a *BBS,* is a place where you can post messages, called *articles,* on a particular topic, and read messages on the same topic that others have posted. It is a place where people with similar interests gather to share news and information, find out what others are thinking, ask questions, and (hopefully) get answers.

BBS articles are similar to e-mail messages, with a few crucial differences:

- E-mail messages are private, or at least, relatively private. BBS articles are public. Anyone who pops in to a BBS can read any article you, or anyone else, has posted. A BBS article is sometimes called a *post,* which emphasizes the public nature of BBS articles.

- E-mail messages are addressed to a specific individual. BBS articles are addressed to the bulletin board itself.

✔ BBS articles remain in the BBS until the BBS manager decides that they have become too old. Usually, articles appear for a week or so, but articles in the busiest bulletin boards may disappear after only a day or two.

✔ You use the Internet Mail program to create and read e-mail messages. To create and read bulletin board articles, you use a separate program, called Microsoft Internet News.

Welcome to Microsoft Internet News

Forum bulletin boards are handled outside of the MSN Program Viewer by the Microsoft Internet News program — hereafter referred to simply as Internet News, with all due respect to Bill Gates & Co. Internet News is also used for the forum guest book and suggestion box. In short, you won't get far in MSN forums unless you learn how to use Internet News.

Why the funny name — *Internet News?* After all, most of the MSN forums don't have anything to do with news. The Internet News program that handles MSN forum bulletin boards and file libraries was originally developed to handle an Internet feature called *newsgroups*. In the Internet, a newsgroup is similar to an MSN bulletin board: it is a place where users all over the world post articles about subjects of common interest.

The original version of MSN had it's own peculiar program for handling bulletin boards. Then Microsoft realized that bulletin boards and newsgroups were really the same thing. In its infinite wisdom, Microsoft decided that in the latest and greatest version of MSN, all bulletin boards would be handled just like Internet newsgroups and accessed with the Internet News program.

Of course, you can still use Internet News to access Internet newsgroups. In the remainder of this chapter, I focus on those features of Internet News which apply to MSN bulletin boards and file libraries. I cover features specific to Internet News later, in Chapter 19.

Accessing a Bulletin Board

To start Internet News to access a bulletin board, follow these steps:

1. Go to the forum that contains the bulletin board you want to access.

To get there, choose MSN Forums from the Communication menu, click Show All Forums, and then click the forum you want to enter. A screen appears, unique to the forum you select.

2. Click the Bulletin Boards button.

A list of the forum's bulletin boards appears. For example, Figure 12-3 shows the list of bulletin boards for the Comedy Connection forum. Comedy Connection actually contains a dozen bulletin boards, but only the first three are visible in Figure 12-3. You can scroll down the page to see the additional bulletin boards.

3. Click the bulletin board you want to enter.

Internet News opens in a separate window, showing all of the articles that have been posted to the BBS. For example, Figure 12-4 shows how Internet News displays articles from one of the Comedy Connection bulletin boards.

In some cases, you may get a dialog with a message such as `There are new newsgroups. Do you want to view them now?` If that happens, ignore the message and click No to access the bulletin board.

Also, the MSN sign-in dialog box may appear. If so, make sure your MSN user ID and password are correct and click OK to sign in to MSN.

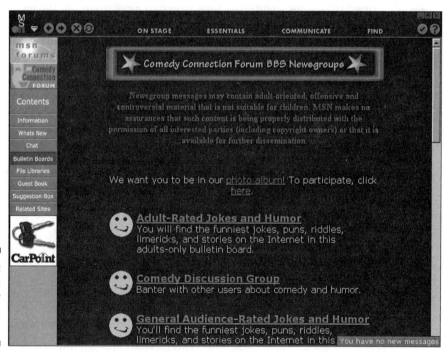

Figure 12-3:
The
Comedy
Connection
forums.

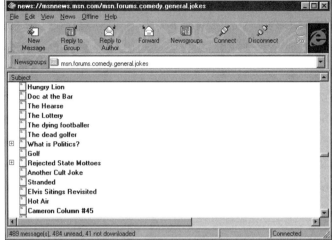

Figure 12-4:
Internet
News
displays a
bulletin
board.

When you are finished using the bulletin board, just close Internet News by choosing the File⇨Exit command or clicking the close button located in the upper right corner of the Internet News window.

Reading Threads

A *thread* is a BBS article, plus any articles that were posted as replies to the original article, articles posted as replies to the replies, and so on. Internet News groups together all of the articles that belong to a thread. A plus sign next to a message title indicates that the article has replies. For example, notice back in Figure 12-4 that the messages *What is politics* and *Rejected state mottos* both have plus signs next to them. That means that there are replies to these messages.

To view the replies, click the plus sign. The plus sign changes to a minus sign and the article's replies are displayed, indented beneath the original article. In some cases, some or all of the replies will also have plus signs. Click these plus signs to reveal replies to the replies. For example, Figure 12-5 shows how the *What is politics* thread appears once all of its replies are expanded.

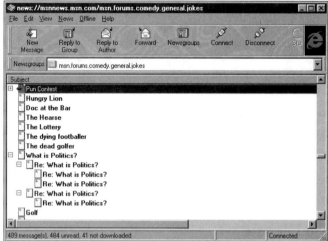

Figure 12-5:
An
expanded
thread.

Reading an Article

To read an article, double-click the article title. The article appears in a separate window, as shown in Figure 12-6. After you finish reading the article, click the article window's Close button to close the window.

To save an article to your computer, choose File➪Save As, or click the Save button.

To print an article, choose File➪Print, or click the Print button.

Figure 12-6:
A bulletin
board
article.

You can go to the next or previous articles by clicking the following buttons:

🖝 Click the Next button to read the next article.

🖝 Click the Previous button to read the previous article.

Replying to an Article

To reply to a BBS posting, follow these steps:

1. Count to ten and then reconsider your reply.

Keep in mind that replying to a BBS is not like replying to e-mail. Only the intended recipient can read an e-mail reply. Any MSN member can read your BBS postings. If you don't really have anything to add to the discussion, why waste time? Go to Step 5.

2. After reading the article you want to reply to, click the Reply to Group button in the toolbar.

A new message window appears, with the subject line already filled in and the original message copied to the bottom of the message area, as shown in Figure 12-7.

3. Type your reply.

Note that composing a reply in Internet News is identical to composing a reply to an e-mail message using Internet Mail. See Chapter 1 for information about composing and editing messages.

4. Click the Send button.

Your article is sent to the newsgroup.

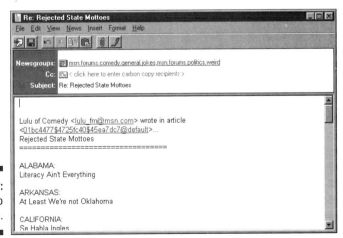

Figure 12-7:
Replying to
an article.

5. You're about to become a published writer.

By default, the complete text of the original article is added to the end of your reply. If the message is long, you may want to delete some, or all, of the original text. If you don't want the original message text to be automatically added to your replies, choose <u>N</u>ews⇨<u>O</u>ptions, click the Send tab, and then deselect the I<u>n</u>clude original message in reply option.

Writing a New Article

When you have finally mustered up the courage to post an article of your own to a BBS, follow these steps:

1. Open the BBS in which you want to post a new article.

Refer back to the section "Accessing a Bulletin Board" for the procedure.

2. Click the New Message button.

A new message window appears.

3. Type a subject for the article in the Subject box.

Make sure that the subject you type accurately reflects the topic of the article — or prepare to get flamed. Being *flamed* doesn't mean that your computer screen actually emits a ball of fire in your direction, singeing the hair off your forearm. It refers to getting an angry — even vitriolic — response from a reader. If your subject line is misleading, at least one MSN user is sure to chew you out for it.

4. Type your message in the message area.

5. If you are worried about your vice-presidential prospects, choose <u>N</u>ews⇨Check Spe<u>l</u>ling.

The spell checker gives you the option to correct any misspelled words.

6. Click the Send button when you're satisfied with your response.

Adding a Signature

Like Internet Mail, Internet News enables you to attach a signature to the end of all your BBS postings. The signature can include any text you wish: Your name, contact information, and perhaps a witty saying. The signature is automatically added to the end of your article postings, so you don't have to type it anew each time.

Here's the procedure for adding a signature to all your BBS postings:

1. Fire up Internet News.

2. Choose the <u>N</u>ews⇨<u>O</u>ptions command.

The Options dialog box appears.

3. Click the Signature tab near the top of the dialog box.

The Signature settings appear, as shown in Figure 12-8.

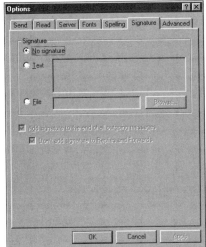

Figure 12-8:
The
Signature
settings.

4. Click the <u>T</u>ext button.

This activates the large text box near the center of the dialog box.

5. Type your signature in the text box.

Try to come up with something clever. For example, **Doug "I Love Dummies" Lowe.**

6. If you do not want the signature automatically added to every article you post, deselect the A<u>d</u>d signature to the end of all outgoing messages checkbox.

If you deselect this check box, your signature will not be automatically added to every article. You can manually attach your signature to any article by clicking the Add Signature button when you create the article.

7. Click OK.

The Options dialog box disappears. The next time you create a message, your signature will automatically be added.

Dealing with Attachments

BBS articles can have *attachments,* which are nontext files such as pictures, sound files, program files, or word processing documents that have been added to an article. To save an attachment as a file on your computer, all you have to do is follow these steps:

1. **Open the article that has the attachment.**

   Unlike Internet Mail, Internet News does not indicate which messages contain attachments by displaying a paper clip next to the subject line. The only way to tell whether a message has an attachment is to open the message.

2. **Right-click the attachment icon.**

   A shortcut menu appears.

3. **Choose the Save As command from the shortcut menu.**

   A standard Save As dialog box appears.

4. **Select the location where you want to save the file.**

   The controls in the Save As dialog box allow you to navigate to any drive or folder.

5. **Check the file name that is proposed for the file.**

   If you don't like it, change the file name.

6. **Click Save.**

   The file is saved. Note that if the file is large, you will have to wait while MSN downloads the file to your computer. A progress bar is displayed to give you an idea of how long the download will take.

You can view an attachment without saving it to disk by double-clicking the attachment.

To add an attachment to an article you want to post, just choose the Insert➪File Attachment command or click the Insert File button, shown in the margin, when you compose the article. Then, select the file you want to attach from the dialog box that appears, and click Attach.

Adding Formatting To Your Articles

Internet News gives you the option of adding fancy formatting, such as **bold** or *italic* type, to your BBS articles. To accommodate this special formatting, Internet News posts its articles in HTML format, using the same formatting codes that are used by pages on the Web.

To enable HTML formatting while composing an article, choose
Format⇨HTML. An additional Formatting toolbar appears in the New
Message window, as shown in Figure 12-9. The Formatting toolbar is identical to the one you use to compose e-mail messages. To find out how to use
it, check out Chapter 10.

Figure 12-9:
Using HTML
formatting
in a
newsgroup
article.

Using Forum File Libraries

MSN is in the process of giving forum file libraries a major overhaul. As a
result, by the time you read this, forum file libraries may look completely
different than they do here — or they may look exactly the same. Most
likely, some forum libraries will resemble the ones shown in this section,
and others will take on a new look as the MSN forums move slowly over to
the new, supposedly more efficient, forum software.

When you access a so-called old style forum file library, you will see a
window such as the one shown in Figure 12-10. This one happens to be a
joke archive in the Comedy Connection forum. You can access forum file
libraries such as this one by clicking the File Library button in any forum,
and then clicking the library you want to open.

 The old style file libraries resemble Windows 95 file folders. In fact, you can
navigate your way through the file libraries folders just as you can through
normal Windows 95 folders. To open a folder, just double-click it. To return
to a previous folder, click the Up One Level button in the toolbar (shown in
the margin).

When you find a file you want to download, double-click the file to open it. A
message window, in which the file itself is represented as an icon, appears.

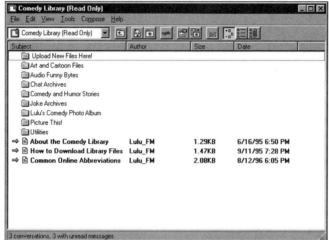

To download the file, double-click the icon and then click the <u>D</u>ownload File button in the dialog box that appears. The file is downloaded to your computer. When the download is complete, MSN plays an obnoxious sound to let you know.

To find the file that you've just downloaded, follow these steps:

1. **Clear your desktop by minimizing open applications.**

2. **Double-click the My Computer icon.**

3. **Double-click the C: drive icon.**

4. **Double-click the folder titled *Program Files*.**

5. **Double-click the folder titled *The Microsoft Network*.**

6. **Double-click the folder titled *Transferred Files*.**

You should then see the file you downloaded in the Transferred Files folder.

Part IV
Great Stuff to Do on The Microsoft Network

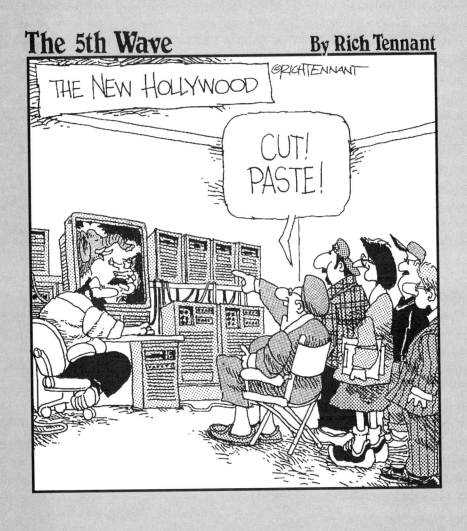

The 5th Wave   By Rich Tennant

THE NEW HOLLYWOOD

CUT! PASTE!

In this part . . .

The four chapters in this part dive into four of MSN's most useful online services. You find out how to manage your finances with Microsoft Investor, how to plan a vacation with the Expedia travel service, how to shop online at the Plaza, Microsoft's electronic shopping mall, and how to buy and sell a car using CarPoint.

Chapter 13

Managing Your Investments with Microsoft Investor

Microsoft Investor is an online investment program that you can use to track your personal fortune. It enables you to keep track of your investments, research the market to help you decide which investments to make, and even enables you to buy and sell stocks and mutual funds online. Whether you're a large or small investor, Investor is a great way to keep track of your stash.

Most of Investor's features are freely available to all MSN users. Some of Investor's features, however, require that you sign up and pay a $9.95 per month subscription fee. In this chapter, I focus on the free features of Investor. If you're a serious investor, you may find that the extra services that are available only to subscribers are well worth the monthly fee.

Getting Started with Microsoft Investor

Microsoft Investor is found in the Essentials section of The Microsoft Network. To start Microsoft Investor, just choose Essentials in the MSN Navigation bar, point to Personal Finance, and then click Investor. Investor comes to life, as shown in Figure 13-1. (The first time you start Investor, you see a Welcome screen and are asked to sit through a four-minute download. When the download finishes, the screen shown in Figure 13-1 is displayed.)

The Investor home page provides a menu of icons which lead you into Investor's main areas. Notice that each of these items also appears on a

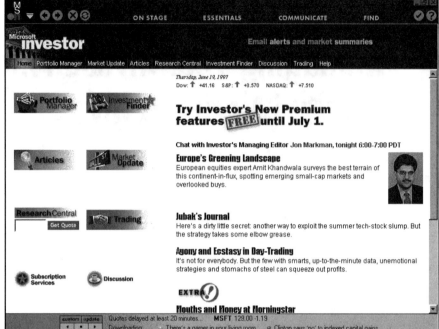

Figure 13-1:
The
Microsoft
Investor
home page.

toolbar near the top of the page. This toolbar is always visible no matter where you are in Investor, so you can always access any of the Investor features with a click of the mouse.

Here are the major Investor features:

✔ **Portfolio Manager:** Enables you to track your personal fortune. All you have to do is tell Portfolio Manager what investments you have made, and you can watch as your fortunes rise and fall.

✔ **Market Update:** Gives you late breaking news about the market. Go to this area to follow the stock exchanges, currency rates, and general business news.

✔ **Articles:** This section of Investor is like an online financial newsletter, with feature articles about the state of the economy, hot investment strategies, and interviews with business leaders.

✔ **Research Central:** When you want to research an investment, Research Central is the place to go. Here, you can get quotes on stocks and mutual funds, historical charts, and company news about selected securities. Those who have popped for the $9.95 monthly subscription fee can get additional information here too, including company profiles, analyst information and recommendations, and financial reports.

✔ **Investment Finder:** Investment Finder is an advanced feature that is available only to those who subscribe to Microsoft Investor and pay the $9.95 per month subscription fee. It enables you to search a huge database of investments to select securities based on criteria such as revenue per employee, P/E ratio, earnings growth, number of left-handed bald-headed customers, and so on.

✔ **Discussion:** Microsoft Investor plays host to several bulletin boards. You need to use the Microsoft News program to participate in these discussion groups. See Chapter 12 for more information.

✔ **Trading:** Although Microsoft is not a licensed broker, Investor includes links to several online brokers. If you have an account with one of these brokers, you can buy and sell securities online.

Getting Stock Quotes

One of the most common uses of Investor is to get a current price on a stock or mutual fund. Stock quotes are handled through the Investor Research Central section.

The quotes you receive from Investor are delayed at least 20 minutes, so the information is not quite up-to-the-minute. What do you expect from a free service?

Getting a quote if you already know the symbol

If you know the symbol of the stock or fund you want, you can get a quote by following these steps:

1. **On the Investor home page, type the stock or fund symbol into the text box that appears immediately below the Research Central icon.**

   For example, to get a quote on Microsoft, type **msft** in the text box.

2. **Click the Get Quote button.**

   The stock quote you requested is displayed, as shown in Figure 13-2.

3. **To get another quote, type a different symbol in the Name or Symbol text box and then click Enter.**

   You don't have to go back to the home page to do this. Just type in another name or symbol and click Enter.

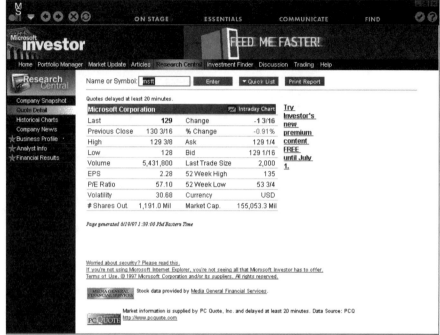

Figure 13-2:
I should
have
bought
Microsoft at
53 3/4.

What if I don't know the symbol?

If you don't know the symbol for the stock or fund you want, don't panic. Just follow these steps:

1. On the Investor home page, type the company or fund name into the text box that appears beneath the Research Central icon.

For example, type **Acme.**

2. Click the Get Quote button.

The Find Symbol dialog box appears, as shown in Figure 13-3.

3. Click the Find button.

Microsoft Investor looks up all of the companies that match the company name you entered, and then displays the results, as shown in Figure 13-4. In many cases, more than one symbol and company name is listed.

4. Click the company you want to look up, and then click OK.

The Find dialog box disappears, and the quote for the company you selected is displayed.

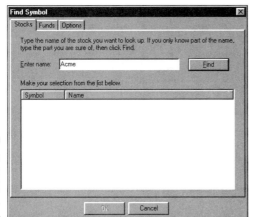

Figure 13-3:
The Find
Symbol
dialog box.

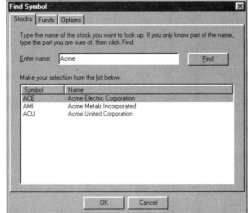

Figure 13-4:
More than
one Acme
company is
listed.

Charting a stock's performance

You can easily display a chart of a stock's or mutual fund's past performance. First, call up the company or fund quote (see the section "Getting a
quote if you already know the symbol," earlier in this chapter). Then click
the Historical Charts button that appears to the left of the quote information. Investor grinds and churns for a moment, and then displays a chart
similar to the one shown in Figure 13-5.

The top part of the chart in Figure 13-5 shows the movement of the stock
price for the past year. The bottom part shows the trading volume for the
same time period.

Figure 13-5:
Charting a
stock.

You can change from a price history chart to a price performance or income growth chart by clicking the Chart button that appears to the right of the chart, and then selecting the type of chart you want to display. You can also change the period shown in the chart from one year to one week, one month, one quarter, three years, five years, or ten years by clicking the Period button and then selecting the time period you want.

To plot a graph for two stocks together, type the symbol for the second stock you want to chart in the Compare with text box, and then click Add. A second stock is added to the chart so that you can compare the performance of the two stocks. You can add additional stocks to the chart in the same manner. When you add additional stocks to the chart, the additional stocks will have a check box next to them. To remove a stock from the chart, all you have to do is click this check box to deselect the stock you want removed.

For even more control over the chart, click the Chart Options button. This brings up a Price Chart Options dialog box, which enables you to set options such as whether or not to show dividends and splits, price limit lines, moving averages, and other helpful chart goodies.

Managing Your Portfolio

You can use Investor to track your entire investment portfolio by using the Portfolio Manager. To access Portfolio Manager, click the Portfolio Manager icon on the Microsoft Investor home page or click Portfolio Manager from the menu bar that appears on all of the Investor pages. Either way, you'll be taken to Portfolio Manager, shown in Figure 13-6.

The following sections show you how to perform the basic tasks you need to use to track your investments using Portfolio Manager.

Setting up an account

When you first start Portfolio Manager, you are set up with two sample accounts, named My Sample Account and My Sample Watch Account. The first thing you should do is delete both of these accounts by following these steps:

1. **Start Portfolio Manager by starting Investor (select Investor from Essentials⇨Personal Finance) and then clicking Portfolio Manager.**

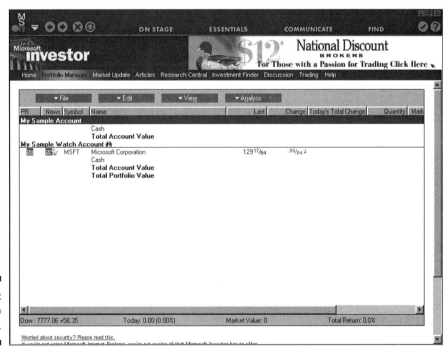

Figure 13-6: Portfolio Manager.

Figure 13-7:
This
annoying
dialog box
appears
when you
delete the
sample
accounts.

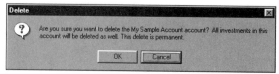

2. **Click the My Sample Account line to select the first sample account.**

3. **Press the Delete key.**

   The Delete dialog box, shown in Figure 13-7, appears.

4. **Click OK.**

   The My Sample Account account is deleted, and the My Sample Watch Account is highlighted.

5. **Press the Delete key again.**

   The Delete dialog box appears again.

6. **Click OK.**

   My Sample Watch Account is deleted.

How secure is Portfolio Manager?

You may be skeptical about keeping track of your confidential financial information using Portfolio Manager, which runs over the Internet. Isn't there a risk that someone else might be able to get your portfolio data and find out how much — or how little — you've stashed away?

Not really. The financial information you enter into Portfolio Manager is never actually transmitted over the Internet. Instead, all of the financial information is kept in a file on your very own hard disk. Not even Bill Gates himself can find out how much Microsoft stock you own.

If you're worried that someone might snoop around your computer and stumble across your financial secrets, you can always assign a password to your portfolio. In Portfolio Manager, click Edit, and then choose Preferences. In the Preferences dialog box that appears, click the Security tab and select High as a Security Level. Then click the Create Portfolio Password Now button and type the password you want to use. You will then have to supply a password each time you access Portfolio Manager.

Now you're ready to create an account for your own portfolio. Follow these steps:

1. **Click File to reveal the File menu, and then choose Ne̲w Account.**

   The Portfolio Manager New Account Wizard dialog box appears, as shown in Figure 13-8.

2. **Click Ne̲xt.**

   The second page of the Wizard appears, as shown in Figure 13-9.

3. **Type a name for your account in the A̲ccount Name text box.**

   For example, type **Retirement account** or **College fund**.

Figure 13-8:
The
Portfolio
Manager
New
Account
Wizard
dialog box.

Figure 13-9:
Give your
account a
name.

4. **Skip the options.**

The other two options on this screen enable you to set up a *Watch Account,* which is an account that tracks investments you don't actually own, and an *Associated Cash Balance* account, which keeps a cash balance for your account. Skip both of these options for now.

5. **Click <u>N</u>ext.**

The last page of the Wizard appears, as shown in Figure 13-10.

6. **Click Finish.**

The account is created and displayed in Portfolio Manager, as shown in Figure 13-11.

Buying a stock or mutual fund

To add an investment to an account, follow the bouncing ball through the steps described in the following procedure:

1. **Click the Edit button to summon the Edit menu, and then choose the Record a <u>b</u>uy command.**

The Record a Buy dialog box, shown in Figure 13-12, appears.

2. **Type the symbol for the investment in the <u>S</u>ymbol text box.**

For example, type **msft** if you want to buy Microsoft.

If you don't know the stock's symbol, click the <u>F</u>ind Symbol button. This summons the Find Symbol dialog box, which was shown back in Figure 13-3. Type the name of the company whose symbol you don't know, and then click <u>F</u>ind. A list of companies appears. Select the one you want, and then click OK to return to the Record a Buy dialog box.

Figure 13-10: The Chart Wizard is finished.

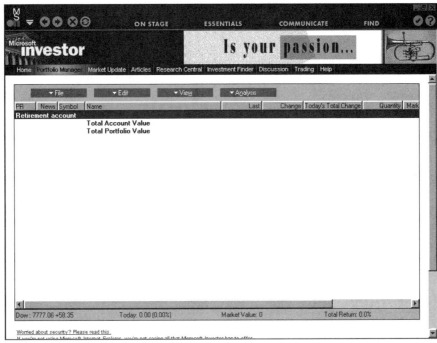

Figure 13-11:
A new
Portfolio
Account, just
waiting for
investments.

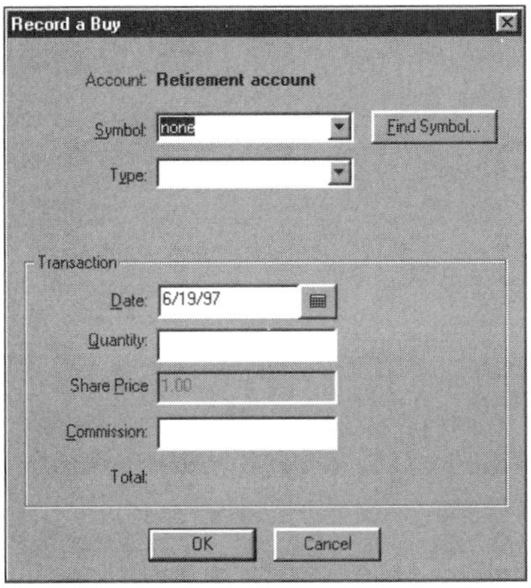

Figure 13-12:
Recording
a buy.

3. **Select the investment type from the Type drop-down list.**

   The investment types include Bond, Certificate of Deposit, Employee
   Stock Option, Index, Money Market Fund, Mutual Fund, Option, or Stock.

4. **Select the Reinvest income if received option if you want income to
   be reinvested.**

5. **Enter the date, number of shares, purchase price, and amount of commission in the appropriate text boxes.**

6. **Click OK.**

The Record a Buy dialog box disappears and a line is added to the account showing the stock you just purchased.

Just my luck. I bought 100 shares of Microsoft at $125 and immediately lost $87.50. Oh well. Investor guarantees that it can track your investments — it doesn't guarantee that your investments will actually make money.

Selling a stock or mutual fund

When you're ready to unload an investment, follow these steps:

1. **In the Portfolio Manager, click the investment you want to sell.**

2. **Click the Edit button, and then choose the Record a sell button.**

The Record a Sell dialog box appears, as shown in Figure 13-13.

3. **If you don't want to sell all of your shares, type the number you do want to sell into the Quantity text box.**

4. **Type the selling price in the Share Price text box.**

Hopefully, this amount is more than what you paid for the investment.

5. **Type any commission amount in the Commission text box.**

6. **Click OK.**

Your portfolio is updated to reflect the sold investment.

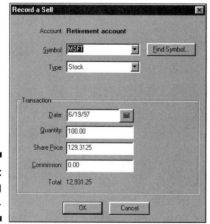

Figure 13-13:
Recording
a sell.

Charting your account

You can create a chart of your portfolio's performance by clicking the Analysis button and then choosing Portfolio Charting from the menu that appears. Initially, the chart will resemble the one shown in Figure 13-14, but you can change the appearance of the chart in several ways.

To change the chart type, click the Chart button, and then choose from one of three chart types that appears: Investment Performance, Investment Value, or Investment Allocation. The default setting is Investment Value.

To change the period of time to be charted, click the Period button, and then choose the time period you want to show. The default setting is YTD.

You can select one of three Chart by options: Account, Security, and Type. If you choose Account, your entire account's value is shown in the chart. If you choose Security, the investment value of each security you own is listed separately. If you choose Type, the various types of investments – stocks, bonds, mutual funds, and so on, is listed separately.

To print the chart, click the Print Chart button. To dismiss the chart so you can return to Portfolio Manager, click the Close button at the upper-right corner of the Portfolio Charting window.

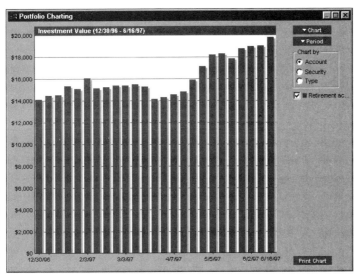

Figure 13-14:
Charting
your
portfolio.

More detail for financial gurus

Portfolio Manager is capable of tracking much detailed information about your investments. By default, the following information is shown from left to right for each security (stock or fund) you buy:

- ✔ An icon that displays when there is an announcement about the security.
- ✔ An icon that appears whenever there is news about the security.
- ✔ The security symbol.
- ✔ The security name.
- ✔ The most recent trading price.
- ✔ The difference between the current price and yesterday's closing price.
- ✔ The total change in value for this investment so far today.
- ✔ The number of shares you own.
- ✔ The market value of your shares.
- ✔ The total gain or loss for this security.
- ✔ The percentage gain or loss for this security.

If this information isn't enough, you can add the following fields to the Portfolio Manager investment listing:

- ✔ Cost basis
- ✔ Average cost
- ✔ Income
- ✔ Price appreciation
- ✔ Total return
- ✔ Total annualized return
- ✔ % of portfolio
- ✔ Last updated
- ✔ Currency
- ✔ Type
- ✔ Price
- ✔ Commissions
- ✔ % Change
- ✔ Volume
- ✔ High
- ✔ Low

- ✔ Open
- ✔ Close
- ✔ 52-Week High
- ✔ 52-Week Low
- ✔ Ask
- ✔ Bid
- ✔ Size of last sale
- ✔ EPS
- ✔ PE Ratio
- ✔ Shares outstanding
- ✔ Market capitalization
- ✔ Volatility
- ✔ Strike price
- ✔ Expiration date
- ✔ Vested value
- ✔ Memo

To add this extra detail, click the Edit button and then choose Columns Displayed from the menu that appears. This summons the Column Settings dialog box, which is shown in Figure 13-15.

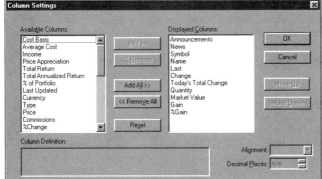

Figure 13-15:
The Column
Settings
dialog box.

From this dialog box, you can add an additional column to the Portfolio Manager display by clicking the column you want to add in the Available Columns list, and then clicking Add. To remove a column, click the column you want to remove in the Displayed Columns list and then click Remove.

To rearrange the order of the columns, click the column you want to change in the Displayed Columns list and then click the Move Up or Move Down button to move the column up or down in the list.

When the columns are set up the way you want, click OK.

Backing up

If you use Portfolio Manager to track your financial information, you should periodically back up your portfolio just in case you accidentally delete your account or mess up a trade. To back up your portfolio, follow these steps:

1. **In Portfolio Manager, click the File button and then choose Backup from the menu.**

   The Save As dialog box, shown in Figure 13-16, appears.

2. **Type a name in the File name text box.**

   I suggest typing something along the lines of **Portfolio Backup**.

Figure 13-16:
Backing up
your
portfolio.

3. Choose a location for the backup.

Funny thing — the Save As dialog box defaults to the Windows folder
for the backup, but if you try to save the backup in the Windows folder,
you get an error message telling you that isn't allowed. Choose a different folder to save your backup.

I suggest you back up to the root directory by clicking the Up One Level
button once, and then clicking the New Folder button and create a new
folder named *Portfolio Backup*. Then save the backup in the new folder.

4. Click OK.

Your backup is saved.

If you accidentally mess up your portfolio and you want to restore from the
backup you made, click File and choose the Restore Backup command.
When the Open dialog box appears, double-click the backup file you previously created.

When you restore a backup file, any changes you made to your portfolio
since the last time you backed up will be lost.

Chapter 14

Planning a Vacation with Microsoft Expedia

. . . .

In This Chapter

▶ Signing up for Expedia

▶ Planning a trip

▶ Purchasing airplane tickets online

▶ Reserving a hotel room

▶ Renting a car

. . . .

*M*icrosoft Expedia is an online travel agent that you can use to plan your next vacation or business trip. With Expedia, you can shop for airline tickets to get the best fare and travel schedule for your trip. And you can reserve hotel rooms and even make car rentals. The only thing Expedia cannot do for you is pack.

Signing Up

Before you can use Expedia to plan a trip, you have to sign up. Expedia doesn't cost anything extra, but member identification is required before you can access the Expedia reservation system. To sign up for Expedia, just follow these steps:

1. **Call up Expedia by pointing to Essentials in the MSN Program Viewer's Navigation bar, pointing to Travel, and then clicking on Expedia.**

   The Expedia home page appears, as shown in Figure 14-1.

Figure 14-1:
The Expedia
home page.

2. Click Travel Agent.

The Travel Agent link is found in the menu bar that appears near the top of the page. When you click it, the page shown in Figure 14-2 appears.

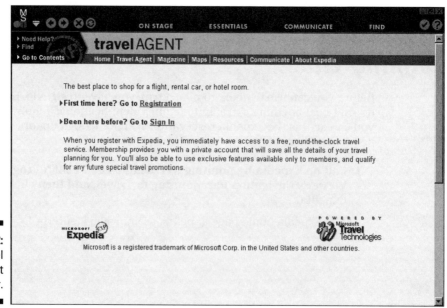

Figure 14-2:
The travel
Agent front
door.

3. **Click Registration.**

   You go to a special Registration Wizard page, shown in Figure 14-3.

4. **Make sure the Secure Connection option is selected, and then click Continue.**

   The Secure Connection option ensures that personal information sent between your computer and the Expedia computers is encrypted so that spies and sinister agents can't intercept it and use it later to blackmail you.

   Next, the Member Information page appears as shown in Figure 14-4.

5. **Fill out all of the information on the Member Information page.**

   The page is big, so be sure to scroll down to see all of it. The Member Information page asks for seven tidbits of information:

   • Your first and last name.

   • Your e-mail address.

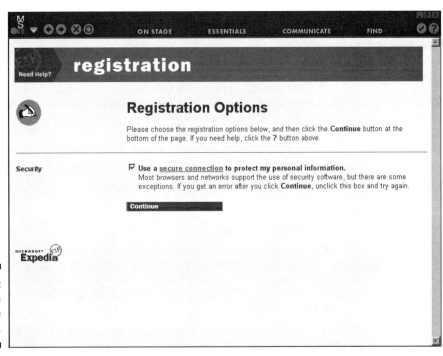

Figure 14-3:
The
Registration
Wizard.

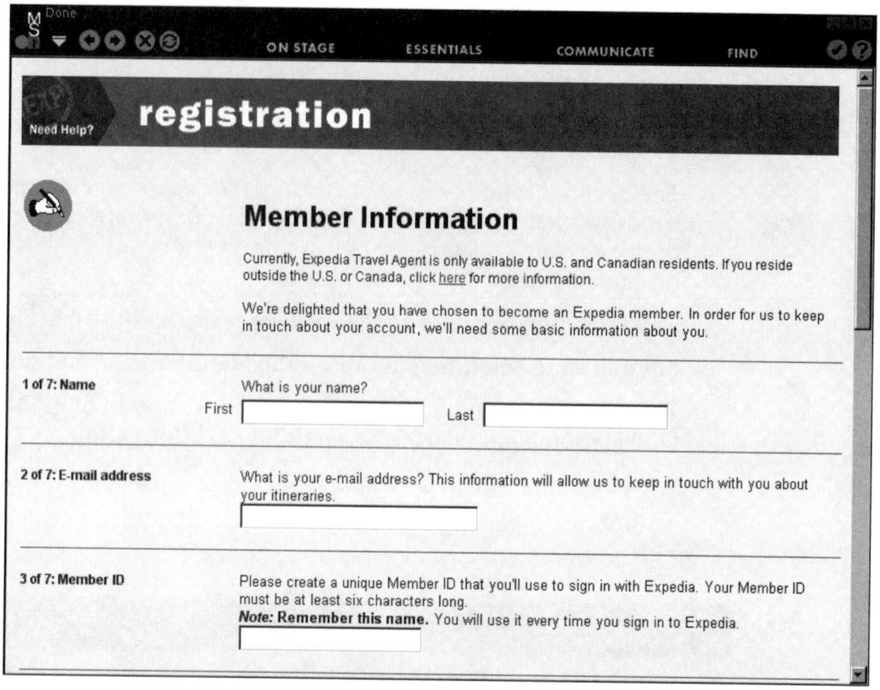

Figure 14-4:
Expedia
needs to
know a
bunch of
stuff
about you.

- A member ID, which you will use later to access the system. Write this down — you'll need to remember this ID.

- A password. Write this one down, also, so you'll remember it.

- The country you live in and your zip code.

- Your local airport.

- Whether or not you want to receive special travel promotions via e-mail.

6. **Click Continue.**

   If all is well, a confirmation page is displayed so that you can verify that the information you gave Expedia is correct. If you forgot to enter information, or if you entered incorrect information (such as an airport that doesn't exist), Expedia redisplays the Member Information page with error messages.

7. **Fix the incorrect entries, if you made any, and then click Continue again.**

8. **Read over the information shown on the confirmation page. If the information is correct, click I ACCEPT. If not, click Change and return to Step 5.**

9. **You're done!**

   You now have an Expedia account set up.

Signing In (After You Have Signed Up)

To access the Expedia Travel Agent once you have signed up, return to Expedia's home page and click Travel Agent again. The screen which was shown back in Figure 14-2 reappears. Then, follow these steps:

1. **Click Sign In.**

   The Sign In screen, shown in Figure 14-5, is displayed.

Figure 14-5:
Expedia
waits for
you to
sign in.

2. Make sure the Expedia Account and Secure Connection options are checked; then click Continue.

You are automatically signed in to Expedia using the member ID and password you created when you signed up. Note that the signing in procedure is automatic; you don't have to actually type in your member ID and password. A page indicating that automatic sign in was successful appears as soon as you are signed in.

3. When the Secure Automatic Sign in Successful page appears, click Continue.

The Travel Agent main page appears at last, as shown in Figure 14-6.

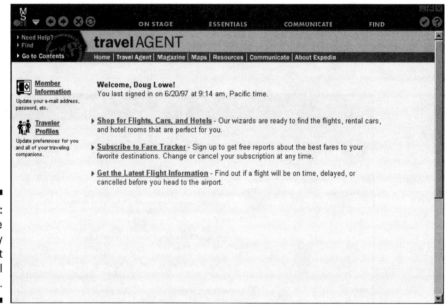

Figure 14-6:
You've finally arrived at the Travel Agent page.

Creating an Itinerary

In Expedia, each trip you plan is called an *itinerary*. Before you can shop for airplane tickets, hotel reservations, or car rentals, you must first create an itinerary. To do so, follow these steps:

1. **From the Travel Agent page (refer to Figure 14-6), click Shop for Flights, Cars, and Hotels.**

   The Select Itinerary page, shown in Figure 14-7, appears.

2. **Click Start a New Itinerary.**

   The New Itinerary page appears, as shown in Figure 14-8.

3. **Shop for airplane tickets, car rentals, and hotel reservations.**

Once you have started a new itinerary, you can complete the itinerary by shopping for airplane tickets, hotel reservations, and car rentals. The steps for these procedures are described in the following sections.

Figure 14-7:
The Select
Itinerary
page.

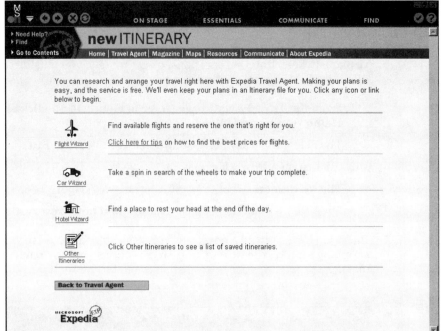

Figure 14-8:
The New
Itinerary
page.

Here are a couple of thoughts to ponder about itineraries, before we get into the detailed procedures for reserving flights, rooms, and cars:

✔ When you have added at least one flight, hotel room, or car rental to your itinerary, an itinerary page is displayed showing your itinerary so far. From this page, you can add additional flights, rooms, or car rentals. You can also print the itinerary by clicking Print, or you can delete the entire itinerary by clicking Delete.

✔ You can add flights, hotels, or cars to your itinerary in any order you wish. And once you've added an item to your itinerary, you can easily go back and change or delete that item.

✔ Expedia can remember your itinerary from one session to another. So you can work on your itinerary today, forget about it for a few days, and then work on it some more.

✔ Expedia can keep track of more than one itinerary for you at a time.

We Can Fly!

The first step in preparing an itinerary is arranging your flight plans. Just follow the bouncing ball through these steps:

1. **From the New Itinerary page, click the Flight Wizard icon.**

   The Flight Wizard comes to life, as shown in Figure 14-9.

2. **Choose Roundtrip, One Way, or Multiple Destinations from the tabs at the top of the page.**

   The procedures for Roundtrip, One Way, and Multiple Destination itinerary trips are similar. The rest of this procedure assumes you are planning a simple round trip itinerary — Los Angeles to New York.

3. **Type the city or airport code you are departing from in the From field.**

   If you know the airport code for the city you'll be traveling from, type the airport code. If you don't know the airport code, just type the city. For this example, I typed *LAX* for the From airport.

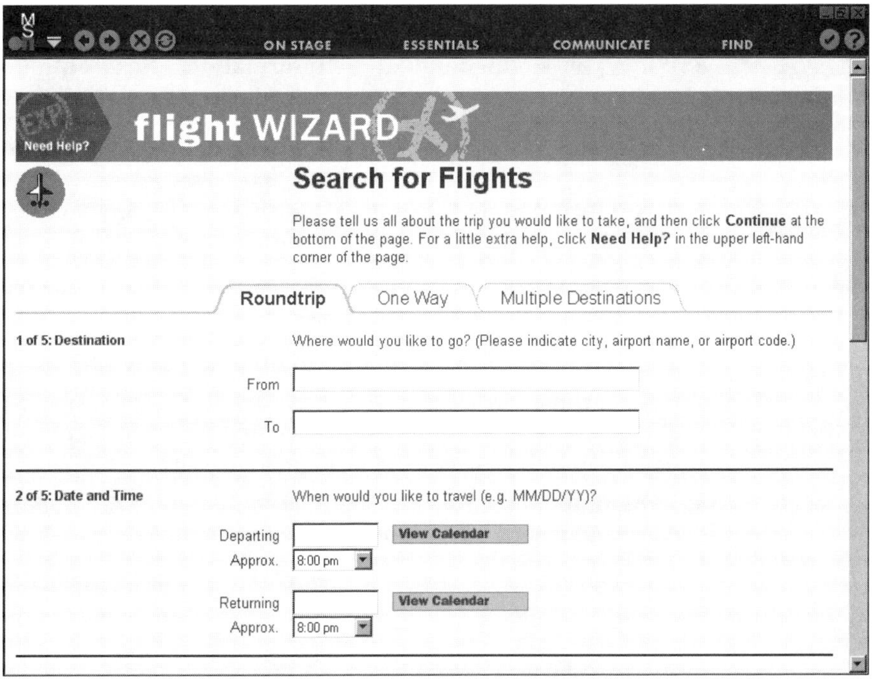

Figure 14-9:
The Flight Wizard is ready to gather information about your flights.

4. Type the city or airport code you are traveling to in the To field.

Again, type the airport code if you know it. If you don't, just type the city. You'll be able to choose from a list of airports for that city later.

5. Type the departure date in the Departing field, and then select your preferred departure time from the drop-down list.

6. Do the same for the return date and preferred arrival time.

7. Scroll down the page and fill out the rest of the information required by the Flight Wizard.

In addition to the cities and departure and return dates, the Flight Wizard needs the following information:

- The number of passengers, and how many of them are adults, children, infants, and seniors.

- Your ticket preferences. In particular, your preferred class (coach, first, or business), airline (any airline or a specific airline), whether or not you want to limit the search to just flights that have no change penalties or advance purchase restrictions, and whether to search for direct flights only.

- What to show first: the best priced flights, or those flights that most closely match your departure and arrival times.

8. When you've filled out all the information, click Continue.

Expedia searches through its massive database of flight information and displays the flights that best match your request, as shown in Figure 14-10.

9. Scroll through the list of flights until you find one you like and then click the Choose and Continue option for that flight.

You are rewarded with a page that lists the details of the flight you have selected, similar to the one shown in Figure 14-11.

10. Carefully read over the details of the flight you have selected.

Pay special attention to the flight restrictions. Make sure you understand whether or not the ticket is refundable, whether or not change or cancellation fees exist, and other restrictions.

11. If the flight is the one you want, scroll down to the bottom of the page and select the You must check here box.

This indicates that you have read and understand the restrictions.

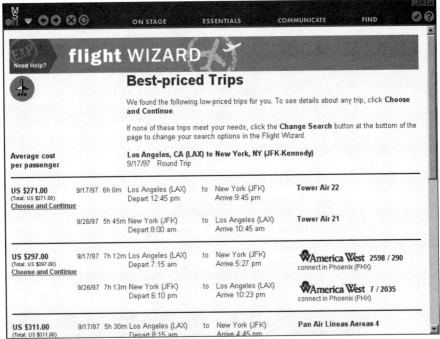

Figure 14-10:
Expedia displays a bunch of flights.

Figure 14-11:
Details for a flight.

12. If you want to reserve the ticket now, click the Reserve button. Otherwise, click the Add to Itinerary button.

If you click the Reserve button, you are taken to a page that gives you the option of holding the ticket 24 hours or actually purchasing the ticket. You'll have to supply your credit card information at this point.

If you click the Add to Itinerary button, the flight is added to your itinerary, but no ticket is reserved or purchased. This is a good way to plan a tentative trip without actually purchasing tickets, but keep in mind that by the time you get around to purchasing the tickets, the flight may by full.

Either way, when you finish the Flight Wizard, the Saved Itinerary page appears, which shows the status of your itinerary so far. Figure 14-12 shows an itinerary with a flight added but not reserved. From this page, you can reserve the flight by clicking Reserve, change the flight information by clicking Change Flights, or delete the flight by clicking Delete.

You are now ready to proceed to the next step: reserving a hotel room.

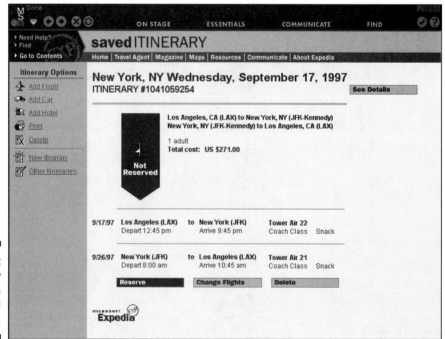

Figure 14-12:
An itinerary with an unreserved flight.

Booking a Room

Unless you plan to sleep on a park bench, you'll want to book a hotel reservation as a part of your itinerary. When you finish making your flight plans, Expedia displays a Saved Itinerary page, which shows the status of your itinerary so far. This page was shown in Figure 14-12. From this page, you can make hotel reservations by following these steps:

1. From the Saved Itinerary page, click Add Hotel.

This fires up the Hotel Wizard, shown in Figure 14-13.

2. Fill in all the information requested by the Hotel Wizard.

The Hotel Wizard needs the following information:

- **The location:** You can indicate that you want a hotel in a city, near an airport, or near a major attraction, such as Disneyland or Yellowstone. If you have added a flight to your itinerary, the city is automatically set to your destination city, but you can change to any city you want.

- **A hotel chain:** If you have a preference, you can select a hotel chain.

Figure 14-13:
The Hotel
Wizard.

You can also direct the Wizard to limit its search to hotels that can be reserved online, and to display the hotels in a map form rather than in a list (this option works only for certain cities).

- **The price range:** Options are: under $75, $75–149, $149–225, over $225, or All. Of course, in New York city, anything under $225 is probably a flea trap.

- **Amenities:** Nonsmoking, wheelchair accessible, restaurant, exercise room, free children, and swimming pool.

3. **When all the information is filled in, click Continue.**

   After a moment of deep thought, Expedia displays a list of hotels that meet your criteria, as shown in Figure 14-14.

4. **Click the hotel you're interested in to display additional information about the hotel.**

   The display will include information such as the types of accommodations, amenities available at the hotel, telephone numbers, and so on.

5. **Click the Check Room Available button to see what rooms are available.**

   The Check Availability page, shown in Figure 14-15, appears.

Figure 14-14: Expedia suggests these fine establishments.

Figure 14-15:
Checking for
available
rooms.

6. **Fill out the information in the Check Availability page.**

   Type in the following information:

   - The number of adults and children staying.
   - The Check In date.
   - The Check Out date.

7. **Click Continue.**

   If rooms are available on the dates you indicated, a list of the available rooms appears, as shown in Figure 14-16.

   If no rooms are available, you'll have to try another hotel or change your dates.

8. **Click the room you're interested in.**

   A page of detailed information about the room will be shown.

9. **To reserve the room, click Reserve. Or, click Add to Itinerary to add the room but not actually reserve it.**

   If you elect to reserve the room, you'll have to supply your credit card information again. If you reserve the room, or just add it to your itinerary, the Saved Itinerary page reappears. This time, the room is indicated on the itinerary.

Figure 14-16:
Lots of
rooms are
available for
this date.

You're done! From the Saved Itinerary screen, you can easily change or cancel your hotel reservation and add additional hotel reservations.

To get around while you're there, you'll want to rent a car.

Renting a Car

To rent a car using Expedia's car rental service, just follow these steps:

1. From the Saved Itinerary page, click Add Car.

The Car Wizard page appears, as depicted in Figure 14-17.

2. Fill in all the information the Car Wizard wants.

The Car Wizard needs to know:

- The location where you want to pick up the car.
- The dates you need the car.
- The type of car you want to rent.
- The company you prefer.

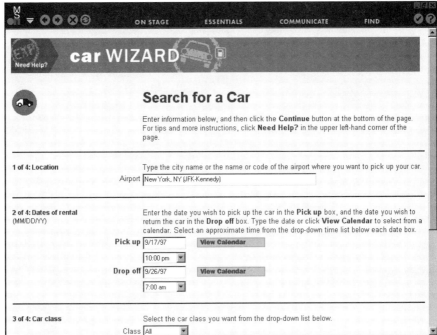

Figure 14-17:
The Car
Wizard.

3. Click Continue.

You get a list of possible rentals, as shown in Figure 14-18.

4. Click the car you want to rent.

Expedia displays a page of detailed information about the car you selected.

5. To reserve the car, click Reserve to reserve the car. Click Add to Itinerary to add the car to your itinerary without actually reserving it.

If you choose to rent the car, you get to type in your name, credit card number, and all that good stuff. Oh boy!

Eventually the Saved Itinerary page reappears with — you guessed it — your car rental information added.

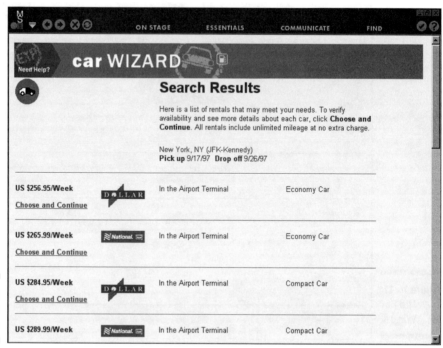

Figure 14-18:
Cars you
can rent.

Chapter 15

Shopping at the Plaza

· ·

· ·

*I*f you enjoy shopping, the MSN Plaza is a great place to hang out. The Plaza is an online shopping mall, and it's small but growing. Currently seven stores are at the Plaza, and all seven of these stores enable you to shop and actually purchase products online. The Plaza is the MSN equivalent of a home shopping network.

Welcome to the Plaza

To get to the Plaza, click Essentials in the MSN Program Viewer Navigation bar, point to Shopping, and then click The Plaza on MSN. The Plaza home page appears, as shown in Figure 15-1.

Figure 15-1:
Welcome to
the Plaza
on MSN.

The Plaza boasts eight stores that allow you to shop and purchase products online. Each store maintains its own online shopping site. Microsoft does not have control over the appearance of these online stores. As a result, each online store has a slightly different look and feel.

In the following sections, I briefly describe the features of the eight online stores. Then I show you how to purchase a product online from Tower Records, which is how you purchase a product from any of the stores.

American Greetings

American Greetings, whose home page is shown in Figure 15-2, is an online gift shop that sells and delivers the following types of gift products:

✔ Personalized greeting cards

✔ Gift baskets

✔ Animated greeting cards that run on PC or Macintosh computers

✔ Chocolates

✔ Ties

✔ Other cool gift ideas

You don't have to sign up to shop at American Greetings, but American Greetings does have a membership option, which enables you create an online address book so you can easily send gifts to your friends.

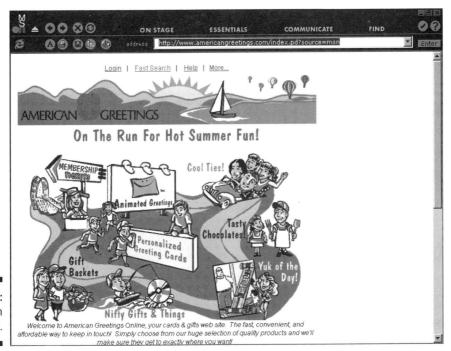

Figure 15-2:
American
Greetings.

AtOnce Software

AtOnce Software is an online software store that you to purchase software and download it immediately to your computer. You can't purchase huge programs, like Microsoft Office, because such programs take hours to download. You can choose from hundreds of smaller but equally useful programs, with moderate prices — typically between $10 and $40. Figure 15-3 shows the AtOnce Software home page.

When you find a program that you want to purchase from AtOnce Software, first check to make sure that the program will run on your computer. Each program includes a list of system requirements so that you can make sure your computer passes muster. Then you simply click the Download & Buy icon to download the software to your computer. The download takes a couple of minutes, depending on the size of the program and the speed of your MSN connection.

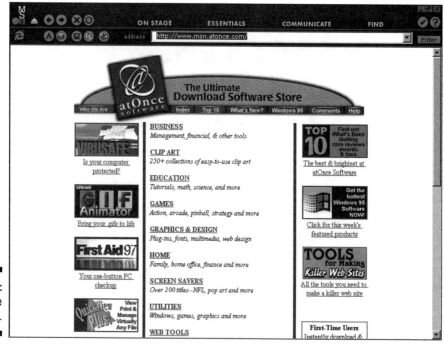

Figure 15-3:
AtOnce
Software.

After the program has been downloaded, AtOnce asks for your credit card information. This information is sent back to AtOnce Software. Then, you will be able to install the software. With this arrangement, you don't have to pay for the software before you have successfully downloaded it.

Avon

The Avon home page, shown in Figure 15-4, sells Avon beauty products online. You can purchase your favorite makeup, skin care products, fragrances, and many other Avon products here. The Avon site also includes a section of beauty tips and ideas compiled by Avon's experts. Here's looking at you!

Disney

The Disney Store Online, shown in Figure 15-5, lets you purchase Disney products over the Internet. The Disney Store Online offers a large selection of videos, CD-ROMs, books, clothing, art, toys, and other products. If you're a Pooh fan (and who isn't?), there's also a collection of more than 50 Pooh products to choose from.

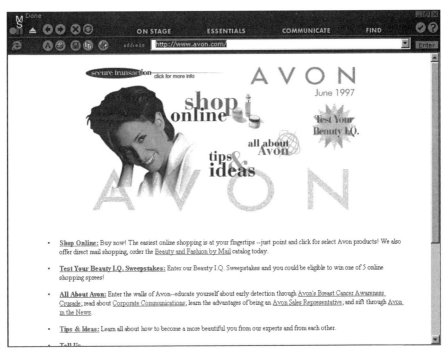

Figure 15-4:
Avon.

Figure 15-5:
The Disney
Store
Online.

1-800-Flowers

With 1-800-Flowers, you can have flowers sent just about anywhere. 1-800-Flowers is the largest florist in the world, with more than 130 company-owned or franchised shops and another 2,500 partner flower shops. You can choose from more than 150 types of flower arrangements and other floral gifts and have the gift delivered almost anywhere. If your order is placed before 12:30 p.m. where the recipient lives, the flowers can be delivered the same day. Otherwise, the flowers are delivered the following day. Figure 15-6 shows the 1-800-Flowers home page.

iQVC

iQVC is the online version of the popular QVC home shopping service. If you don't like to shop on cable TV, you can now purchase from QVC via the MSN Plaza. iQVC features a huge variety of high quality products, selling everything from books to barbecue tools. Figure 15-7 shows the iQVC home page.

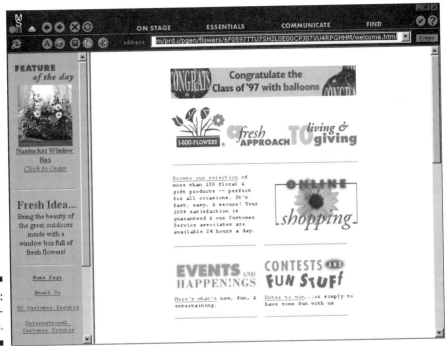

Figure 15-6:
1-800-
Flowers.

Figure 15-7:
iQVC.

The Scandinavian Pavilion

There's more to Scandinavia than Vikings and fjords. The Scandinavian Pavilion is an online store devoted to bringing you the very best Scandinavian products, from toys to watches to dinnerware. See Figure 15-8.

Tower Records

Tower Records offers thousands of CDs of all types that you can purchase online. You can search Tower's database by artist, title, song, or producer to find just the CD you're looking for. Figure 15-9 shows the Tower Records home page. For more information about buying online from Tower Records, see the next section, "Let's Go Shopping."

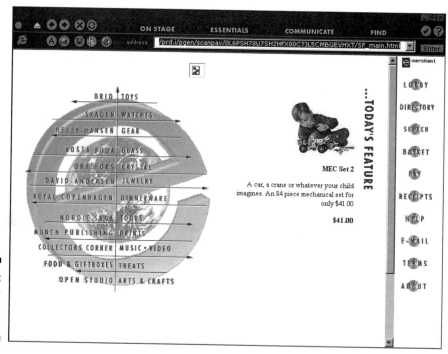

Figure 15-8: The Scandinavian Pavilion.

Let's Go Shopping

Although each of the stores on the Plaza has a slightly different procedure for online shopping, all of them take a similar approach. As you browse through the online catalogs or product listings, you can add items to a virtual shopping basket. When you have made all of your selections, you proceed to the virtual checkout, where you confirm that you want to purchase the items in your shopping basket and then provide your credit card number and shipping address. At any time up until checkout, you can change or remove items from your shopping basket, or you can empty your shopping basket altogether.

To give you an idea of how this online shopping works, the following paragraphs describe the process of purchasing a CD from Tower Records. Keep in mind that, although the other shops vary in details, they all follow a similar approach.

The best way to shop at Tower is to search its massive database for your selections. For example, suppose you want to buy a Spike Jones CD. You'd start by searching the database for all Spike Jones titles. To search the Tower database, scroll down the home page to find the search fields shown in Figure 15-10.

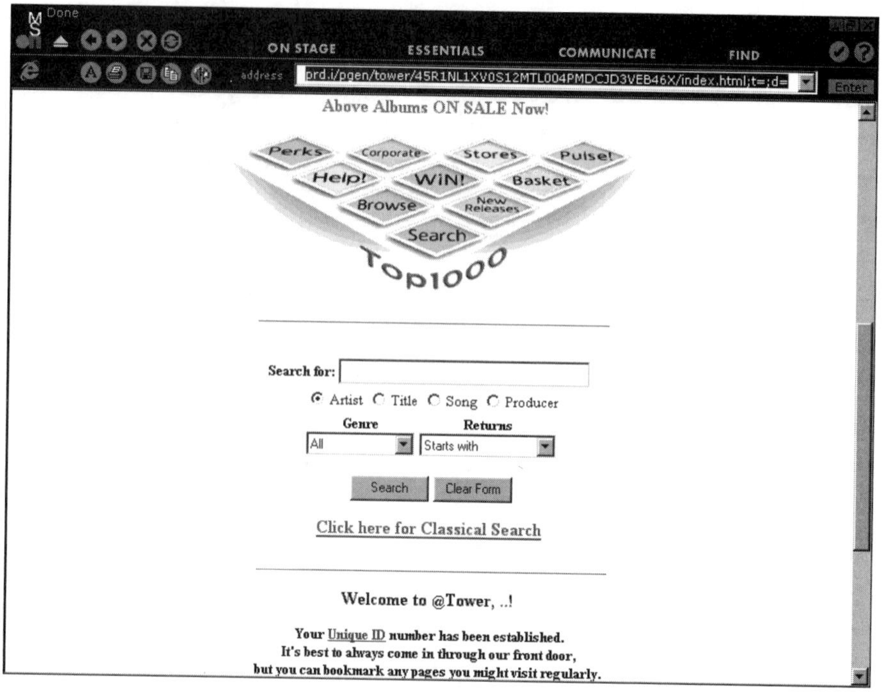

Figure 15-10:
Searching
the Tower
database.

To search for Spike Jones albums, type **Spike Jones** into the Search for text box, make sure that the Artist option is selected, and then click Search. After a moment, a list of all the Spike Jones albums Tower carries is displayed, as shown in Figure 15-11. Notice the albums with stars next to them, which indicate that Tower has those albums in stock and ready to ship.

To inspect an individual album, click the album you're interested in. A page similar to the one in Figure 15-12 appears. You can see it in the figure, but if you scroll down, the page lists a lot of information about this album, including a list of all the songs on the album.

To add the album to your shopping basket, click the ADD TO BASKET button. This places the item in your virtual shopping basket.

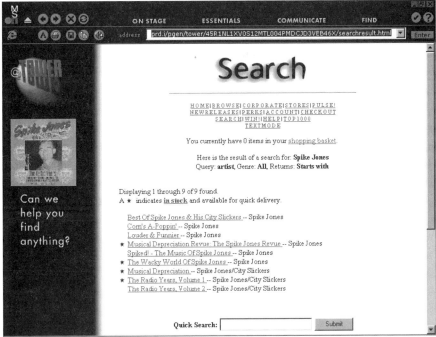

Figure 15-11:
Look how many Spike Jones albums Tower carries!

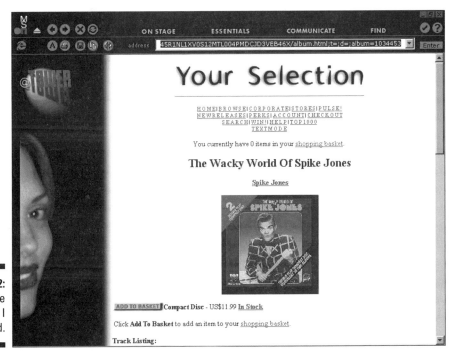

Figure 15-12:
This is the album I need.

You can then search for additional albums to add to your basket. When you have collected all the albums you want, click CHECKOUT, which, by the way, appears on most of the pages in the Tower shopping site. This takes you to a Checkout page where you can use a Secure or Unsecure checkout mode. I suggest you click Secure checkout to prevent online thugs from stealing your credit card number. The Checkout screen shown in Figure 15-13 appears next.

Scroll down this form and supply the following information:

- ✔ Your name and address
- ✔ Your phone number and e-mail address
- ✔ The shipping address, if it's different from the billing address
- ✔ An optional gift message

When you've filled in the information, click the Proceed to Next Page button. A page which enables you to choose your shipping method appears. You can then click the Proceed to Final Page button. The final checkout page appears, where you must enter your credit card number.

To complete the order, click the Submit Order button. Your order is processed and sent as soon as possible.

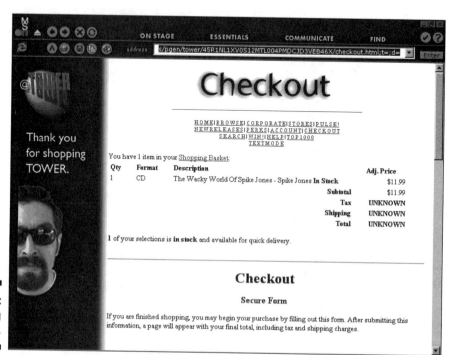

Figure 15-13:
Checking
out.

Chapter 16

Car Shopping with CarPoint

● ●

In This Chapter

▶ Researching information about new cars

▶ Getting secret dealer invoice information

▶ Figuring monthly car payments

▶ Buying a car through the CarPoint online car buying service

● ●

*I*f you like cars, you'll love Microsoft CarPoint. It's chock full of information about new cars from every manufacturer. If you're in the market for a new car, you can find all the details about the car you're interested in, including a complete listing of dealer invoice prices. You can even buy your next car through the CarPoint network of no-hassle dealers.

Even if you're not in the market for a new car, CarPoint is a lot of fun. You can find out what's hot and what's not, read interesting articles about the auto industry, and catch test drive reviews of the latest cars.

Welcome to CarPoint

To start CarPoint, point to Essentials in the Navigation bar, point to Automobiles, and click CarPoint. The CarPoint home page appears, as shown in Figure 16-1.

Figure 16-1:
The
CarPoint
home page.

You can access all of the CarPoint features from the CarPoint home page. Throughout CarPoint, a Navigation bar appears at the top of each page. At the right side of this toolbar are three buttons:

✔ **Find:** Enables you to search for a car based on criteria such as the car type, safety rating, gas mileage, and so on. The Find button is described later in this chapter, in the section "Searching for the Perfect Car."

✔ **Home:** Returns you to the CarPoint home page. Use this button when you're lost deep within the bowels of the CarPoint pages and you want to get back to the home page.

✔ **Help:** Displays information about how to use CarPoint.

The CarPoint home page contains links to CarPoint features and services, most of which are described in the remaining sections in this chapter.

Checking Out a New Car

To get information about a particular make and model of car, start by selecting the vehicle category. The CarPoint new car information is organized into six categories of vehicles:

✔ Passenger Cars

✔ Luxury Cars

✔ Sports Cars

✔ Vans & Minivans

✔ Sport Utilities

✔ Pickup Trucks

Click the button for one of these six categories to display general information about the category and a list of vehicle models. For example, Figure 16-2 shows the Sport Utilities page. This page includes news about new Sport Utility vehicles, a history of Sport Utilities, and a list of 35 Sport Utility vehicles. (The controls that appear next to the picture of the car's interior in Figure 16-2 let you display a 360-degree view of the car. See the section "Take a Look Inside," later in this chapter, for information about how these controls work.)

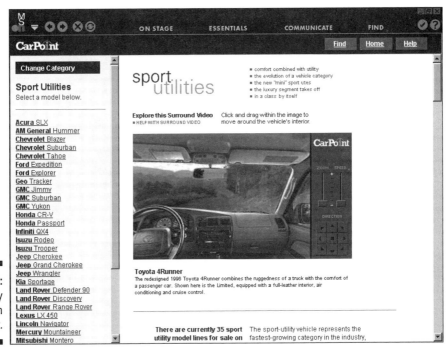

Figure 16-2: Sport Utility vehicles on CarPoint.

You can click any of the vehicles listed on the category page to see information about that particular model. For example, Figure 16-3 shows the AMC Hummer page. Arnold Schwarzenegger supposedly owns *two* of these monsters.

The menu to the left of the photograph of the vehicle is the same for all vehicles in CarPoint. This menu offers the following links:

- ✔ **Description:** A description and photo of the vehicle. This is the page that is initially displayed when you call up a vehicle.

- ✔ **Pricing information:** The retail and dealer invoice price for each model of the vehicle.

- ✔ **Safety features:** A list of the safety features, such as airbags and antilock brakes, that are standard and optional on each model of the vehicle.

- ✔ **Convenience features:** A list of convenience features, such as air conditioning, cruise control, and power door locks, that are available for each model of the vehicle.

Figure 16-3:
The AMC
Hummer.

✔ **Specifications:** Information, such as the engine displacements, horse-power, gas mileage, wheelbase, length, and so on.

✔ **Repair and maintenance:** An estimate of the cost for repairs and maintenance of the vehicle over a five-year period.

✔ **Competitors:** A list of similar vehicles available from other manufacturers.

✔ **Photo Gallery:** Enables you to view a collection of photographs of the vehicle.

✔ **Free Reports:** Enables you to view two reports for the vehicle: a detailed price list, which includes retail and dealer invoice costs not only for the base vehicle models but also for options, and a detailed test-drive review.

The price list report is worth its weight in gold. Armed with this report, you can determine the exact price that the dealer has paid for the car you want to buy, including all options. You can then add whatever amount you think the dealer is entitled to in profit on the car, and then stick with that figure as your offer.

✔ **Dealer Locator:** Locates a dealer in your area where you can see the car.

Take a Look Inside

Many of the vehicles featured in CarPoint include a special Surround Video which enables you to view the car's interior in a unique 360-degree presentation. To see if a Surround Video is available for the car, click the Photo Gallery link. If an icon labeled *CarPoint Surround Video* appears on the Photo Gallery page, click the icon. The Surround Video takes a minute or so to download.

Figure 16-4 shows the Surround Video for the AMC Hummer. After the Surround Video finishes downloading, it automatically starts panning around to show you a complete 360-degree view of the car's interior. You can change the view to a different direction by clicking on the view controls that appear in the lower right corner of the Surround Video, or you can click and drag the mouse anywhere in the video image to change the panning direction. Don't forget to look up and down.

You can also use the Zoom and Speed slider controls to zoom in for a closer look. or to change the video's panning speed. Be careful, though: If you set the speed too high, you'll get dizzy and may need to roll down the window.

Figure 16-4:
A Surround
Video view
of the
Hummer's
luxurious
interior.

How Much Car Can I Afford?

CarPoint includes a nifty automobile payment calculator that enables you to determine what the monthly payments will be for your car loan. Or you can use it to determine the maximum amount you can borrow to keep the payments at a certain amount.

To access the payment calculator, return to the CarPoint home page by clicking Home in the Navigation bar at the top of any CarPoint page. Then click the Payment Calculator icon. The payment calculator comes to life, as shown in Figure 16-5.

Notice that the payment calculator includes four lines: the car's purchase price, the loan's interest rate, the number of months for the loan, and the loan's monthly payment. Initially, the purchase price is set to $20,000, the interest rate is 9.0 percent, the loan term is 48 months, and the down payment is set to 20 percent. This makes the monthly payment a paltry $398.16.

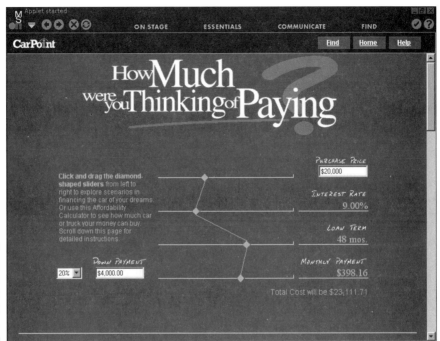

Figure 16-5:
The
CarPoint
payment
calculator.

You can change any of these four loan variables by dragging the diamond that appears on the line to the left or right. For example, if you want to see what the same car would cost per month if you financed it for 60 months instead of 48, drag the diamond on the loan term line to the right. The monthly payment changes from $398.16 to $332.13. Or, suppose you can get 4.5 percent financing. Drag the loan term diamond back to 48, and then drag the interest rate diamond left until it reads 4.5 percent. The monthly payment changes to $364.85.

Notice also that the payment calculator includes a text box for the down payment amount. You can type the down payment you wish to make, or you can set the down payment percentage, which is the drop-down list box that appears to the left of the Down Payment text box, to 0, 5, 10, 15, or 20 percent and let the payment calculator calculate the down payment amount for you.

The initial setting for the down payment percentage is 20 percent. The down payment is subtracted from the purchase price to set the actual amount of the loan used to calculate the monthly payment. In other words, if the purchase price shows $20,000, the actual loan is for $16,000 — $20,000 less the $4,000 down payment.

To use the payment calculator to see how much car you can afford for a given monthly payment, drag the interest and loan term diamonds to the best terms you can get for your loan; then drag the monthly payment diamond to the largest monthly payment you can afford. The purchase price diamond changes to reflect the car price you can afford.

For example, suppose you can get a 7.0 percent 60-month loan and you can afford $325 in monthly payments. Drag the interest rate diamond to 7.5 percent, the loan term diamond to 60 months, and the monthly payment diamond to $325. The purchase price will jump to $21,834. You won't be able to afford that $60,000 Hummer, but you should be able to get a decently equipped Ford Taurus.

Buying a Car Through CarPoint

If you're actually ready to buy a car, you may want to try out the CarPoint buying service. The Buying Service consists of a network of dealers who have been screened by CarPoint and have agreed to provide you with their best competitive price on the car you request, with no hassles and no haggling. If you like the price, you can buy the car. If you don't, you can walk away.

To use the CarPoint Buying Service, go back to CarPoint's home page and then click the Buying Service icon. The CarPoint Buying Service page appears.

To buy a car with this service, all you do is type in your zip code and click the Begin Processing button. A form appears in which you type your name and phone number and indicate the car make, model, color, and options you want.

When you have filled out the form, click the Submit button, which appears at the bottom of the form. The form is e-mailed to a CarPoint Sales Consultant in your area, who will contact you within 48 hours (except on weekends) with a firm price quote and tell you whether the car is available immediately or will have to be ordered. If you like the price, you can arrange to purchase the vehicle that day. If you don't like the price, you can say "Thanks, but no thanks," and hang up with no further obligation.

Part V
Internet Excursions

The 5th Wave By Rich Tennant

"You know, I liked you a whole lot more on the Internet."

In this part . . .

Taking the plunge into the Internet — that vast, sprawling collection of computers commonly known as the *Information Superhighway* — is one of the main reasons many people sign up to use MSN. Unfortunately, many folks don't realize that the Internet is at the deep end of the MSN pool.

The water is colder down at the deep end of the pool, and you'd better know how to swim. Help is here, though. You can think of these chapters as your swimming lessons for the Internet. You won't learn how to do the butterfly stroke, or triple-back-flip-two-and-a-half-gainer dives, but you will at least discover how to dog paddle your way through Internet newsgroups and the World Wide Web.

Chapter 17

What Is the Internet?

*I*nternet access is one of the most sought after features in online services these days. A few years ago, online services including MSN provided poor access to the Internet, with only a few of the Internet's complete range of features available at high cost. Things have changed, however. The Microsoft Network is now an excellent and cost effective method of accessing the Internet. MSN prices are competitive even with small local internet providers, and MSN service can't be beat.

What Is the Internet?

The Internet is the largest computer network in the world. The mother of all computer networks, the Internet links tens of millions of computer users throughout the world. Most people are referring to the Internet when they say, "Information Superhighway."

Strictly speaking, the Internet is a network of networks. As of January 1995, the Internet consists of close to 71,000 separate computer networks, linked so that a user on any of the 71,000 networks can reach out and touch a user on any of the other networks. These networks connect nearly five million computers.

The World Wide Web refers to the most popular portion of the Internet, in which information is displayed in attractive, graphically formatted pages which can be accessed by any of the millions of users who have an Internet connection.

The Internet consists of several distinct types of networks:

- ✔ **Government agencies:** Such as the Library of Congress and the White House
- ✔ **Military sites:** Did you ever see *War Games?*
- ✔ **Educational institutions:** Such as universities and colleges
- ✔ **Businesses:** Such as IBM and Microsoft
- ✔ **Internet service providers:** Which enable individuals to access the Internet
- ✔ **Commercial online services:** Such as CompuServe, America Online, and, of course, MSN

Boring Internet History You Can Skip

The Internet has a fascinating history, if such things interest you. There's no particular reason you should be interested in such things, of course, except that a superficial understanding of how the Internet got started may help you understand and cope with the way it exists today. Here goes.

The Internet traces its beginnings back to a small network called ARPANET, built by the Department of Defense in 1969 to link defense installations. ARPANET was soon expanded to include not only defense installations, but universities as well. In the 1970s, the ARPANET split into two networks, one for military use (MILNET) and one for nonmilitary use (the original ARPANET). The two networks were connected using a networking link called IP, the Internet Protocol, because it enabled communication between two networks.

The good folks who designed the Internet Protocol had the foresight to realize that soon more than two networks would want to be connected. In fact, they left room for tens of thousands of networks to join the game, which is a good thing because it wasn't long before the Internet began to grow.

By the mid-1980s, ARPANET was beginning to reach the limits of what it could do. In came the National Science Foundation (NSF), who set up a nationwide network designed to provide access to huge supercomputers — those huge scientific computers used to discover new prime numbers and calculate the orbits of distant galaxies. The supercomputers themselves were never put to much use, but NSFNET, the network that was put together to support the supercomputers, was put to use. NSFNET replaced ARPANET as the new backbone for the Internet.

Then out of the blue, the whole world seemed to gain interest in the Internet. Stories about it appeared in *Time* and *Newsweek*. The 'Net began to grow so fast that even NSFNET couldn't keep up, so private commercial networks got into the game. Fortunately, as an Internet user, you don't have to care a whit about what network links are used to connect computers on the Internet. MSN takes care of all those details for you, so you can easily access the Internet with just a click of the mouse.

Just How Big Is The Internet?

The Internet is no longer owned or controlled by one organization. Because of this fact, no one truly knows how big the Internet is. Several organizations attempt to periodically determine the size of the Internet. One such organization is Network Wizards, which completed its last survey in January of 1997. Network Wizards found that 828,000 separate computer networks are represented on the Internet in the form of domain names, with 16.1 million host computers. The same survey showed a mere 240,000 domains and 9.4 million hosts in January of 1996, so the size of the Internet has nearly doubled in just one year. To depict its growth another way, a new computer was added to the Internet every six seconds. (Don't be spooked by the terms *domain name* and *host*. A *domain name* is merely the technical-sounding name for a network that is attached to the Internet. For example, microsoft.com is the domain name for Microsoft. A *host* is just a computer which is connected to the Internet.)

Each domain can support a single user, or — in the case of a domain such as AOL.COM (America Online) or COMPUSERVE.COM (CompuServe), and of course MSN.COM (The Microsoft Network), perhaps millions of users. No one really knows how many actual users are on the Internet. The indisputable point is that the Internet is big and getting bigger every day.

In case you're interested, you can check up on the latest Internet statistics from Network Wizards by accessing their Web site, http://www.nw.com.

What Does the Internet Have to Offer?

The Internet offers information and services similar to those of MSN, but it offers more of them — more bulletin boards, file libraries, and chat rooms. The Internet has evolved into its present form over the past three decades. As a result, the Internet is strewn with holdouts from the past: command languages, cryptic names, and other oddities.

The following sections describe the various services that are available on the Internet.

Internet e-mail

E-mail is the main reason most people use the Internet. As an MSN user, you'll find that Internet e-mail works the same as MSN e-mail: You read incoming mail and compose outgoing mail using Microsoft Internet Mail. Internet Mail is smart enough to figure out when you are addressing a new message to an Internet user, rather than another MSN user, so you don't have to do anything special to send mail via the Internet.

Mailing lists

A mailing list is simply a list of the e-mail addresses of a group of people who are interested in a particular subject. The mailing list itself has an e-mail address. When you send e-mail to the mailing list address, your message is redistributed to everyone else on the list. To get on a mailing list, you send an e-mail message to the list's administrator. You can *subscribe* to a mailing list at no cost, except for the charges you incur by downloading all the mail you receive as a result.

As you read on about other Internet services, you may wonder why anyone would bother with mailing lists. That's a very good question. The main reason mailing lists continue to thrive is that a large number of people have Internet e-mail as their only Internet service. Other services such as newsgroups and FTP (described later in this chapter) are not available to them, so mailing lists are a lifesaver. As more users gain full access to the Internet, mailing lists will fade in popularity.

Usenet newsgroups

Newsgroups are the Internet's equivalent to the MSN bulletin boards. If you want to get technical, bulletin boards are the MSN equivalent to Internet newsgroups. Newsgroups are places where users with common interests gather to share ideas.

For technical reasons you don't need or want to know, Internet newsgroups are distributed over what is called Usenet. As a result, you sometimes see the terms *Usenet* and *newsgroups* used together.

The MSN bulletin boards are based on the same technology that is used for Usenet newsgroups, and you use the same program to access both: Microsoft Internet News. If you know how to use MSN bulletin boards, you already know most of what you need to know to access news-groups. Most, but not all. Enough tricks to getting around newsgroups remain to be uncovered, however, so I devote the next chapter to the subject.

File Transfer Protocol (FTP)

File Transfer Protocol (FTP) is the Internet's way of moving files around. FTP allows a computer to make its files available to the Internet so that other users can download the files to their own computers. Hundreds, if not thousands, of computers make their files available for downloading on the Internet. These computers are called FTP sites. Many of these FTP sites allow anyone to access their treasures, but access to some of them is restricted to a lucky few.

Internet Relay Chat (IRC)

The Internet Relay Chat (IRC) is the Internet's version of MSN chat rooms, where users gather to shoot the breeze. IRC allows Internet users across the globe to communicate with one another, kind of like a giant conference call. You can read more about the MSN chat rooms in Chapter 14.

Telnet

Telnet is a way of connecting to another computer on the Internet and running programs on that computer, as if your computer were a terminal attached to that computer. Telnet is one of the many Internet services that is rapidly losing popularity as the World Wide Web becomes more popular.

Gopher

Gopher is an attempt at making the entire Internet easy to use by presenting its services as a series of menus. Choose an option from one menu, and Gopher presents another menu with more options, followed by more menus and more options, and so on, until you finally get to something useful, such as an FTP site or a newsgroup.

Gopher was fairly popular in the late 1980s, but when the World Wide Web was invented, most users realized that the Web was an even better way to make the Internet easy to use. As a result, Gopher has all but vanished.

World Wide Web (WWW)

The World Wide Web, affectionately known as *the Web,* is the newest method of accessing information on the Internet. Think of it as a graphical interface to Internet information, with an important twist: The Web is filled with special hypertext links, which let you jump from one Internet locale to another. The Web is explained carefully in Chapter 18, so don't worry if you haven't a clue what this definition means. All in good time.

How Much of the Internet Can You Access from MSN?

MSN enables you to access almost all the services available on the Internet. The original MSN software, which was released along with Windows 95, only provided access to Internet e-mail and newsgroups. MSN Version 2.0 provides full access to all of the Internet's services.

If you've heard that MSN is not a very good way to access the Internet, rest assured that this may have been the case a year ago — but this isn't the case any longer. MSN provides complete access to the Internet at a reasonable cost.

Understanding Internet Addresses

Just as every user of The Microsoft Network must have a member ID, everyone who uses the Internet must have an Internet address. Because the Internet has so many computers and so many users, a single member ID is not sufficient. As a result, Internet addresses are constructed using a method called the *Domain Name System* (DNS).

An Internet address for an individual user follows a format that goes like this:

```
username@organization.category
```

As you can see, the address is broken down into three parts, described in reverse order in the following paragraphs.

> ✔ **Category:** The category is a two- or three-character suffix that indicates the broad category into which the user's computer system falls. The six categories used in the United States are summarized in Table 17-1.

✔ **Organization:** The organization name is the name of the organization, institution, or agency. For example, `ibm.com` is a commercial organization named IBM, `mit.edu` is an educational institution named MIT, and `nasa.gov` is a government agency named NASA.

✔ **Username:** This name is assigned to the user at his or her computer, and is the Internet's equivalent to the MSN member ID. If you are an employee of `nasa.gov` and you log in to NASA's computer as Buzz, your full Internet address would be `Buzz@nasa.gov`.

Table 17-1	Categories Used in Internet Addresses
Domain	*Explanation*
edu	Education
mil	Military
gov	Government
com	Commercial
net	Network
org	Organizations that don't fit one of the other categories

Occasionally, Internet addresses are more complicated. This development happens when large organizations want to divide their networks into two or more groups. For example, a university may break its network down by department. Thus, the history department may be `his.gadolphin.edu`, whereas the track team may be `track.gadolphin.edu`.

When pronouncing Internet addresses, the @ symbol is pronounced *at*, and the period is pronounced *dot*. Thus, the address `Buzz@nasa.gov` is pronounced *Buzz at NASA dot gov*.

Warning: The Internet May Make You Blush

MSN has fairly strict guidelines about the kind of information you can and cannot post. Although Microsoft insists that it does not want to play the role of censor, some guidelines are provided about what is acceptable and what is not. These guidelines do not exist on the Internet, where you can find everything from discussions of model railroading and origami to pictures of men and women engaged in unmentionable acts. Because no one is really in charge of the Internet, no guidelines or regulations about what can or cannot be posted exist.

Fortunately, the Internet does have a very effective form of policing, in which the basic rule is that anything posted on the Internet must be posted in an appropriate area. As a result, you rarely find anything offensive on the Internet unless you go looking for it. If you post an offensive picture in a model railroading newsgroup, you will probably receive an endless deluge of hate mail and *flames* (angry e-mail messages deriding you), and your message will undoubtedly be removed by the newsgroup administrator.

The Internet culture has a very libertarian attitude towards censorship: If you don't like it, don't read it. Unfortunately, MSN isn't quite up to speed yet on your ability to prevent your children from accessing offensive information on the Internet. I discuss what few parental safeguards are in place in Chapter 22, and you find ten suggestions for protecting your kids from Internet smut and unscrupulous Internet users in Chapter 25. For now I offer a stern lecture: Do not let your kids mess around with MSN Internet services unsupervised.

Chapter 18

Surfing the Web

. . . .

. . . .

*T*he World Wide Web — usually referred to simply as *the Web* — is where the most interesting things are happening on the Internet today. In fact, to most people, the Web *is* the Internet. Fortunately, you don't have to do anything extra to gain access to the Web. If you have a Microsoft Network (MSN) account, you already have full access to the Web and all that it has to offer. The Web is but a few mouse clicks away.

There are two ways to surf the Web from MSN. The easiest, but most limited, way is to simply click your way into the Web directly from the MSN Program Viewer. When you do, Web pages appear within the MSN Program Viewer window, almost as if the Web pages were actually a part of MSN's services. You can jump back and forth between MSN and the Web with ease. In fact, it is sometimes hard to tell whether a particular page you are viewing is a part of MSN or the Web.

The second, and more sophisticated, way to surf the Web is to use Microsoft's dedicated Web browsing program, Internet Explorer. Internet Explorer is automatically installed on your computer when you sign up for The Microsoft Network, so you don't have to do anything special to set up Internet Explorer. It takes a few more mouse clicks to get into Internet Explorer, and Internet Explorer has a slightly different look and feel than the MSN Program Viewer. The added benefits Internet Explorer has to offer, however, make it worthwhile to use Internet Explorer, rather than the MSN Program Viewer, to surf the Web.

The first section of this chapter shows you how to access Web pages from the MSN Program Viewer, and the rest of the chapter is devoted to using Internet Explorer. Internet Explorer is a fairly complicated program — complicated enough that I've written an entire book on it, entitled

Internet Explorer 3 For Dummies (from IDG Books Worldwide, Inc., naturally). If you really want to learn how to use Internet Explorer, you'll certainly want to pick up a copy of that book. My family, my pets, and I will be forever in your debt.

Exploring the Web from the MSN Program Viewer

The easiest way to venture into the Web from MSN is to call up the MSN Find page by choosing Find⇨Search MSN and the Web, and then searching for a word or phrase that interests you. The MSN Find service lists not only MSN pages by Web pages as well. For example, Figure 18-1 shows the results of a search for the word *Turtle*. As you can see, Find did not find any information on MSN about turtles. However, it did find three Web sites devoted to various types of turtles.

To access a Web page from the MSN Find service, just click the Web page you want to visit. The web page will be accessed and displayed directly within the MSN Program Viewer window, as shown in Figure 18-2.

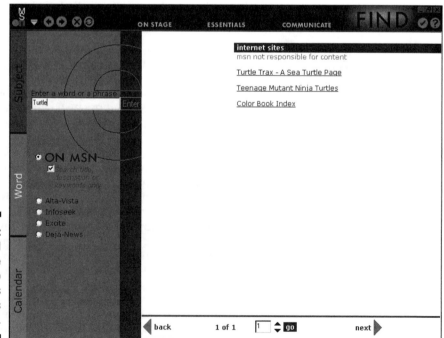

Figure 18-1:
The MSN Find service locates Web pages as well as MSN pages.

Figure 18-2:
The MSN
Program
Viewer
displays
Web pages
with ease.

When you display a Web page in MSN Program Viewer, the Internet toolbar is automatically revealed. In fact, this is the only way to tell when you've left MSN to visit an Internet page. I describe this toolbar in Chapter 3, but I'll list each of this toolbar's buttons here:

Button	What the Button Does
	Summons an Options dialog box which lets you control various aspects of the MSN operation. These options are described separately in Chapter 21.
	Increases the size of text displayed in the Program Viewer window.
	Prints the current page.
	Saves the current page on your computer's hard drive.
	Copies the current page to the Clipboard.
	Lets you change the character set. This is useful if you stumble upon a foreign language page that displays as gibberish on your screen.
Enter	Same as pressing the Enter key.

Here are a few tips to keep in mind when browsing Web pages from MSN's Program Viewer:

✔ The address of the Web page you are viewing is displayed in the address text box in the Internet toolbar. If you know the address of a Web page you want to visit, you can go to that page by typing its address in the address text box and then clicking the Enter button.

✔ You can return to MSN at any time by choosing any menu option from the Navigation bar menus: On Stage, Essentials, Communicate, or Find. You can also go back to MSN by clicking the Back button in the Navigation bar. You may have to click the Back button several times to get all the way back to MSN.

✔ The only indication that you are viewing a Web page rather than an MSN page is that the Internet toolbar appears. If you hide the Internet toolbar by clicking the Hide Internet toolbar button (the button with the upward pointing arrow, located next to the OnMSN logo at the top left corner of the MSN Program Viewer window), there is no visual distinction between MSN and Web pages.

Starting Internet Explorer

If you're a serious Web surfer, you'll want to skip the MSN Program Viewer in favor of Microsoft's more advanced Web browser, Internet Explorer. Internet Explorer offers you a fuller array of toolbar buttons, plus all of its commands are available from the menu bar, whereas the MSN Program Viewer doesn't have a menu bar at all. Fortunately, Internet Explorer is automatically installed on your computer when you install the Microsoft Network software. So all you have to do to launch Internet Explorer is follow these simple steps:

The Internet

1. Double-click the Internet icon that appears on your desktop, as shown in the margin.

Internet Explorer grinds and churns for a moment and then displays the Connect To dialog box, as shown in Figure 18-3.

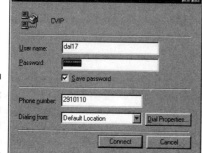

Figure 18-3:
The
Connect To
dialog box.

If you are already connected to your online service or Internet Service Provider when you double-click the Internet icon, the Connect To dialog box will not be displayed. Instead, you can skip forward to Step 4.

2. If your user name and password do not appear in the Connect To dialog box, type them in now.

Normally, the Connect To dialog box shows your user name and password, so you won't need to type them in here. To make sure that the Connect To dialog box remembers your password, check the Save password checkbox.

3. Click the Connect button to connect to MSN or your Internet Service Provider (ISP).

Your computer uses the modem to dial the phone number of MSN or your ISP. If the modem volume is turned up, you hear a dial tone, the familiar tones as the number is dialed, two or three rings, and then a few moments of rather obnoxious squealing as the modems establish their connection.

Note that if you use an Internet Service Provider (ISP) other than MSN, this step will connect you to your ISP, not MSN. Either way, though, you will be able to access the Internet.

4. You're done!

The Internet Explorer window opens, as you see in Figure 18-4.

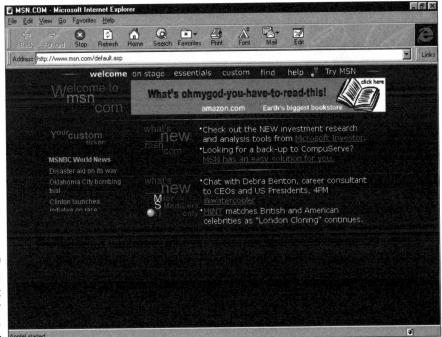

Figure 18-4:
The Internet Explorer window.

When Internet Explorer starts up, it automatically takes you to the MSN home page, which allows you to access many of The Microsoft Network features from Internet Explorer. In fact, across the top of the MSN home page are links designed to resemble the MSN Program Viewer Navigation bar: On Stage, Essentials, Custom, Find, and Help. You can click these links to go to Web pages that provide access to several MSN features.

Making Sense of the Internet Explorer Screen

Before telling you how to actually explore the Internet, let me show you all of the bells and whistles that Microsoft has loaded on the Internet Explorer window. Figure 18-5 shows the Internet Explorer window once again — this time with the more important parts labeled for easy identification.

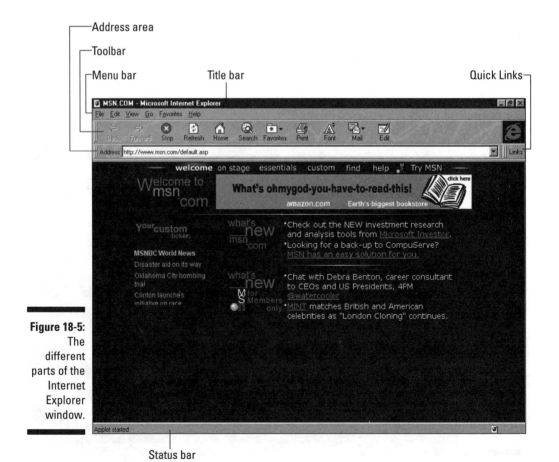

Figure 18-5: The different parts of the Internet Explorer window.

The following items on the Internet Explorer screen are worthy of note:

- ✔ The *title bar,* at the very top of the window, always displays the name of the Internet page you are currently viewing. For example, in Figure 18-5, the page name is *MSN.COM.*

- ✔ The *menu bar* is just below the title bar, as it is in any Windows program. Internet Explorer's deepest secrets are hidden within the menus located on the menu bar. Several of these menus are familiar: File, Edit, View, and Help. Two of the menus, Go and Favorites, provide features that are unique to Internet Explorer. These features are described later in the chapter.

  The menu bar mainly distinguishes Internet Explorer from the MSN Program Viewer. The MSN Program Viewer has no menu bar.

- ✔ Beneath the menu bar is the *toolbar,* which contains buttons you can click to perform common functions. The purpose of each of these buttons is summarized in Table 18-1.

- ✔ Beneath the toolbar is an *address area* which displays the Internet address of the page currently displayed. The drop-down list also reveals addresses of pages you've recently visited. If you don't understand Internet addresses, don't worry. I explain them in a moment, in the sidebar labeled "URLs make me hurl."

- ✔ To the right of the address area are Internet Explorer's *Quick Links,* which let you access any of five of your favorite Internet locations with just a single mouse click. To save space, the links themselves are temporarily hidden from view. To display them, click the word Links in the toolbar. Quick Links overlays the space occupied by the address area. To restore the address area, by click the word Address.

- ✔ The *status bar* is located at the bottom of the window. It periodically displays useful information, such as what Internet Explorer is trying to do, or how much progress it has made downloading a large file.

- ✔ The *scroll bars,* located at the right and bottom of the window, appear and disappear as needed. Whenever all of the information on a Web page cannot be displayed in the window, a scroll bar appears so that you can scroll through the information. You don't see a scroll bar on Figure 18-5.

Table 18-1	Internet Explorer Toolbar Buttons
Button	**What the Button Does**
⇦ Back	Moves back to the most recently displayed page.
⇨ Forward	Moves forward to the page you most recently visited.
⊗ Stop	Cancels a time-consuming download.
Refresh	Forces Internet Explorer to obtain a fresh copy of the current page.
🏠 Home	Takes you to your start page.
Search	Takes you to your search page.
Favorites	Displays your favorite places list, just as the Favorites button does in the MSN Program Viewer.
Print	Prints the current page.
A Font	Changes the font size.

Following the Links

The easiest way to get around the Web is by following the links. A *link* is a bit of text or a graphic on one Web page that leads to another Web page. A link may lead to another page at the same Web site or to a page at a different Web site.

You can easily identify the links on a Web page because they are displayed in a different color than the rest of the text, and they're underlined. For example, back in Figure 18-4, <u>Microsoft Investor</u>, <u>MSN has an easy solution for you</u>, <u>@watercooler</u>, and <u>MINT</u> are links to other Web pages. (Note that you can change the colors and underlining via the <u>V</u>iew⇨<u>O</u>ptions command.)

In addition to text links, many Web pages contain *graphical links* — graphics that you click to jump to another Web page. Unlike *text links,* graphical links are not identified with a special color or underlining. You can spot graphical links by watching the mouse pointer as you drag the mouse over the graphic. If the mouse pointer changes from an arrow to a pointing finger, you know you've found a link.

Going Directly to a Web Page

What if a friend gives you the address of a Web page you want to check out? No problem. To visit a specific Web page for which you know the address (URL), all you have to do is follow these simple steps:

1. **In Internet Explorer, click the mouse anywhere in the large address text box located in the toolbar.**

2. **Type the address of the Web page that you want to display.**

   An Internet address is often referred to as a URL. See the sidebar "URLs make me want to hurl" for information about Web addresses and URLs.

3. **Press Enter.**

   Internet Explorer chugs and churns for a moment, and then displays the page.

If you type an address for a Web page that does not exist, you'll get a dialog box similar to the one in Figure 18-6. Most likely, you made a typing mistake. Click OK, correct the error, and then try again. Other possibilities are that you were given the wrong address, the address has changed, or the Web page no longer exists.

Figure 18-6:
Uh-oh.

URLs make me want to hurl

In World Wide Web terminology, the address for a Web page or other Internet resource is called a *URL*, which stands for *Uniform Resource Locator*. Everything of importance on the Internet has a URL. A URL consists of three parts, written as follows:

```
protocol://host address/resource
name
```

✔ **Protocol:** Written as *http* for Web pages. Http stands for *HyperText Transfer Protocol*, but that won't be on the test.

✔ **Host address:** The Internet address of the computer on which the Web page resides (for example, www.msn.com).

✔ **Resource name:** A name used to retrieve a specific Web page. In many cases, this name contains additional slashes that represent directories on the host system.

Here are examples of complete URLs:

```
http://www.msn.com/default.asp
http://www.yahoo.com
http://www.hq.nasa.gov/office/
    olmsa/imagarch/index.htm
```

Internet Explorer is smart enough to know that if you leave off the *http://* part, you want to access a Web page. You can omit the *http:* and the first two forward slashes when typing a Web page address into Internet Explorer. The following addresses will work in Internet Explorer:

```
www.msn.com/default.asp
www.yahoo.com
www.hq.nasa.gov/office/olmsa/
    imagarch/index.htm
```

Searching the Web

If you don't know the URL of a Web site you want to visit, you'll need to use one of the Internet's many search services to locate the information you need. The easiest way to search for information on the Internet is to click the Search button in Internet Explorer's toolbar. This takes you directly to Microsoft's famous all-in-one search page, which is pictured in Figure 18-7.

As you can see, the all-in-one search page enables you to search the Internet using any of several popular search services. All you have to do is type the word or phrase you want to search for in the appropriate box, and then click the Search button for the service you want to search.

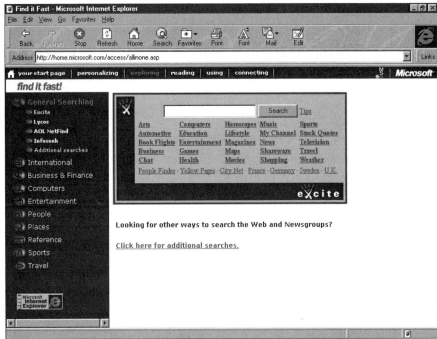

Figure 18-7:
The
Microsoft
all-in-one
search
page.

To use the all-in-one search page to search for information on the Web, follow these steps:

1. Click the Search button on the toolbar.

The all-in-one search page appears, as was shown in Figure 18-7.

2. Pick a search service.

If you're new to Internet searching, just start with the first one on the list: Excite. As you gain experience with the Internet, try each of the search services and decide for yourself which one you like best.

3. Type the word or phrase you're looking for in the text box.

For example, type the word **turtle** in the text box.

4. Click the Search button.

Your search request is submitted to the search service you selected.

5. Whistle "Dixie."

You'll probably be able to make it through the song at least once before the results of the search are displayed. The format in which the search results are displayed depends on which search service you choose.

6. If you find a link that looks promising, click the colored, underlined phrase.

Internet Explorer follows the link to the page you select.

7. If nothing looks promising, click the Next Results button.

Each search service displays only a certain number of *hits* at a time, typically 10 or 15. If none of the hits on the first page looks promising, scroll to the bottom of the page and look for a link or button that says something like *Next Results*. Click this button or link to display additional results for the search.

Here are things to keep in mind when searching:

✔ If no search results appear, try again using a different search word or phrase. For example, try **ninja** instead of **turtle**. Or, try using one of the other search services.

✔ When picking search words, try to use words that are specific enough that you don't end up with thousands of hits, but general enough to encompass the topic you're trying to find. *Turtle* comes up with almost 25,000 hits in the Excite search engine. That's a bit much to look through.

✔ Most of the search services list their results in sorted order, with the pages that most closely match your search criteria listed first. In particular, if you search on two words, those pages in which both words appear will be listed before pages in which just one of the words appears.

✔ Don't forget that you can always use the Back button in the toolbar to return to the all-in-one search page. Depending on how far you've traveled in your quest, you may have to click the Back button several times to return to the search page.

The Microsoft all-in-one search page isn't the only way to search the Web. If you prefer, you can go directly to any of several popular search services. The best of these services are listed in "Serious Web Directories," in Chapter 19.

Changing Your Web Start Page

Normally, Internet Explorer defaults to www.msn.com as its start page, but Internet Explorer enables you to designate any Web page on the Internet to be your start page. For example, if the only Internet Web page you are interested in is the David Letterman's Top Ten List page, you can set the Top Ten List page to be your Web start page.

The start page is also the Web page that reappears when you click the Home button on the toolbar.

To change your starting Web page, follow these steps:

1. **Navigate your way to the Web page you want to use as your new starting page.**

2. **Choose the View⮕Options command.**

   The Options dialog box appears.

3. **Click the Navigation tab.**

   The Navigation options appear, as shown in Figure 18-8.

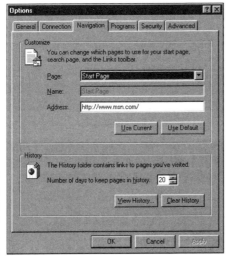

Figure 18-8:
Setting the
Start page
option.

4. **Make sure the Page field indicates Start Page.**

   If necessary, use the drop-down list to select Start Page.

5. Click the Use Current button.

The start page is set to the current page.

6. Click OK to dismiss the Options dialog box.

You're done!

You can change back to the default start page by choosing View⊃Options to summon the Options dialog box. Next, click the Navigation tab at the top of the Options dialog box and click the Use Default button. Then click OK.

Quick Links

Internet Explorer has a Favorites menu that works just like the Favorites button in the MSN Program Viewer. Favorites are a great way to keep track of all of the Web pages you visit periodically. Internet Explorer provides an even more convenient method of quickly visiting up to five of your absolute favorite Web sites: *Quick Links*. Quick Links lets you place your five favorite Web sites on a Links toolbar that can be accessed with just a few clicks of the mouse.

When you first install Internet Explorer, the Quick Links toolbar is configured with default links which take you to various Microsoft Web pages. You'll want to change these default links to your own favorites.

Accessing Quick Links

To access Internet Explorer's Quick Links feature, all you have to do is summon the Quick Links menu. Ordinarily, the Quick Links toolbar is obscured by the Address toolbar. To reveal the Quick Links toolbar, click the word Links near the top right of the Internet Explorer window. This reveals the Quick Links menu bar, as shown in Figure 18-9.

To go to one of the Quick Links, just click its button. To show the Address toolbar again, click the word Address to the left of the Quick Links toolbar.

Figure 18-9:
Getting
quickly to
your top
five Web
sites.

Quick Links menu bar

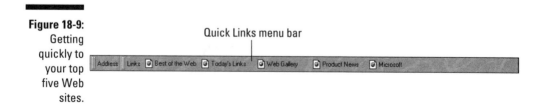

Creating your own Quick Links

Internet Explorer allows you to customize the Quick Links toolbar so that the five Quick Links point to any Web page you wish. Follow these steps to customize any of the Quick Links:

1. **Find a Web page that you want to make one of your Quick Links.**

2. **Choose View⇨Options to summon the Options dialog box and click the Navigation tab.**

   This displays the Navigation options. Refer back to Figure 18-8.

3. **Select the Quick Link you want to set from the Page drop-down list.**

   There are five Quick Link pages you can set: Quick Link 1, Quick Link 2, and so on, up to Quick Link 5.

4. **Click the Use Current button to establish the current page as the Quick Link.**

5. **Type a name for your Quick Link in the Name field.**

6. **Click OK.**

   The Quick Links toolbar shows the Quick Link you just created.

To restore a Quick Link to its default setting, call up the Navigation options as described in Step 2, select the Quick Link you want to restore, click the Use Default button, and click OK.

Chapter 19
Web Sites You Shouldn't Miss

*T*he World Wide Web is a vast collection of information scattered across the globe. This chapter is a listing of some of my favorite Web sites. The list is by no means complete, but it should be enough to get you started. If nothing else, it should at least help you appreciate the diversity to be found on the Web!

Serious Web Directories

Internet Explorer has a default Web search service, Microsoft's own all-in-one search page, which lets you locate information on the Web. But despite its name, Microsoft's all-in-one search page is not even close to a complete catalog to the Web. Several better and more complete search services are available. They are described here. Note that not all Web search services work the same. Some — such as Yahoo! — are like a vast table of contents to the Web, in which Web sites are organized by categories. Others — like Lycos — are more like an index, where you can look up any page that contains a given word.

AltaVista

```
http://www.altavista.digital.com
```

AltaVista is a search service created by Digital Equipment Corporation, one of the largest computer companies in the world. AltaVista uses a special program called a spider which automatically reads and catalogs three million Web pages every day. The AltaVista catalog lists more than 30 million Web pages. The AltaVista home page is shown in Figure 19-1.

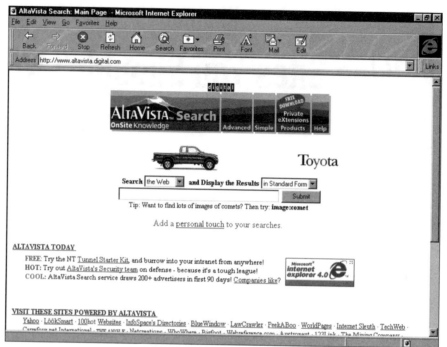

Figure 19-1:
The Alta
Vista
search
page.

Excite

http://www.excite.com

Excite is a search service that includes not only Web sites but also Usenet newsgroup articles. Excite's opening page appears in Figure 19-2.

In addition to ordinary search capabilities, Excite offers:

- ✔ More than 25,000 reviews of Web sites, which are arranged by category. To access these reviews, click the category you want to search in the *Channels by Excite* section of the Excite page.

- ✔ The News icon near the top of the page takes you to a list of the day's top news stories, with links to related Web sites.

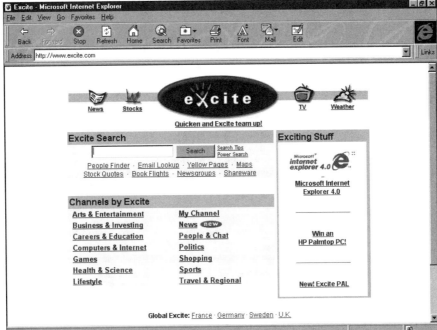

Figure 19-2:
Excite's exciting search page.

Infoseek

`http://www.infoseek.com`

Infoseek enables you to browse through subject category listings or search by keywords. Infoseek is not limited to the Web; it also enables you to search Usenet newsgroups, e-mail addresses, news stories from Reuters News, and a catalog of Frequently Asked Question (FAQ) files from popular newsgroups. Infoseek's main page appears in Figure 19-3.

Lycos

`http://www.lycos.com`

Lycos is a huge Web index that is affiliated with Carnegie Mellon University. It is primarily a keyword search tool, which means you can look up pages by words that are contained on the page. For example, you can find any page that contains the word "Butterfly." Lycos also includes categories you can browse. Because it has so many pages in its database, Lycos is my personal favorite search service. Figure 19-4 shows the Lycos opening page.

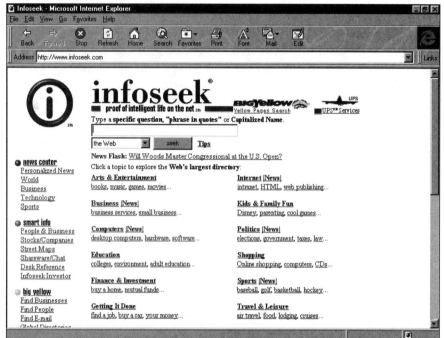

Figure 19-3:
Infoseek
and ye
shall find.

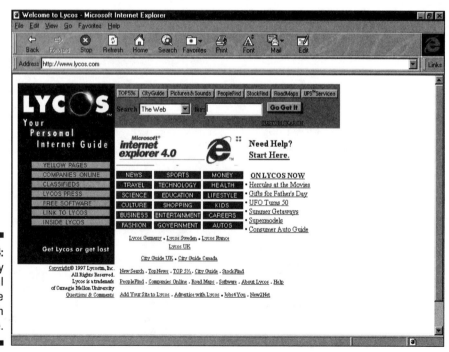

Figure 19-4:
Lycos: My
personal
favorite
search
service.

Where did the name Lycos come from? It's derived from the Latin word for Wolf Spider.

Yahoo!

`http://www.yahoo.com`

Yahoo! is one of the most popular search services. It contains tens of thousands of listings, organized into categories such as Art, Business and Economy, Computers and Internet, Education, and so on. You can browse through the Yahoo! categories, or search for specific pages by keyword. The Yahoo! opening page appears in Figure 19-5.

To search for a keyword in Yahoo!, type the word or words you want to search for in the text box, and then click the Search button. You can also click the *options* link to display a page that gives you more selective control over your searches.

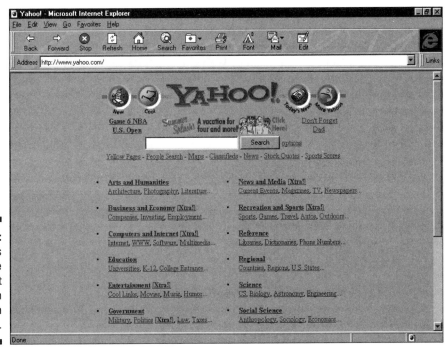

Figure 19-5:
Yahoo! is one of the hottest search services on the Web.

Yahoo! includes other links to services you may find interesting:

- **New:** Click New to see a list of new entries in the Yahoo! database. Note that on a typical day, 2,000 or more entries are added to Yahoo!'s database.
- **Cool:** Click Cool to see a list of sites that the Yahoo! staff thinks are worth checking out.
- **Today's News:** Click Today's News to see a list of newsworthy items, sorted into categories such as Business, Technology, World, Sports, Entertainment, Politics, and Weather.
- **More Yahoos:** Click More Yahoos to see a list of other services offered by Yahoo.

Yahoo! was founded by two college students at Stanford University. Rumor has it that Yahoo! stands for *Yet Another Hierarchical Officious Oracle,* but the two student founders deny it.

Computer Companies

Nearly all of the major computer hardware and software companies have Web pages. Most of these Web sites include valuable information, such as answers to frequently asked questions, or updates that correct software problems. This information can often save you the trouble of making a phone call to the company's support lines. The following sections describe the Web sites for the largest computer companies.

Microsoft

`http://www.microsoft.com`

Microsoft has one of the most active pages on the World Wide Web. It serves as a portal to all kinds of information and support provided free by Microsoft. The opening page for Microsoft's Web site is shown in Figure 19-6.

Microsoft figured you would want to visit its Web site so often that they built a link right into Internet Explorer 3.0. All you have to do is click Links to reveal the Quick Links toolbar, and then click Microsoft.

Microsoft's Web site offers many different features, including product information, schedules of upcoming events, and press releases, and product support.

Figure 19-6:
The
opening
page of
Microsoft's
Web site.

IBM

```
http://www.ibm.com
```

IBM's Web page, shown in Figure 19-7, is almost like an online magazine, with frequently updated articles describing current issues facing IBM, new products, or important events. Because this information changes frequently, you want to visit `www.ibm.com` frequently if you're an IBM follower.

IBM is an outrageously large organization and so is their Web site. The best way to get around it is to click Search and do a keyword search to look for the information you need.

Novell

```
http://www.novell.com
```

Novell is one of the leading suppliers of networking software for PCs. If your computer is attached to a network that runs Novell's NetWare software, you may need to cry to Novell for help. You can do it online via Novell's Web page, illustrated in Figure 19-8.

Figure 19-7:
IBM's
Web site.

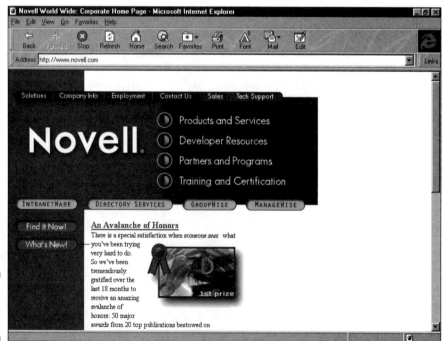

Figure 19-8:
Novell's
Web page.

Click Tech Support to search a large database of questions and answers, download updated software, or display pages for specific Novell products. In addition, the complete text of Novell's software manuals is available online.

Other computer companies on the Web

Quite a few other computer companies have pages on the Web. Table 19-1 lists a few of them. For the sake of completeness, Table 19-1 also lists the companies I've already described.

Table 19-1	Computer Companies with Web Pages
Company	*URL*
Apple	`http://www.apple.com`
Borland	`http://www.borland.com`
Compaq	`http://www.compaq.com`
Corel	`http://www.corel.ca`
Creative Labs	`http://www.creaf.com`
Dell	`http://www.del.com`
Delrina	`http://www.delrina.com`
Hewlett-Packard	`http://www.hp.com`
IBM	`http://www.ibm.com`
Intel	`http://www.intel.com`
Lotus	`http://www.lotus.com`
Microsoft	`http://www.microsoft.com`
NetScape	`http://www.netscape.com`
Novell	`http://www.novell.com`
Packard Bell	`http://www.packardbell.com/`
Symantec	`http://www.symantec.com`
WordPerfect	`http://www.wordperfect.com` (WordPerfect is now owned by Corel.)

Government Stuff

Your tax dollars at work! Yes, the federal government is everywhere on the Web. Just about every government agency has its own Web site, where you can find both propaganda and genuinely useful information. It's up to you to sift the wheat from the chaff.

If you dig deep beneath the flashy opening pages of many of these Web sites, you can often find information that is otherwise hard to obtain, such as the status of a bill that is before the House, or a case before the Supreme Court. Enjoy!

The White House

http://www.whitehouse.gov

The opening Web page for the White House Web site is a door to interesting information about the First Family — including the First Cat — and the executive branch of government. Figure 19-9 shows the White House Web page.

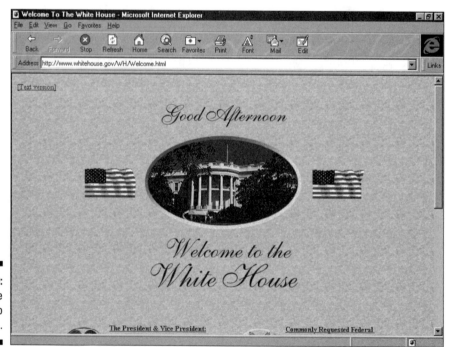

Figure 19-9:
The White House Web page.

Here are just a few of the interesting things you can do at the White House home page:

✔ Read about the accomplishments of the current administration. Just remember not to believe everything you read!

✔ Get the latest press releases direct from the White House press staff.

✔ Take a virtual tour of the White House.

✔ Send e-mail to the President or Vice President.

✔ Find links to other federal government sites.

Congress

    http://www.house.gov

    http://www.senate.gov

Not to be outdone by the White House, both the House of Representatives and the Senate also have their own Web sites. Figure 19-10 shows the opening page of the House Web site; the Senate Web site is similar.

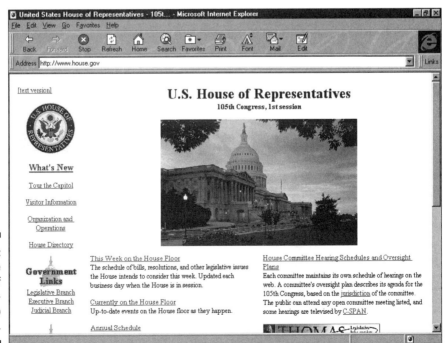

Figure 19-10:
The House of Representatives Web page.

Here are some of the services that are available from the House and Senate Web pages:

- ✔ The complete text of all bills introduced during the current congress. (If you read this stuff, you'll be doing more than many of the representatives who actually vote on it!)

- ✔ Information about the status of current bills, amendments, voting records, committees, and so on.

- ✔ The names, addresses, and phone numbers of all legislators.

- ✔ Information about visiting Capitol Hill.

- ✔ A schedule of legislative activity.

The Library of Congress

```
http://www.loc.gov
```

The Library of Congress Web page, shown in Figure 19-11, is one of my favorite pages anywhere on the Web. Apparently I'm not alone; www.loc.gov is one of the most frequently accessed sites on the Internet.

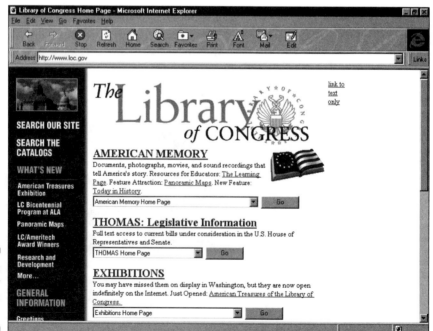

Figure 19-11: The Library of Congress Web page.

In addition to allowing you to search through its vast catalogs of books, this Web page provides special exhibits of the Library's fascinating collections. For example, the following special exhibits were available in June 1997:

- African-American Culture and History
- Creating French Culture: Treasures from the Bibliothèque Nationale de France
- Declaring Independence: Drafting the Documents
- Dresden
- 1492: An Ongoing Voyage
- The Gettysburg Address
- Revelations from the Russian Archives
- Rome Reborn: The Vatican Library and Renaissance Culture
- The Russian Church and Native Alaskan Cultures
- Scrolls from the Dead Sea
- Temple of Liberty: Building the Capitol for a New Nation
- Women Come to the Front (about the role of women in the Great War)
- Frank Lloyd Wright
- American Treasures of the Library

Plus, the Library of Congress is constructing a digital library called *American Memory*, which includes, among other items of interest, documents from the Continental Congress and Constitutional Convention, digitized images of Walt Whitman's notebooks, thousands of photographs from the Civil War, and early motion pictures that can be downloaded and played on your computer.

The Smithsonian Institution

```
http://www.si.edu
```

Take a tour of the nation's museum by checking out the Smithsonian Institute's Web site. From the Web page, you can visit any of the Smithsonian's 18 museums, including the National Air and Space Museum, the National Museum of American History, the National Museum of American Art, and the National Zoo. You can also visit Smithsonian research institutions and make use of a travel planner that helps you plan a trip to the nation's capital.

A visit to any of the museums leads you to digitized images of the museum's most priceless treasures. For example, you'll find images of the Apollo 11 Command Module, which is displayed in the entrance gallery of the National Air and Space museum along with other milestone aircraft, including the Wright Brother's original flyer and The Spirit of St. Louis. You can also find information about forthcoming exhibits. For example, Figure 19-12 shows a Web page that describes a planned exhibit about the *Star Wars* film trilogy.

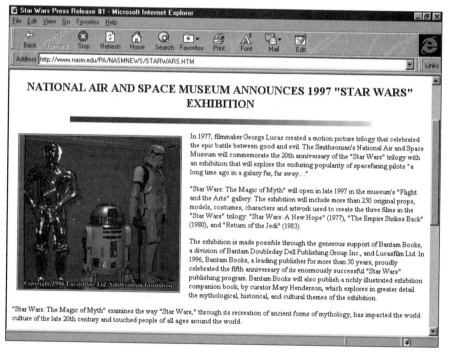

Figure 19-12:
Even the
Smithsonian
Institution is
swept up in
the Star
Wars craze.

Other Government Sites

Table 19-2 lists URLs for a variety of popular agencies of the federal government.

Table 19-2	Your Tax Dollars at Work
Government Agency	*URL*
Census bureau	`http://www.census.gov`
Central Intelligence Agency	`http://www.odci.gov`
Department of Agriculture	`http://www.usda.gov`
Department of Commerce	`http://www.doc.gov`
Department of Defense	`http://www.af.mil/dod-www.html`
Department of Education	`http://www.ed.gov`
Department of Energy	`http://www.doe.gov`
Department of Health and Human Services	`http://www.os.dhhs.gov/`
Department of Housing and Urban Development	`http://www.hud.gov`
Department of Justice	`http://www.usdoj.gov`
Department of the Interior	`http://www.doi.gov`
Department of the Treasury	`http://www.ustreas.gov`
Department of Veterans Affairs	`http://www.va.gov`
Environmental Protection Agency	`http://www.epa.gov`
Federal Aviation Administration	`http://www.faa.gov`
Federal Bureau of Investigation	`http://www.fbi.gov`
Federal Communications Commission	`http://www.fcc.gov`
Federal Emergency Management Association	`http://www.fema.gov`
Federal Trade Commission	`http://www.ftc.gov`
Internal Revenue Service	`http://www.ustreas.gov/treasury/bureaus/irs/irs.html`
National Science Foundation	`http://www.nsf.gov`
National Security Agency	`http://www.nsa.gov:8080`

(continued)

Table 19-2 *(continued)*

Government Agency	URL Address
Peace Corps	`http://www.clark.net/pub/peace/PeaceCorps.html`
Securities and Exchange Commission	`http://www.sec.gov`
Small Business Administration	`http://www.sbaonline.sba.gov`
Social Security Administration	`http://www.ssa.gov`
U.S. Patent and Trademark Office	`http://www.uspto.gov`
United States Postal Service	`http://www.usps.gov`

Fun and Generally Weird Pages

Not everything on the Web is deadly serious. The following sections are just a sample of some of the fun stuff you can find.

Games Domain

`http://www.gamesdomain.com`

Games Domain, illustrated in Figure 19-13, is one of the most complete gaming Web sites you'll find. The Games Domain maintains its own library of downloadable games, with more than 5,000 games available online. That should be enough to keep you playing for awhile!

In addition to links to downloadable games, Games Domain also includes *Frequently Asked Questions* (FAQ) files for more than 100 games, plus links to hundreds of other game-related Web sites.

If you find yourself stuck in a game, you can also check out one of the *walkthroughs,* which provide complete solutions for more than 200 computer games. Of course, reading one of these walkthroughs will spoil the game for you, so read them only if you are really stuck.

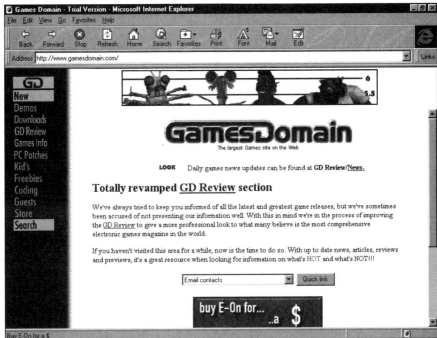

Figure 19-13:
The Games
Domain.

Internet Anagram Server

http://www.wordsmith.org/anagram

An *anagram* is a word or phrase that is made up of the same letters as another word or phrase. For example, the letters in my name, "Doug Lowe," can also be used to spell *Wood Glue* or *We Go Loud!*

The Internet hosts several Web sites that will generate anagrams for you for any word or phrase. The best of these is the Internet Anagram Server, as shown in Figure 19-14. All you have to do is type a word or phrase into the text box and press Enter. After a few moments, a long list of anagrams for the word or phrase will be displayed. I'm not kidding: In many cases, thousands of possible anagrams will be displayed. Most will be nonsense; the trick is to search through the list to find something that makes sense.

In addition to creating anagrams, the Internet Anagram Server also includes general information about anagrams and a link to the Usenet anagram discussion group, alt.anagrams.

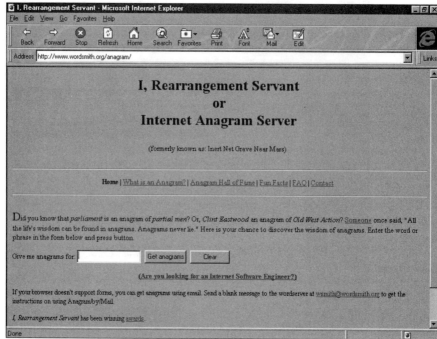

Figure 19-14:
I, Rear-
rangement
Servant.

The Dilbert Zone

http://www.unitedmedia.com/comics/dilbert/

If you're a Dilbert fan, you'll appreciate The Dilbert Zone. It features the latest Dilbert comic strip, plus interesting information about Dilbert and his creator, Scott Adams. You'll also find information about Dilbert books, early sketches of Dilbert that were rejected, and other miscellaneous Dilbert news.

The Dilbert Zone is just one of the many comic strips that are available online from United Media. Check out the United Media Web page at http://www.unitedmedia.com/comics/ for links to a dozen or so popular comics, including The Born Loser, Marmaduke, and Peanuts.

Shakespearean Insult Server

```
http://www.nova.edu/Inter-Links/cgi-bin/bard.pl
```

> ✔ Thou fawning rump-fed puttock.
>
> ✔ Thou quailing fen-sucked pignut.
>
> ✔ Thou beslubbering idle-headed harpy.
>
> ✔ Thou reeky fool-born hedge-pig.

If these insults, culled from the work of the immortal Insult Master himself, tickle thy fancy, then check out the Shakespearean Insult Server. This Web page spews out a new Shakespearean insult every time you view the page.

To obtain a new insult, click the Refresh button. You can drag the mouse over the insult to select it, press Ctrl+C to copy it to the clipboard, switch to a word processing document (or, better yet, the Microsoft Exchange mail editor), and press Ctrl+V to paste the insult into your text.

The Late Show with David Letterman

```
http://www.cbs.com/lateshow
```

Couldn't stay up late enough last night to watch the *Late Show with David Letterman?* Check out this Web page to get the current Top 10 list, and access an archive of past Top 10 lists. You can also find information about guests and news about the show. See Figure 19-15 for a look at the Letterman Web page.

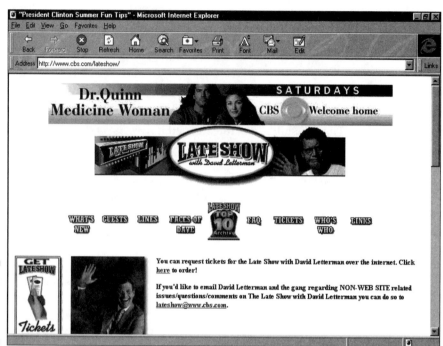

Figure 19-15:
The
Letterman
Web page.

Chapter 20

Check Out the Newsgroups

. . . .

In This Chapter

▶ Understanding newsgroups

▶ Browsing newsgroups with Microsoft Internet News

▶ Reading and writing messages to newsgroups

▶ Downloading pictures and other binary files from newsgroups

. . . .

*I*nternet Newsgroups are where the most lively, entertaining, and informative discussion happens on the Internet. Newsgroups are similar to Microsoft Network bulletin boards — so similar, in fact, that you use the same program to access both. Chapter 12 showed you how to use Microsoft Internet News to access MSN bulletin boards. In this chapter, I'll show you how to use Internet News for it's original intended purpose: accessing Internet newsgroups.

What is a Newsgroup?

A *newsgroup* is a place where you can post messages, called *articles,* about a particular topic and read messages that others have posted about the same topic. It is an area where people with similar interests gather to share news and information, find out what others are thinking, ask questions, get answers, and generally shoot the breeze.

The Internet has thousands of newsgroups — yea, *tens* of thousands — on topics ranging from astronomy to the Civil War. You can find a newsgroup for virtually any subject that interests you.

Newsgroups come in two basic types:

> ✔ **Moderated newsgroups:** In a moderated newsgroup, one person is designated as a *moderator,* who has complete control over what does and does not appear in the newsgroup. Articles are submitted to the moderator for his or her review, and are not posted to the newsgroup until the moderator approves them.

The moderator establishes the criteria for which articles get posted to the newsgroup. For some newsgroups, the criteria may be that the article must somehow be related to the subject of the newsgroup. Other newsgroups use more stringent criteria, enabling the moderator to be more selective about what gets posted. As a result, only the best postings actually make it into the newsgroup. This supervision may seem stifling, but, in most cases, it dramatically improves the quality of the newsgroup articles.

✔ **Unmoderated newsgroups:** In an unmoderated newsgroup, anyone and everyone can post an article. Unmoderated newsgroups are free from censorship, but they are also often filled with blatant solicitations, chain letters, and all sorts of noise.

What is Usenet?

Usenet refers to a collection of newsgroups that are distributed to *news servers* (computers that run special software). Each Internet Service Provider (ISP) provides its own news server so that you can access the newsgroups that are a part of Usenet. The Microsoft Network is no exception: MSN provides access to a Usenet server named NetNews.msn.com.

In theory, the Usenet servers share their new postings with one another, so that all of the servers contain the most recent postings. In practice, Usenet servers are never really quite up-to-date, nor are they always in sync with one another. You find that when you post an article to a newsgroup, a day or so may pass before your article propagates through the Usenet so that it appears on all of the servers throughout Usenet. Likewise, replies to your articles may take awhile to show up on the MSN Usenet server.

How Newsgroups are Organized

Usenet boasts thousands of newsgroups. Each newsgroup has a unique name that consists of one or more parts separated by periods. For example, soc.culture.assyrian is a newsgroup that discusses Assyrian culture, sci.polymers contains information on the scientific field of polymers, and rec.food.drink.beer is a place to discuss your favorite brew.

The following sections describe three broad categories of newsgroups.

Basic Usenet newsgroups

The basic Usenet newsgroups are divided into seven broad categories, as indicated by the first part of the newsgroups name. The seven categories are described in the following list:

- comp: Discussions about computers. Many of the participants in the comp newsgroups wear pocket protectors and glasses held together by tape, so be careful.

- news: Discussions about the Usenet itself, such as help for new Usenet users, announcements of new newsgroups, and statistics about which newsgroups are most popular.

- rec: Recreational topics, such as sports, fishing, basket weaving, and model railroading.

- sci: Discussions about science.

- soc: Social topics, where people gather to shoot the breeze or to discuss social issues.

- talk: Newsgroups that favor long-winded discussions of topics such as politics and religion.

- misc: Topics that don't fit in any of the other categories.

Within these categories are many subcategories. The best way to get the feel for how these categories are organized is simply to spend an hour or so browsing through them.

Regional newsgroups

An entire structure of *regional newsgroups,* which share regional interests rather than subject-matter interests, also exists. These regional newsgroups are indicated by a short — usually two or three letters — prefix, such as aus (Australia) or can (Canada). Most states have regional newsgroups designated by the state's two-letter abbreviation (CA for California, WA for Washington, and so on).

Alternative and other newsgroups

Finally, you find the so-called *alternative* newsgroups. These newsgroups are identified by the following prefixes:

✔ alt: Hundreds of newsgroups using this prefix discuss topics that range from bizarre to X-rated to paranoid. These newsgroups are not officially sanctioned by Usenet, but some of the most popular newsgroups fall into this category. The most visited of the alt newsgroups fall under alt.binaries. These newsgroups contain binary files, such as pictures, sounds, and actual programs, that are specially encoded to be sent via Usenet's text-only messages. Fortunately, Internet News is able to automatically decode these attachments, so you don't have to worry about using a separate program to do so.

✔ bit: Bitnet is the network that supports Internet mailing lists. A mailing list is like a newsgroup, except that all messages are exchanged via e-mail. The bit newsgroups are the bitnet mailing lists presented in newsgroup form.

✔ biz: This prefix denotes a business related newsgroup.

✔ bionet: Newsgroups with this prefix discuss topics related to biology.

Because the content of newsgroups, particularly the alt newsgroups, can be offensive, MSN does not automatically grant you access to all of them. See the section "Obtaining Full Access to Internet Newsgroups," later in this chapter for more information.

Accessing Internet Newsgroups

To get started with Internet News, follow these steps:

1. Click the Start button in the taskbar and then choose Programs⇨Internet News.

Internet News comes to life.

2. Choose the News⇨Newsgroups command.

You can also click the Newsgroups icon in the toolbar. Either way, the Newsgroups dialog box appears, as shown in Figure 20-1.

3. Click the NetNews icon located in the list of news servers.

This connects you to the MSN Usenet news server and displays a list of all the newsgroups.

4. Click the newsgroup you want to access.

There are thousands of newsgroups available, so you'll have to scroll through the list to find the newsgroup you want.

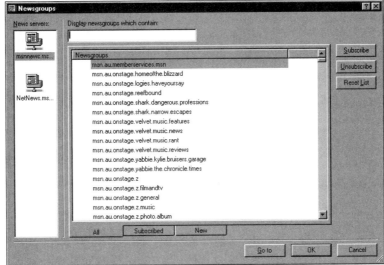

5. Click Go to.

The newsgroup you selected will be opened, as shown in Figure 20-2. In this case, I've opened one of my favorite newsgroups, `alt.folklore. urban`, which contains discussions about commonly told stories, which usually have little basis in fact but are nevertheless accepted by most people as true.

If you find a newsgroup that you think you'll visit frequently, click the Subscribe button. This adds the newsgroup to the list of newsgroups that appears in the main Internet News window in the Newsgroups drop-down list box. This is where your current newsgroup is listed.

You can type a word or phrase in the Display newsgroups text box to display only those newsgroups whose names contain the word or phrase you type. For example, Figure 20-3 shows a list of all newsgroups that contain the word *startrek*. As you can see, Usenet plays host to some pretty strange *Star Trek* fans.

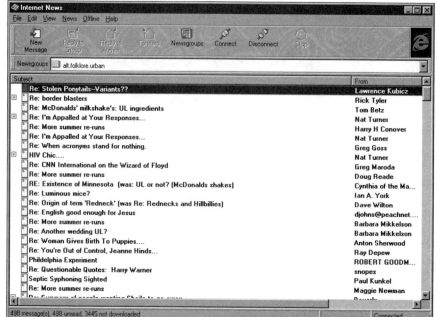

Figure 20-2:
Internet
News
displays a
newsgroup.

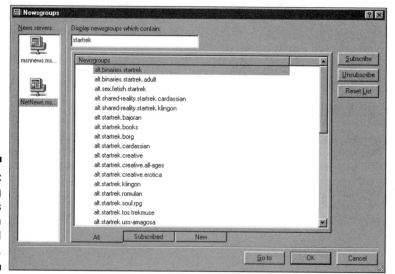

Figure 20-3:
Displaying
newsgroups
that contain
the word
startrek.

Reading Article Threads

A *thread* is a newsgroup article, plus any articles that were posted as replies to the original article, articles posted as replies to the replies, and so on. Microsoft Internet News sorts together all of the articles that belong to a thread. Initially, only the first message in a thread is listed in Internet News. A plus sign next to a message title indicates that the article has replies. To see the replies to the original message, you need to expand the thread. When you no longer want to see the replies, you can collapse the thread so that only the original message is shown.

The following are ways you can expand or collapse threads:

✔ Click the plus sign to reveal the replies to an article.

✔ Click the minus sign to hide replies.

✔ Choose View➪Expand to expand a thread.

✔ Choose View➪Collapse to collapse an expanded thread.

Reading an Article

To read an article, double-click the article title. The article appears in a separate window. After you finish reading the article, click the article window's close button to close the window.

Here are other actions you can take while reading an article:

 ✔ Read the next article.

 ✔ Read the previous article.

 ✔ Print the article.

 ✔ Save the article as a text file on your hard disk.

 ✔ Forward the article to someone via e-mail.

 ✔ Post a reply. See the next section, "Replying to an Article," for more information.

 ✔ E-mail a reply to the author of the article.

Replying to an Article

To reply to a newsgroup article, follow these steps:

1. **Count to ten, and then reconsider your reply.**

   Keep in mind that replying to a newsgroup is not like replying to e-mail. Only the intended recipient can read an e-mail reply. Anyone on the planet can read your newsgroup reply. If you don't really have anything to add to the discussion, why waste time? Go to Step 5.

2. **After reading the article you want to reply to, click the Reply to Group button on the toolbar.**

   A new message window appears, with the subject line already filled in.

3. **Type your reply.**

4. **Click the Send button.**

   Your article is sent to the newsgroup.

5. **You're about to become a published writer.**

By default, the complete text of the original message is added to the end of your reply. If the message is long, you may want to delete some or all of the original text. If you don't want the original message text to be automatically added to your replies, choose <u>N</u>ews⇨<u>O</u>ptions, click the Send tab, and then deselect the I<u>n</u>clude original message in reply option.

Hold the spam

No, I'm not referring to that canned meat product that was the butt of many jokes in the old TV series, *M*A*S*H*. I'm talking about a particular type of annoying newsgroup message. A *spam* is a message that has been bogusly posted to more than one — perhaps dozens — of newsgroups, all at the same time, in an effort to generate hundreds of responses. Spams often have subject headers like *Make money fast* or *Free X-rated pictures in your mailbox!*

The best way to deal with spams is to ignore them. You see, the main problem with spams is that they generate hundreds of responses, which may also generate hundreds of responses. Most of the responses are along the lines of "Quit spamming us, you idiot," but the responders don't realize that they themselves help the spammer by keeping his or her bogus thread alive. Better to ignore the spam altogether so it goes away.

Writing a New Article

When you have finally mustered up the courage to post an article of your own to a newsgroup, follow these steps:

1. **Open the newsgroup to which you want to post a new article.**

2. **Click the New Message button.**

   A new message window appears.

3. **Type a subject for the article in the Subject box.**

   Make sure that the subject you type accurately reflects the topic of the article — or prepare to get flamed. (Being *flamed* doesn't mean that your computer screen actually emits a ball of fire in your direction, singeing the hair off your forearm. It refers to getting an angry — even vitriolic — response from a reader.) If your subject line is misleading, at least one Internet user is sure to chew you out.

4. **Type your message in the message area.**

5. **If you are worried about your vice-presidential prospects, choose News⇨Check Spelling.**

   The spell checker gives you the option to correct any misspelled words.

6. **Click the Send button when you're satisfied with your response.**

Dealing with Attachments

Internet newsgroups are text only; you cannot attach binary files, such as program, picture, and sound files, to newsgroup messages. Internet users are very resourceful, however, and they long ago figured out a way to get around this dilemma. They invented a technique called *encoding* that converts a binary file into a series of text codes, which can be posted as a newsgroup article. Such an article looks completely scrambled when you see it. However, you can save the article to a file on your hard disk and then run the saved file through a special decoding program that converts it back to its original form, whether it's a program, picture, or sound file.

With Internet News, the decoding routine is built in, so you don't need a separate program. To save a binary file that has been attached to a newsgroup article, all you have to do is follow these steps:

1. **Open the article that has the attachment.**

   Unlike Internet Mail, Internet News does not indicate which messages contain attachments by displaying a paper clip next to the subject line. The only way to tell whether a message has an attachment is to open the message.

2. **Right-click the Attachment icon.**

   A shortcut menu appears.

3. **Choose the Save As command from the shortcut menu.**

   A standard Save As dialog box appears.

4. **Select the location where you want to save the file.**

   The controls in the Save As dialog box allow you to navigate to any drive or folder.

5. **Check the filename that is proposed for the file.**

   If you don't like it, change it.

6. **Click Save.**

   The file is saved.

You can view an attachment without saving it to disk by double-clicking the attachment. This opens the attachment in a separate window so you can see it.

Obtaining Full Access to Internet Newsgroups

Because some of the material found on the Internet's newsgroups is adult in nature, The Microsoft Network does not initially grant you access to all of it. Instead, it prevents you from accessing certain Internet newsgroups which contain adult content. Before you can access these groups, you must first request and be granted full Internet access.

To request full Internet access, all you have to do is send e-mail to Postmaster@msn.com. In your e-mail message, say that you are requesting full Internet access. You'll soon receive an e-mail message containing a form which you can fill out and return. After the form has been processed, you'll be granted access to all of the Internet newsgroups.

Part VI

Customizing Your MSN Journey

The 5th Wave — By Rich Tennant

"IT'S ANOTHER DEEP SPACE PROBE FROM EARTH, SEEKING CONTACT FROM EXTRATERRESTRIALS. I WISH THEY'D JUST INCLUDE AN E-MAIL ADDRESS."

In this part . . .

This is the part to turn to when you're tired of working with MSN as it works out of the box, and you want to customize it to more closely suit your working style. In these chapters, you discover how to customize MSN's various settings, with special emphasis on controlling access to MSN and Internet content that you may find offensive.

Chapter 21

Opting for Options

. . . .

. . . .

*Y*ou use the MSN Properties dialog box to set the myriad of preference options that affect the way the MSN Program Viewer browses The Microsoft Network and the World Wide Web. Of course, you can't use this command to pick your *real* preferences, such as playing golf instead of toiling with your computer. But you can do stuff that's almost as much fun, such as changing the colors used to display links you've already visited, or changing the amount of disk space MSN uses to store downloaded graphics.

Note: I am aware that for some people golf is a more frustrating pastime than using their computers. For others, golf is more boring than reading the MSN online help. If you're one of those poor, unenlightened souls who think golf is more boring, feel free to substitute your favorite non-golf pastime.

What's With All the Options?

There are two ways to get to the Internet Properties dialog box:

- ✔ Point the mouse at the OnMSN icon that appears in the top-left corner of the MSN Program Viewer window, and then choose Internet Properties from the menu that appears.

- ✔ Click the down arrow that appears next to the OnMSN icon to reveal the full Internet toolbar, and then click the Internet Explorer icon (the funny looking *e*).

Either way, you'll be rewarded with the Internet Properties dialog box that has four tabs: General, Connection, Security, and Advanced. To switch from one tab to another, just click the tab label at the top of the dialog box.

Here's the lowdown on the four tabs that appear in the Options dialog box:

✔ **General:** Contains options that affect the general operation of the MSN Program Viewer.

✔ **Connection:** Indicates which dial-up connection to use to establish the connection to MSN.

✔ **Security:** Enables you to indicate if you want to be warned before doing something that may jeopardize your computer's security, and enables you to filter out pages with questionable content.

✔ **Advanced:** Contains options that just didn't fit anywhere else.

To set any of these options, follow this general procedure:

1. **Point to the OnMSN icon and choose the Internet Properties command from the menu that appears.**

   Or click the Internet Explorer icon in the Internet toolbar. Either way, the Internet Properties dialog box appears.

2. **Click the tab that contains the option you want to set.**

   If you're not sure which tab to click, just cycle through them all until you find what you're looking for.

3. **Set the options however you want.**

   Most of the options are check boxes that you click to select or deselect. Some options require that you select a choice from a drop-down list, and some have the audacity to require you to actually type something as a proof of your keyboard proficiency.

4. **Repeat Step 3 until you've exhausted your options, or you're just exhausted.**

5. **Click OK.**

   You're done!

Saluting the General Options

These options started out as Private options, but quickly re-upped and now, after years of dedicated service, have been promoted to the rank of General. You'd better snap-to whenever you call up these options, shown in Figure 21-1.

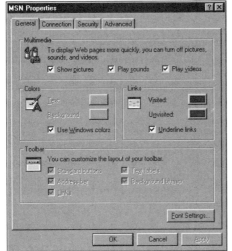

Figure 21-1:
The
General
options.

The following list enumerates the General options:

✔ **Multimedia:** Enables you to indicate whether graphics, sounds, and video should be automatically downloaded whenever a page is displayed. Disabling any or all of these options improves the MSN performance, but robs you of the spectacular effects of pictures, sounds, and animations. You'll probably find that MSN is all but unusable if you disable pictures because MSN pages tend to present their information using pictures. On the other hand, disabling sounds and videos can be a big timesaver and won't diminish the usefulness of MSN much.

✔ **Colors:** Enables you to set the colors to use for text and background.

✔ **Links:** Enables you to change the color used to display links you've already visited and links you haven't yet traversed.

✔ **Toolbar:** In the full-fledged Internet Explorer program, these options enable you to control the appearance of the toolbar. For the MSN Program Viewer — which is really just a special version of Internet Explorer — Microsoft doesn't want you fiddling with these options. As a result, they are grayed out.

Cajoling the Connection Options

The Connection options, shown in Figure 21-2, enable you to specify which dial-up connection is used to connect to the Internet. You may find yourself turning to this tab frequently if you have more than one Internet provider, and you often switch from one to another. You'll also turn to this tab if you decide to change providers.

If you have not yet created a dial-up connection for your Internet provider, click the Add button. This launches a Wizard that creates a connection for you. Just follow the steps through the Wizard to create the connection. You need to make up a name for the new connection you are creating (any name will do), and you must supply the phone number for the connection. When you have created the new connection, it automatically becomes the default connection used to connect to MSN.

If your Internet Service Provider charges you by the hour for connect time, consider checking the Disconnect If Idle For option. With this option selected, if you accidentally walk away from your computer without disconnecting from MSN, the MSN Program Viewer automatically disconnects after a certain amount of time. The default time setting is 20 minutes, which seems about right to me.

If your computer is connected to a local area network and you access the Internet through the network, you may need to configure a *proxy server*. If so, click the Proxy Server check box and then click the Change proxy settings button and enter the proxy settings. (These settings will be supplied to you by your network administrator.)

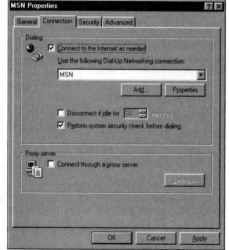

Figure 21-2:
The
Connection
options.

Striving with Security Options

Figure 21-3 shows the Security options, which are designed to protect you from Internet sites with offensive content, protect your privacy, and to warn you about potential security problems.

The following three security features are covered by the Security options:

✔ **Content Advisor:** This is the feature that enables you to screen out Internet sites which have potentially offensive content. It is covered in more detail in Chapter 22.

✔ **Certificates:** These are the best method of ensuring secure communications between two Web sites. *Certificates* are specially encoded documents that are like identification badges. They are exchanged by the two Web sites. The certificates can guarantee that the computer you are connected to is who it claims to be, and vice versa.

✔ **Active Content:** These features enable you to select Microsoft's hot new ActiveX technology, which enables Web designers to fill their pages with all sorts of interesting new controls. If you want to visit pages that use ActiveX, select all of these options. Because more and more Web sites — including most of the MSN pages — rely on ActiveX, deselecting these options results in frequent and annoying warning messages. I suggest you select these options. You can also choose to enable or disable Java programs, which are a different way of creating interesting Web pages. You should probably leave this setting enabled.

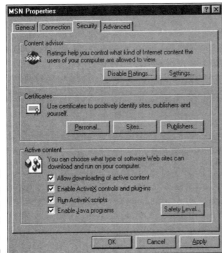

Figure 21-3:
The
Security
options.

Arguing with the Advanced Options

The Advanced options, shown in Figure 21-4, enable you to set several options that govern the MSN Program Viewer operation.

Among the options found with the Advanced options are:

✔ **Warnings:** Notify you whenever certain actions are about to occur, such as sending information over an unsecured line. Most of these warnings are annoying, so you'll probably end up deselecting these sooner or later.

✔ **Temporary files:** Enable you to manage the temporary files that are downloaded by MSN to your hard disk. By default, MSN will pick a default size that depends on the size of your hard drive. On my computer, with a 5GB hard drive, the default setting is 2 percent. The more disk space you allocate to MSN, the less often MSN is forced to download files that you've already seen. This means that MSN will seem to run faster. Of course, the tradeoff is that increasing the amount of disk space MSN can use decreases the amount of free disk space on your computer.

To change the temporary files options, click the Settings button, which summons the Settings dialog box shown in Figure 21-5. Adjust the temporary files settings and then click OK.

If your hard disk runs out of free space, you can empty the Temporary Internet Files folder by clicking the Empty Folder button. When you empty this folder you will notice delays, as Internet Explorer downloads files that were previously stored on your disk. But you will regain the disk space that was used by these files.

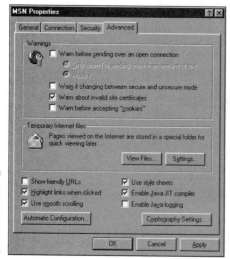

Figure 21-4:
The
Advanced
options.

✔ **Show Friendly URLs:** This option affects how the MSN Program Viewer displays Web addresses in the Internet toolbar. If this option is selected, MSN abbreviates URLs by eliminating the portions of the address that refer to the current page. This usually shortens the URLs and makes them easier to read. For example, suppose you are currently viewing a page whose URL is `http://www.somewhere.com`, and the page has a link to `http://www.somewhere.com/goodstuff.htm`. With Show Friendly URLs selected, the URL is displayed as simply `goodstuff.htm`.

✔ **Highlight links when clicked:** With this option enabled, MSN draws a box using dashed lines around a link when you click it. This is a fairly inconsequential option, so don't bother changing it.

✔ **Use smooth scrolling:** You may have noticed that MSN scrolls its windows differently than most other applications. MSN uses an animated effect that makes scrolling appear smoother. On slower computers, you may want to deselect this option to improve performance.

✔ **Use Style Sheets:** Style sheets are a new Internet feature that Web authors can use to create splashy Web pages. By all means leave this option selected.

✔ **Enable Java JIT compiler:** This is another option you should leave selected. It enables Web pages that have special scripts called *Java programs* to run more efficiently.

✔ **Enable Java logging:** If you are a Java expert, you can use this option to enable the Java log, which records all Java activity.

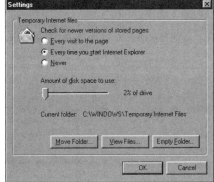

Figure 21-5:
Adjusting
the
temporary
file settings.

Chapter 22

Exercising Your Parental Controls

● ●

In This Chapter

▶ Understanding Web site ratings

▶ Activating the MSN Content Advisor

▶ Determining your blush threshold

▶ Picking a secret password

▶ Requiring password access to restricted sites

● ●

*A*lthough MSN and the Internet can be a great resource for kids, both can also be unsafe places for kids to hang out unsupervised. Although MSN is fairly tame, the Internet is anything but tame. For every museum, library, and government agency that springs up on the Internet, a corresponding adult bookstore, sex shop, or smutty magazine seems to appear. What's a parent to do?

Fortunately, MSN has a built-in feature called Content Advisor that enables you to restrict access to off-color MSN and Internet sites. Content Advisor uses a system of ratings similar to the ratings used for movies. Although this system isn't perfect, it goes a long way toward preventing your kids from stumbling into something they shouldn't.

About Internet Ratings

Internet ratings work much like motion picture ratings, because they let you know what kind of content you can expect at a given Internet site. The Internet ratings are assigned voluntarily by the publisher of the Web site.

Although movie ratings give you an overall rating for a movie (G, PG, PG-13, R, or NC-17), the motion picture ratings system doesn't give you a clue about *why* a movie receives a particular rating. For example, does a PG-13 rating mean that a movie is filled with foul language, almost explicit sex, or excessive violence? It can be any of these, or all of these.

By contrast, Internet ratings give specific information about several categories of potentially offensive material. Several different rating systems are currently being developed. The system used by MSN was developed by a nonprofit organization called the *Recreational Software Advisory Council* (RSAC). RSAC assigns a rating of zero to four for each of the following four categories:

- ✔ Violence
- ✔ Nudity
- ✔ Language
- ✔ Sex

Table 22-1 shows the specific meaning for each RSAC rating number.

Table 22-1	What the RSAC Ratings Mean			
Rating	*Violence*	*Nudity*	*Language*	*Sex*
0	Harmless conflict; some damage to objects	No nudity or revealing attire	Inoffensive slang; no profanity	Romance, no sex
1	Creatures injured or killed; damage to objects; fighting	Revealing attire	Mild expletives	Passionate kissing
2	Humans injured or killed; with small amount of blood	Partial nudity, nonsexual anatomical references	Expletives	Clothed sexual touching
3	Humans injured or killed; blood and gore	Nonsexual frontal nudity	Strong, vulgar language; obscene gestures	Nonexplicit sexual activity
4	Wanton and gratuitous violence; torture; rape	Provocative frontal nudity	Crude or explicit sexual references	Explicit sexual activity; sex crimes

With MSN, you can set a threshold value for each of the four categories. Any attempt to access a Web page that has a rating higher than the threshold value will be blocked.

The RSAC ratings system was developed by a group of recognized experts in the effects of the media on children. For more information about RSAC, check out their Web site at `http://www.rsac.org`. Figure 22-1 shows the RSAC's home page, where you can learn more about RSAC. If you're a Web publisher, you can also find out how to provide a rating for your site.

Limitations of Internet Ratings

Before I show you how to activate and configure the MSN Ratings feature, I want to be sure I don't lull you into a false sense of security, thinking that after you activate the ratings feature, you won't have to worry about your kids getting into trouble on MSN or the Internet. Here are a few limitations of the RSAC rating system:

✔ Ratings are voluntary. No one can guarantee that a Web publisher will give his or her site an accurate rating.

Figure 22-1:
The Recreational Software Advisory Council's home page.

✔ Currently, MSN ratings apply only to MSN sites and Web sites. Some of the nastiest Internet content, however, is found not on the Web, but in Usenet newsgroups. Microsoft is working on a way to extend controls to newsgroups, but for now, RSAC ratings apply only to Web sites.

✔ Not all Web sites are rated. In fact, most are not. MSN enables you to either ban all sites that are not rated, or allow full access to these sites. Neither option is good: If you ban sites that are not rated, you'll ban most Web sites; If you allow access to sites that are not rated, you let some garbage in. Sigh.

✔ Kids are clever. You can rest assured that some kids will figure out a way to bypass the ratings feature altogether. No security system is totally secure.

Activating Content Advisor

Out of the box, MSN does not check for Web site ratings. To screen out offensive Web sites, you first activate the Content Advisor. Just follow these steps:

1. **Point at the OnMSN icon in the MSN Program Viewer window, and then choose the Internet Properties command from the menu that appears.**

   The Internet Properties dialog box appears.

2. **Click the Security tab.**

   The Security options appear, as shown in Figure 22-2.

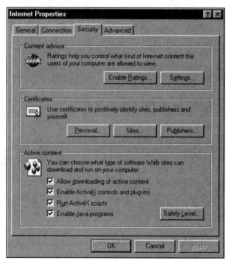

Figure 22-2:
The
Security
options.

3. Click the Enable Ratings button.

MSN asks you to create a supervisor password in the dialog box shown in Figure 22-3.

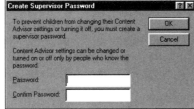

Figure 22-3:
Creating a
supervisor
password.

4. Think up a good password.

Read the nearby sidebar, "What's the password?," to get guidelines for creating a good password.

5. Type the password once into the Password field, and then type it again into the Confirm Password field.

The password is not displayed on-screen as you type it, so MSN requires you to type your password twice, just to make sure that you don't make a typing mistake.

6. Click OK.

The following message is displayed in its own little dialog box:

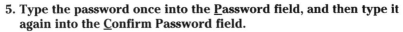

7. Click OK.

The Internet Properties dialog box reappears. You can tell that Content Advisor has been turned on because the Enable Ratings button has been changed to Disable Ratings.

8. Click the Settings button.

The Supervisor Password Required dialog box appears, as shown in Figure 22-4.

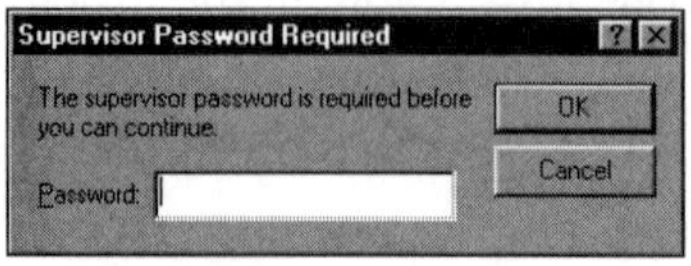

Figure 22-4:
Content
Advisor
asks for
your
password.

9. **Type the password and then click OK.**

   The Content Advisor dialog box appears, as in Figure 22-5.

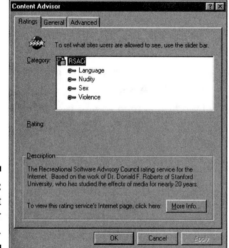

Figure 22-5:
The Content
Advisor
dialog box.

10. **Set the rating for each category by clicking the category and then adjusting the slider bar for the rating you want to use.**

    The slider bar magically appears after you click the category. For example, Figure 22-6 shows the slider bar that appears after you click the Language category. A description of each rating level appears beneath the slider bar. This description changes as you move the slider bar.

11. **After you have set the ratings to appropriate levels for your kids, click OK.**

    You are returned to the Options dialog box once again.

12. **Click OK to dismiss the Options dialog box.**

    Finally! You're finished!

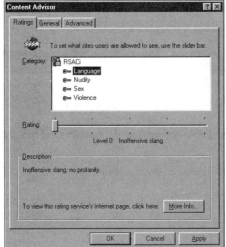

Figure 22-6:
Setting the rating for the Language category.

After you activate Content Advisor, the Content Advisor dialog box you see in Figure 22-7 appears whenever someone attempts to access a Web site that your ratings do not allow.

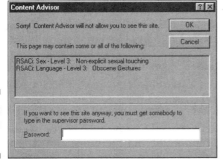

Figure 22-7:
Caught in the act!

You can deactivate Content Advisor at any time by calling up the Security options (Choose <u>V</u>iew➪<u>O</u>ptions and then click the Security tab) and clicking the Disable Ratings button. You will be required to enter the password.

If you deactivate the ratings so you can use MSN and the Internet without restriction, don't forget to activate them again when you're finished!

What's the password?

The Internet Ratings feature is only as good as the password you pick. Make sure that you don't pick a password that can be easily guessed. Here are passwords to avoid:

- Your name or your kids' names
- The names of your pets
- The name of your boat
- Your birthday or anniversary
- Your car license plate number
- The password you use to access the Internet

- Any other word or number that is important to you which your kids can easily figure out

The best passwords are random combinations of letters and numbers. Of course, they're also the hardest to memorize. Next best are randomly chosen words. Just open the dictionary to a random page, point to a random word, and use it.

Above all, do not write the password down on a stick-on note attached to the computer monitor! If you write the password down, put the piece of paper in a secure place where only *you* can find it.

Dealing with Unrated Sites

Internet Ratings are a great idea, but unfortunately, not all Web sites are rated. When you enable Content Advisor, MSN bans access not only to sites whose ratings are above the threshold you set, but also to any site that is not rated.

Because most Web sites on the Internet are unrated, MSN lets you ease the ban on unrated sites. Here is the procedure:

1. **Point at the OnMSN icon in the MSN Program Viewer window, and then choose the Properties command from the menu that appears. When the Internet Properties dialog box appears, click the Security tab.**

   The Security options appear. Refer to Figure 22-2 for a look at the Security options.

2. **Click the Settings button.**

   You are asked for your password. Type the password and then click OK. The Content Advisor dialog box appears.

3. **Click the General tab.**

   You see the General Internet Ratings options, as shown in Figure 22-8.

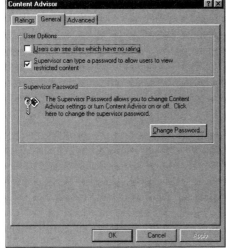

Figure 22-8:
The
General
Internet
Ratings
options.

4. **Select the Users can see sites which have no rating check box.**

5. **Click OK to dismiss the Content Advisor dialog box.**

   The Options dialog box reappears.

6. **Click OK to dismiss the Options dialog box.**

Now, you can view unrated sites without the constant Sorry! Your ratings do not allow you to see this site message.

To restrict access to unrated sites once again, repeat the procedure, except this time deselect the Users can see sites which have no rating check box in Step 4.

The General options dialog box also allows you to change the supervisor password. Click the Change Password button. A dialog box appears, into which you can type a new password. As before, you must type the password twice to make sure you that don't make any typing errors.

Normally, you can view a restricted site by typing in the supervisor password. If you want to disable this feature so that restricted sites cannot be viewed even if you do know the password, deselect the Supervisor can type a password option.

Part VII
The Part of Tens

The 5th Wave   **By Rich Tennant**

"He should be all right now. I made him spend two and a half hours on a 'prisoners' chat line.'"

In this part . . .

If you keep this book in the bathroom, the chapters in this part are the ones that you'll read the most. Each of these chapters consists of ten (more or less) things that are worth knowing about various aspects of using MSN. Without further ado, here they are, direct from the home office in Fresno, California.

Chapter 23

Ten Things That Often Go Wrong

● ●

In This Chapter

▶ Old version of MSN

▶ Modem connection not working

▶ Forgotten passwords

▶ Strange error messages

▶ Disappearing MSN windows

▶ Vanishing downloaded files

▶ Cut off from MSN in the middle of a big download

▶ Favorite MSN or Web page lost

▶ No answer

▶ Threat of nuclear war

● ●

*A*ctually, probably more like 10,000 things can go wrong, but this chapter describes some of the things that go wrong most often.

I Don't Have the Latest and Greatest MSN!

Microsoft has mailed out billions and billions of copies of their free MSN CD-ROM, but in case you didn't get yours, you can easily request one. Just go online to the MSN Web site:

```
www.msn.com
```

Click the Try MSN icon. A Web page appears where you can fill out a request for a free MSN CD-ROM. The CD-ROM comes with a free one-month trial so that you can check out what MSN has to offer.

I Can't Get Connected!

You double-click the MSN icon, the Connect To dialog box appears, and you type in your name and password, but that's as far as you get. For an unknown reason, you are unable to connect to MSN. Arghhhhh!

Many, many things can be wrong here. Here are a few general troubleshooting procedures that should help you solve the problem, or at least narrow it down:

✔ Make sure that the modem is securely connected to the telephone wall jack and that the correct jack is on the back of the modem. Phone cables sometimes jar loose or go bad, so replacing the phone cable may solve the problem. If you're not sure which jack is the correct one, you'll have to consult the manual that came with the modem.

✔ Make sure that the modem is not in use by another program, such as a fax program or the Windows 95 Hyperterminal program.

✔ Make sure that your teenager isn't talking on a phone that shares the same phone line as the modem (this happens to me all of the time).

✔ Try calling your MSN access number on a regular phone and see if it answers. If you get a busy signal or it just continues to ring, something may be wrong with the local access number. Try again later, and call the MSN customer service if the problem persists.

✔ Double-check the phone number in the Connect To dialog box.

✔ Sometimes removing and reinstalling the modem within Windows 95 will solve the problem. Click the Start button and choose the Settings➪Control Panel command. Double-click on the Modems icon, click the modem to select the modem, and then click the Remove button. Then click Add and follow the Install a New Modem wizard to reinstall the modem.

✔ The MSN CD-ROM contains an excellent connection troubleshooting program. Insert the MSN CD-ROM into your CD-ROM drive. When the MSN window opens, click Get help connecting the MSN.

✔ Make sure that the modem is configured to use the proper communications port within your computer. This problem is most likely to occur if you just installed the modem, or if the modem has never worked right.

To change the communications port setting, follow these steps:

1. **Click the Start button and choose the Settings➪Control Panel command.**

2. **Double-click on the Modems icon.**

3. **Click the Properties button.**

4. Change the <u>P</u>ort setting for the modem.

5. Click OK twice.

6. Try again.

I Forgot My Password!

Didn't I tell you to write it down and keep it in a safe place? Sigh. If you really did forget your password, and you didn't write it down anywhere, you have to call Microsoft for assistance. If you can convince them that you really are who you say you are, they'll allow you to reset your password.

So you don't find yourself in this mess again, make sure that the <u>S</u>ave Password option on the Connect To dialog box is selected. This way you don't have to always type your password. Write down your password and store it in a secure location. Here's a list of several not-so-secure places to hide your password:

✔ In a desk drawer, in a file folder labeled *Not My Internet Password*.

✔ On a magnet stuck to the refrigerator. No one, including you, will ever be able to pick it out from all the other junk stuck up there.

✔ On the inside cover of this book, in Pig Latin, so that no one will be able to understand it.

✔ Carved on the back of a park bench.

✔ On the wall in a public bathroom.

✔ Tattooed backward so that you can read it in a mirror.

I Received a Weird Error Message

This happens sometimes when you try to follow a link to a cool Web page, or you type in a URL of your own and press Enter. Instead of being greeted with the expected Web page, you get this message:

```
Cannot open the Internet site http://www.whatever.com
             An unexpected error has occurred.
```

The unexpected error means that for one reason or another, the Web page you tried to access can't be found. Several possible explanations exist:

✔ The Web page you are trying to display may no longer exist. The person who created the Web page may have removed it.

✔ The Web page may have been moved to a new URL. Sometimes you'll get a message telling you about the new URL, and sometimes you won't.

✔ The Web site that hosts the Web page may be having technical trouble. Try again later.

✔ The Web page may be just too darn popular, causing the server to be busy. Try again later.

The MSN Program Viewer Window Disappeared!

You know you are signed in to MSN, but you can't seem to see it anywhere. The window has mysteriously vanished!

Here are a few things to check before giving up in despair:

✔ Find the taskbar, that Windows 95 thingy that usually lurks down at the bottom of your screen. The taskbar has a button for every window that's open. Find the MSN window in the taskbar and click on it. That should bring the window to the front. (If the taskbar isn't visible, you have to move the mouse all the way to the bottom edge of the screen to make it appear. Also, if you've moved the taskbar, it may be on the top, left, or right edge of the screen rather than the bottom.)

✔ If no MSN window appears in the taskbar, you may have closed MSN but remained connected to the Internet. To make MSN come alive again, double-click on the desktop MSN icon. Because you are already connected to MSN, you don't have to go through the Connect To dialog box again.

✔ You may have been disconnected from MSN. Normally when this happens, a dialog box appears, informs you that you have been disconnected, and offers to reconnect you.

If the dialog box doesn't appear, you can reconnect on your own. Select the Start➪Programs➪Accessories➪Dial Up Networking command, and then double-click on the icon for your MSN connection.

You can tell if you're connected to the MSN by looking for the little modem icon in the right corner of the taskbar. If the icon is present, you are connected. If the icon is missing, you're not.

I Can't Find a File I Downloaded!

Don't worry. The file is probably around, and you're just not looking in the right place. MSN offers a Save As dialog box, which you must complete before downloading a file. Presumably you know where the file has been saved, but it's all too easy to click OK when this dialog box appears.

Fortunately, all you have to do is right-click a graphic object or a text link, and then choose the Save As command from the menu that appears. This will summon the Save As dialog box, which will by default open the same folder the dialog box was last opened to. Just check the Save In field at the top of the dialog box to find out what folder you saved your file in, and then click Cancel to dismiss the Save As dialog box, without actually saving anything.

If you cannot remember the name of the file you downloaded, here's a trick that may help you find it:

1. **Open a My Computer window for the folder in which you saved the file.**

   Click My Computer, and then navigate your way through your drives and folders until you come to the one you saved the file in.

2. **Click the Details View button.**

3. **Choose View⇨Arrange Icons⇨By Date.**

   The file is sorted into date sequence, and the newest files appear at the bottom of the list.

4. **Look at the files at the bottom of the list.**

   Hopefully, one of these files rings a bell.

I Was Disconnected in the Middle of a Two-Hour Download with Only Ten Minutes to Go!

Wow. Tough break. Unfortunately, MSN doesn't have any way to restart a big download and pick up where you left off. The only solution is to download the entire file again.

Don't blame me, I'm just the messenger.

I Can't Find My Favorite Web Page!

I've faced this problem myself. The Internet is such a large place that it's easy to stumble into a Web page you really like, but then not find it later.

The best way to avoid such frustration is to add any cool Web page you stumble across to your Favorites list the moment you stumble across it. You can always find the Web page again by choosing the Favorites command. If you later decide that it's not such a great page after all, you can always delete it from Favorites.

I'm Still Stuck

If you've consulted MSN online help and still can't get an answer to a question, you may need to call the MSN technical support line. The MSN technical support phone numbers are a closely guarded secret, but you can find them by following this procedure:

1. **Insert the MSN CD-ROM into your CD-ROM drive.**

2. **When the MSN window appears, click the Get help connecting to MSN button.**

3. **Click Member Support Phone Numbers.**

4. **Click your country or region (United States, Canada, Europe, whatever).**

5. **Write down the numbers.**

6. **Call MSN Technical Support**

I've Started a Nuclear War

If you're minding your own business, enjoying a nice game of Global Thermonuclear War at `http://www.wargames.com`, and you suddenly hear air raid sirens and see mushroom clouds on the horizon, don't panic. See if you can interest the computer in a nice game of chess instead.

Really, this isn't your fault. Nothing you do can start a nuclear war from the Internet. Experienced computer users have been trying to start nuclear wars on the Internet for years, and no one has succeeded — at least not yet.

Chapter 24

Ten Microsoft Network Commandments

In This Chapter

"Fear not! For I bring you glad tidings of great joy. For behold, a software giant shall conceive and bring forth a new online service, and its name shall be called The Microsoft Network! And this shall be a sign unto you, that you shall find the network lying as an icon upon your desktop. And you shall double-click it, and behold, the network shall be given unto you!"

— Networks 1:1

And so it came to pass that these Ten Microsoft Network Commandments were handed down from generation to generation, to be worn as frontlets between the computer nerds' eyes (where their glasses are taped). Obey these commandments, and all shall go well with your computer, your children's computers, and your children's children's computers.

I. Thou Shalt Treat Thy Network Neighbor As Thou Wouldst Thyself Be Treated

This commandment is the online equivalent of the Golden Rule, and it is the core of network etiquette, or *Netiquette* as it is called.

II. Thou Shalt Not Allow Thy Children to Use MSN Unsupervised

Suffer the little children and forgive them not, for theirs is the network. But don't let them go online unsupervised. The online world is fraught with peril for children. Teach your children the safety rules found in Chapter 25, and monitor their use of the MSN. Be especially wary about granting Internet access to the kids.

III. Thou Shalt Not Abuse HTML Formatting

Yes, MSN enables you to send e-mail messages and newsgroup articles formatted using HTML. But opening a message written in 32-point Aardvark Bold and being able to see only three or four words at a time is really annoying. Just because you *can* use goofy formatting doesn't mean you *should*.

IV. Thou Shalt Not Upload Anything Thou Dost Not Have Permission to Upload

Using your scanner to scan a picture from *Life* magazine and uploading it to MSN would be great. It would also be illegal. Pictures in books, magazines, and other publications are always copyrighted. Uploading them to an online service or the Internet is a clear violation of the copyright.

The same applies to commercial software. Don't upload the latest version of Quake or Tie Fighter. These and most other programs are copyrighted and cannot be uploaded.

V. Thou Shalt Not Inquire as to Personal Information

Don't pop into a chat room and start asking personal questions, such as a person's phone number, address, or credit card numbers — unless you want Federal agents surrounding your house the next day.

VI. Thou Shalt Not Spam

Spam is unwanted e-mail sent to a bunch of URLs all at once, or unwanted newsgroup articles posted to a bunch of newsgroups all at once. Don't be a spammer.

VII. Thou Shalt Not Forget to Check Bulletin Boards Upon Which Thou Hast Posted Articles

If you post a message to a BBS or a newsgroup, be sure to check back each day for awhile to see whether anyone answers your post.

VIII. Thou Shalt Not Flame Thy Neighbor

Plenty of flaming goes on already. Don't add to the fray.

IX. Thou Shalt Register Thy Shareware

Shareware is not free. Instead, shareware is an alternative distribution method for software: a try-before-you-buy system in which you download the software and use it long enough to decide whether you like it and intend to use it. Then you either register the software by sending the author the requested registration fee, or delete the software from your computer.

X. Remember Thy Password, and Keep It a Secret

Write your password down somewhere, but not somewhere obvious. Never, under any circumstances, give your password to someone on MSN or the Internet, or to someone who calls you and says that he or she must "verify your account" or other gibberish.

Chapter 25

Ten Safety Tips for Kids on the 'Net

In This Chapter

▶ Safety tips for kids and their parents

▶ Ways to help keep the Internet a safe place for everyone

*M*SN and the Internet are inherently risky places for kids — and adults. Along with pictures of Neil Armstrong on the moon, your kids can just as easily find pictures you probably don't want them to see. While chatting online can be fun and enlightening, it can also be unhealthy, and possibly even dangerous.

This chapter lists ten important safety tips that you should drill into your kids' heads before you allow them to go online.

I really don't want to be an alarmist. Overall, the online world is a fairly wholesome place. Don't be afraid to let your kids venture online, but don't let them do it alone. Make sure that they understand the ground rules.

Do Not Believe People Are Who They Say They Are

When you sign up for MSN, you can type anything you want for your user ID. No one makes you tell the truth in e-mail, newsletter, or chats. Just because someone claims to be a 16-year-old female is not reason enough to believe that they are. That person can be a 12-year-old boy, a 19-year-old girl, or a 35-year-old Martian.

Never Give Out Your Address, Phone Number, Real Last Name, or Credit Card Number

If you're not sure why this rule exists, refer to the section titled "Do Not Believe People Are Who They Say They Are."

Never Pretend to Be Someone You're Not

The flip side of not believing who people say they are, is that people may believe that you *are* who you say you are. For example, if your daughter is a 13-year-old and claims to be a 17-year-old, she may be inviting trouble.

We all like to gloss over our weaknesses. When I'm online, I don't generally draw attention to the fact that a substantial portion of my hair is gone and I'm a bit pudgy around the waistline (well, okay, I'm a *lot* pudgy around the waistline). But I don't represent myself as a super athlete or a rock star, either. I just try to be myself.

Save Inappropriate E-Mail to a File

Tell your kids that if someone sends them inappropriate e-mail — not something that makes them feel angry or upset, but something that seems downright inappropriate — they can use the File⇨Save As command to save the message as a file. They can then show the e-mail to you.

Save Inappropriate Chat to a File

Tell your kids to save the chat to a file if someone is vulgar or offensive in an online chat. They can then show the file to an adult. Microsoft Chat enables them to save the chat to a file by using the File⇨Save command.

Watch Your Language

The Internet isn't censored. In fact, it can be a fairly rough place. Crude language abounds, especially on Usenet. But that doesn't mean your kids need to contribute to the endless flow of colorful metaphors. Tell them to watch their language while chatting online or posting messages.

Don't Obsess

Going online can be fun, but there's more to life than surfing the net. The best friendships are the ones in which your kids actually spend time in the presence of other people. If you find them spending hour upon hour online, maybe you should have them cut back a bit.

Report Inappropriate Behavior to an Adult

If something seems amiss in their online experience — for example, if they think someone is harassing them, or if someone asks them questions of a questionable nature — have your kids tell you.

You can then complain by sending mail to the administrator of the perpetrator's service provider. If the perpetrator is clever, you may not be able to figure out his or her true e-mail address, but often you can. If your kids receive harassing mail from `idiot@jerk.com`, try sending a complaint to `postmaster@jerk.com`.

If You Feel Uncomfortable, Leave

Tell your kids not to stick around in a chat session if they feel uncomfortable. They should just leave. Similarly, tell them not to bother to reply to inappropriate e-mail messages or newsgroup articles.

Parents: Be Involved with Your Kids' Online Activities

Don't let your kids run loose online! Get involved with what they are doing. You don't have to monitor them every moment they are online. Just be interested in what they are doing, what friends they have made over the network, what they like, and what they don't like. Ask them to show you around their favorite Web pages.

Good Terms to Know

• •

ActiveX: The new Web-based object technology by Microsoft, which enables intelligent objects to be embedded in Web documents to create interactive pages. See also *object linking and embedding*.

address book: A file that stores the e-mail addresses of the people with whom you correspond regularly.

AFK: *Away from keyboard,* an abbreviation commonly used when chatting.

America Online: A popular online information service that also provides Internet access. America Online is often referred to as AOL. To send e-mail to an AOL user, address the message to the user's America Online name, followed by the domain name (@aol.com). For example, if the user's AOL name is Barney, send an e-mail message to Barney@aol.com.

anniversary date: The day of the month you enrolled in MSN. Microsoft helps you celebrate your anniversary each month by billing your credit card.

anonymous FTP: An FTP site that allows access to anyone, without requiring an account.

AOL: See *America Online*.

applet: A program written in the Java language and embedded in a Web page. Applets run automatically whenever a user views the Web page that contains the applet.

article: A message posted to a Usenet newsgroup.

ASCII: The standard character set for most computers. Internet newsgroups are *ASCII-only,* meaning that they can support only text-based messages.

attach: To send a file along with an e-mail message or newsgroup article.

attachment: A file attached to an e-mail message or newsgroup article.

AVI: The Microsoft standard for video files that can be viewed in Windows. AVI is one of the most popular video formats on the Web, but other formats, such as QuickTime and MPEG, are also widely used.

bandwidth: The amount of information that can flow through a network connection. Bandwidth is to computer networks what pipe diameter is to plumbing: the bigger the pipe, the more water can flow at one time.

baud: See *bits per second*. (Actually, a technical difference does exist between *baud* and *bits per second*, but only people with pocket protectors and taped glasses care.)

BBS: See *bulletin board*.

binary file: A non-ASCII file, such as a picture, sound, video, or a computer program.

BITNET: A large network connected to the Internet. BITNET stands for "Because It's Time Network" and connects colleges and universities in North America and Europe. BITNET mailing lists are presented as Usenet newsgroups under the `bit` hierarchy.

bits per second (bps): A measure of how fast your modem can transmit or receive information between your computer and a remote computer, such as an Internet Service Provider. You won't be happy browsing the Internet using anything less than a 14,400 bps modem (commonly referred to as a *14.4 modem*). The term *Kbps* is often used to designate thousands of bits per second. Thus, 28,800 bps and 28.8 Kbps are equivalent.

BRB: *Be right back,* an abbreviation commonly used in chat rooms.

browser: A program that you can use to access and view the World Wide Web. The MSN Program Viewer is actually a browser based on the Microsoft Internet Explorer.

bulletin board (BBS): An MSN service that enables you to post articles and read other articles posted by other MSN users, similar to an Internet newsgroup.

cache: An area of your computer's hard disk used to store recently down-loaded data from the network so that the data can be redisplayed quickly.

cappuccino: An Italian coffee drink.

certificate: An online form of identification which gives one computer assurance that the other computer is who it says it is. Certificates are most often used for online financial transactions. For example, when you purchase an item from a mail order company over the Internet, the mail order company offers a certificate to convince the MSN Program Viewer that the company is on the up and up. Similarly, MSN offers a certificate to the mail order company so that the company knows that you can be trusted. Certificates are a relatively new phenomenon on the Internet.

chat: The Microsoft Network equivalent to a conference call: A chat is an online conversation between two or more users who are on MSN at the same time. When you send a message to a chat, everyone in the chat can immediately see your message and respond.

chat history: Microsoft Chat keeps a copy of all messages that have been sent during a chat. The chat history begins the moment you join the chat, and continues until you exit. You can scroll back through the chat history to review sent messages, and you can save a chat history to a file if you want to keep a permanent record of a chat.

chat room: A place where chats on a particular topic take place. Most MSN forums have at least one chat room dedicated to the forum's topic. Some forums have several rooms.

Chaucer: A dead English dude who didn't spell very well.

Coke machine: A coin-operated device that dispenses Coke and other Coca-Cola products (computer geeks apparently don't like Pepsi). The latest rage in the computer science departments of many universities is to hook the Coke machine up to a Web server so that users all across the globe can find out how much Coke and Diet Coke remains in the machine. Go figure.

compressed file: A file that has been processed by a special compression program, which reduces the amount of disk space required to store the file. If you download the file to your computer, you must decompress the file, using a program such as WinZip or PKUNZIP, before you can use it.

CompuServe: A popular online service that also provides Internet access. To send Internet mail to a CompuServe member, address the mail to the user's CompuServe user ID — two groups of numbers separated by a comma, and followed by @compuserve.com. You must use a period instead of a comma in the user ID, however. For example, if the user ID is 55555,1234, send mail to 55555.1234@compuserve.com. You have to use the period because Internet e-mail standard doesn't allow for commas in e-mail addresses.

connect time: The amount of time you are connected to MSN. Microsoft allows you a certain number of hours per month before it starts charging you extra money.

Content Advisor: The MSN feature that enables you to block access to sites that may contain offensive material.

cookie: A file that a Web server stores on your computer. The most common use for cookies is to customize the way a Web page appears when you view it. MSN leaves cookies all over your computer. Don't worry: Cookies don't bite.

cyberspace: An avant-garde term used to refer to the Internet.

data center: A big room filled with computers. Microsoft maintains a huge data center in Redmond, Washington, where the MSN computers are housed.

decode: To reconstruct a binary file that was encoded by the _uuencode_ scheme, used in e-mail and newsgroups. Internet Mail and Internet News automatically decode encoded files.

decompression: The process of restoring a compressed file to its original state. Decompression is usually accomplished with a program such as WinZip or PKUNZIP. You can download the shareware version of PKUNZIP at `www.pkware.com`.

decryption: See _Tales from Decrypt._ Just kidding. Decryption is the process of unscrambling a message that has been encrypted (scrambled up so that only the intended recipient can read it). See **encryption**.

Department of Justice (DOJ): An evil government agency that wants to shut down The Microsoft Network. Boo! Hiss!

DNS: _Domain Name Server._ The system that enables us to use almost intelligible names, such as `www.microsoft.com`, rather than completely incomprehensible addresses, such as `283.939.12.74`.

domain: The last portion of an Internet address (also known as the _top-level domain_), which indicates whether the address belongs to a company (`com`), an educational institution (`edu`), a government agency (`gov`), a military organization (`mil`), or another organization (`org`).

domain name: The address of an Internet site, which generally includes the organization domain name followed by the top-level domain, as in `www.idgbooks.com`.

download: To copy a file from another computer to your computer using a modem.

Eform: A special type of document that displays a form on your screen, gathers information from you, and then e-mails the information back to MSN to be processed.

e-mail: _Electronic mail,_ an MSN service that allows you to send and receive messages to and from other Internet users.

emoticon: Another word for a smiley face you create with keystrokes you find around the house.

encode: A method of converting a _binary file_ to ASCII text, which can be sent by e-mail or posted to a newsgroup or BBS. When displayed, encoded information looks like a stream of random characters. But when you run the encoded message through a decoder program, the original binary file is reconstructed. Internet Mail and Internet News automatically encode and decode messages, so you don't have to worry about using a separate program for this purpose.

encrypt: Scrambling a message so that no one can read it, except of course the intended recipient, who must *decrypt* the message before reading it. See *decrypt*.

ETLA: *Extended Three Letter Acronym.* A four-letter acronym. Computer nerds think this is funny.

Explorer: A Windows 95 program that enables you to view the contents of folders alongside a hierarchical representation of the computer's folders. It's the Windows 95 version of the old Windows 3.1 Program Manager and File Manager.

e-zine: An electronic magazine published online on the Internet or on MSN.

FAQ: A *frequently asked questions* file. Contains answers to the most commonly asked questions. Always check to see if a FAQ file exists for a BBS or Usenet newsgroup before asking basic questions. If you post a question on an Internet newsgroup and the answer is in the FAQ, you'll get flamed for sure.

favorites: A collection of Web page addresses that you visit frequently. MSN allows you to store your favorite Web addresses in a special folder so that you can recall them quickly.

File Transfer Protocol (FTP): A system that enables the transfer of program and data files over the Internet.

flame: A painfully brutal response to a dumb posting on a BBS or Internet newsgroup. On some newsgroups, just having `aol.com` in your Internet address is cause enough to get flamed.

forum: A collection of MSN pages, bulletin boards, chat rooms, and other services that are related to a particular topic. All forums have a dedicated *forum manager*.

forum manager: The person who oversees a forum. The forum manager decides which bulletin boards, chat areas, and other services will be available on the forum, and tries to keep discussions on topic.

freeware: Software that you can download and use without paying a fee.

FTP: See *File Transfer Protocol*.

FTP site: An Internet server that has a library of files available for downloading using FTP.

GIF: *Graphic Interchange Format.* A popular file format for picture files. The GIF format uses an efficient compression technique that results in less data loss and higher quality graphics than other formats, such as PCX.

home page: The introductory page at a Web site; sometimes refers to the entire Web site. Not to be confused with *start page*.

host computer: A computer to which you connect via the Internet.

HTML: *HyperText Markup Language.* A system of special tags used to create pages for the World Wide Web.

HTTP: *HyperText Transfer Protocol.* The protocol used to transmit HTML documents over the Internet.

hyperlink: Text or a graphics in a Web page that you click to retrieve another Web page. The new Web page may be on the same Web server as the original page, or it may be on an entirely different Web server halfway around the globe.

hypermedia: A variation of hypertext in which hyperlinks can be text, graphics, sounds, and videos. The World Wide Web is based on hypermedia, but the term *hypertext* is often loosely used.

hypertext: A system in which documents are linked to one another by text links. You click a text link, to retrieve a linked document. See also *hypermedia*.

IBM: A big computer company.

Internet: A vast worldwide collection of networked computers; the largest computer network in the world.

Internet address: A complete address used to send e-mail to someone over the Internet. Your Internet address consists of your user ID followed by @msn.com. For example, if your user ID is Jclampet, your internet address is Jclampet@msn.com.

Internet Explorer: The Microsoft program for browsing the World Wide Web and other Internet resources, such as FTP and Gopher. Internet Explorer comes free with MSN.

Internet Relay Chat (IRC): See *IRC.*

Internet Service Provider (ISP): Also known as *ISP.* A company that provides access to the Internet. MSN is an ISP.

IP: *Internet Protocol.* The data transmission protocol that enables networks to exchange messages; serves as the foundation for communications over the Internet.

IRC: *Internet Relay Chat.* A system that enables you to carry on live conversations, known as *chats,* with other Internet users; the Internet equivalent of MSN's chat rooms.

ISDN: A digital telephone line that can transmit data at 128 Kbps. ISDNs still costs a bit too much for the average home user. Watch, though — the price will come down.

ISP: See *Internet Service Provider.*

Java: An object-oriented programming language designed to be used on the World Wide Web. Java is created by Sun Microsystems and can be used to add interactivity to Web pages.

JPEG: *Joint Photographic Experts Group.* A popular format for picture files. JPEG uses a compression technique that greatly reduces a graphics file size, but also results in loss of resolution. For photographic images, this resolution loss is usually not noticeable. Because of its small file size, JPEG is a popular graphics format for the Internet.

KB: An abbreviation for *kilobyte* (roughly 1,024 bytes).

Kbps: A measure of a modem's speed in thousands of bits per second. The two most common modem speeds are 14.4 Kbps and 28.8 Kbps.

LAN: See *Local Area Network.*

lawyer joke: The original lawyer joke was told by Shakespeare, in King Henry IV, Part II: "The first thing we do, let's kill all the lawyers." The Comedy Connection forum is a good place to find other lawyer jokes on MSN.

link: See *hyperlink.*

Local area network (LAN): Also referred to as a *LAN.* Two or more computers that are connected to one another to form a network. A LAN enables computers to share resources, such as disk drives and printers. A LAN is usually located within a relatively small area, such as a building or on a campus.

LOL: *Laughing out loud.* A common abbreviation used to express mirth or joy when chatting online, in e-mail messages, or in newsgroup articles.

lurk: To read articles in a newsgroup without contributing your own postings. Lurking is one of the few approved forms of eavesdropping. Out of politeness, it's always a good idea to lurk for awhile in a newsgroup before posting your own articles.

mailing list: An e-mail version of a newsgroup. Any messages sent to the mailing list server are automatically sent to each list subscriber.

MB: *Megabyte.* Roughly a million bytes.

Microsoft: The largest software company in the world. Among other things, Microsoft is the maker of MS-DOS, Windows 95, and the Microsoft Office suite, which includes Word, Excel, PowerPoint, and Access. Oh, and I almost forgot — The Microsoft Network.

MIME: *Multipurpose Internet mail extensions.* One of the standard methods for attaching binary files to e-mail messages and newsgroup articles. See also ***uuencode***.

modem: A device that enables your computer to connect with other computers over a phone line. Most modems are *internal* — they are housed within the computer's cabinet. *External* modems are contained in their own boxes and must be connected to the back of a computer using a serial cable.

moderated newsgroup: A newsgroup whose postings are controlled by a moderator, which helps to ensure that articles in the newsgroup follow the guidelines established by the moderator.

moof: The phenomenon of being suddenly disconnected from MSN for no apparent reason.

moof monster: A mythical creature who dispenses the dreaded moof at its own discretion, without regard to one's station in life.

MPEG: *Motion Picture Experts Group.* A standard for compressing video images based on the popular JPEG standard used for still images. Internet Explorer 3.0 includes built-in support for MPEG videos.

MSN: The Microsoft Network, a commercial online service.

MSNBC: A combined production of Microsoft and NBC that presents news and information both online and on cable TV.

MSN Program Viewer: The program you use to access The Microsoft Network. MSN Program Viewer is a special version of the Microsoft Internet Explorer.

Netiquette: Electronic etiquette; the standards of politeness that are observed by civilized network users.

Netscape: The company that makes the popular *Netscape Navigator* browser software for the Internet. Internet Explorer and Navigator are currently duking it out for the title of *Most Popular Web Browser.* Although Navigator currently has the lead, Internet Explorer is gaining fast.

Newsgroup: An Internet bulletin board area where you can post and read messages, called *articles*. There are thousands of different newsgroups on almost every conceivable subject. Microsoft even runs its own newsgroups where you can find answers to your questions about Microsoft products.

News Alert: An MSNBC feature that monitors news as it breaks.

News Offline: An MSNBC feature that automatically e-mails you a customized newspaper every day.

news server: A host computer that stores newsgroup articles. You must connect to a news server to access newsgroups. MSN has several news servers at your disposal.

Object Linking and Embedding (OLE): Commonly known as *OLE*. A funky feature of Windows that enables you to embed documents, or portions of documents, from other programs into a document. For example, you can embed an Excel spreadsheet in a Word document. When you double-click the spreadsheet object, Excel takes over to let you edit the spreadsheet.

OIC: *Oh, I see.* A commonly used abbreviation in chats or e-mail messages.

OLE: See ***object linking and embedding***.

online: Connecting your computer to the network.

participant: Someone who participates in a chat. See also ***spectator*** and ***host***.

PKZIP: A popular shareware program used to compress files or to expand compressed files. You can get your copy at www.pkware.com.

PMJI: *Pardon me for jumping in.* A commonly used abbreviation in newsgroup articles.

posting: Adding an article to a newsgroup.

PPP: *Point to Point Protocol.* The protocol that allows you to access Internet services.

Program Viewer: See ***MSN Program Viewer***.

protocol: A set of conventions that govern communications between computers in a network.

public domain: Computer software or other information that is available free of charge. See also ***shareware***.

ROFL: *Rolling on the floor laughing.* A common abbreviation used in chats, newsgroup articles, and e-mail messages. You'll see frequent variations, such as ROFLPP and ROFLMAO. Figure those out yourself.

RSAC: *Recreational Software Advisory Council,* the group that provides the framework for rating online content.

server: A computer that provides services to other computers on the Internet or on a local area network. Specific types of Internet servers include news servers, mail servers, FTP servers, and Web servers.

service provider: See *Internet Service Provider*.

shareware: A software program that you can download and try — free of charge. The program is not free, however. If you like the program and continue to use it, you are obligated to send in a modest registration fee. See *public domain*.

signature: A fancy block of text that users routinely place at the end of their e-mail messages and newsgroup articles.

smiley: A smiley face or other *emoticon* created from keyboard characters; used to convey emotions in otherwise emotionless e-mail messages or newsgroup postings. Examples include:

- ✔ **:-)** Feelin' happy
- ✔ **:-D** Super-duper happy
- ✔ **8^)** Glasses-wearing happiness, or perhaps a smiling Orphan Annie (Leapin' Lizards!)
- ✔ **;-)** Conspiratorial wink
- ✔ **:-o** You surprise me
- ✔ **:-(** So sad
- ✔ **:-|** Apathetic

spectator: Someone who is allowed into a chat room to listen, but is not allowed to converse. In most chat rooms, this classification is a kind of penalty box for participants who have been unruly. See also *participant* and *host*.

Taskbar: A Windows 95 feature that displays icons for all open windows, a clock, and the Start button, which you use to run programs. Normally, the Taskbar appears at the bottom of the screen, but it can be repositioned at any edge of the screen you prefer. If the Taskbar is not visible, try moving the mouse to the very bottom of the screen, or to the left, right, or top edge of the screen.

TCP/IP: *Transmission Control Protocol/Internet Protocol.* The basic set of conventions that the Internet uses to enable different types of computers to communicate with one another.

Telnet: A protocol that allows you to log in to a remote computer as if you were actually a terminal attached to that remote computer.

TIFF: *Tagged Image File Format.* A format for picture files. TIFF files are large compared with other formats such as JPEG and GIF, but preserve all of the original image's quality. Because of its large file size, TIFF files aren't that popular on the Internet.

thread: An exchange of articles in a newsgroup. Specifically, an original article, all of its replies, all of the replies to replies, and so on.

TLA: *Three letter acronym.* Ever notice how almost all computer terms can be reduced to a three letter acronym? It all started with IBM. Now you've got MSN, URL, AOL, and who knows what else. Of course there's a TLA for *Three Letter Acronym.* I guess I shouldn't complain; this book is being published by IDG.

Uniform Resource Locator (URL): A method of specifying the address of any resource available on the Internet, used when browsing the Internet. For example, the URL of IDG Books Worldwide is www.idgbooks.com.

upload: Copying a file from your computer to the Internet.

URL: See *Uniform Resource Locator.*

Usenet: A network of Internet newsgroups that contains many of the most popular newsgroups. Internet News can be used to access Usenet newsgroups.

uuencode: A method of attaching binary files such as programs or documents to mail messages and newsgroup articles. The other method is called MIME.

Vidcam: A video camera attached to a Web server that allows you to view the camera's image over the Net. This setup is kind of a crazy thing to do, but seems to be the rage. See also *Coke machine.*

virus: An evil computer program that slips into your computer undetected, tries to spread itself to other computers, and may eventually do something bad, like trash your hard disk. Because MSN does not include built-in virus detection, I suggest you consider using one of the many virus protection programs available if you are worried about catching a virus.

WAN: See *Wide Area Network.*

Web: See *World Wide Web*.

Web browser: A program that can find pages on the World Wide Web and display them on your home computer. The MSN Program Viewer and the Microsoft Internet Explorer are both examples of Web browsers.

Web page: A document available for display on the World Wide Web. The document may contain links to other documents located on the same server or on other Web servers.

Web server: A server computer where Web documents are stored so they can be accessed on the World Wide Web.

Wide Area Network (WAN): A computer network which spans a large area, such as an entire campus, or perhaps a network that links branches of a company in several cities.

WinSock: Short for *Windows Sockets*. The standard by which Windows programs are able to communicate with TCP/IP and the Internet. Fortunately, you don't have to know anything about WinSock to use it. In fact, you don't even have to know you're using it at all.

Windows 95: The newest version of the Microsoft Windows operating system. Windows 95 is the main operating system for Internet Explorer, although versions of Internet Explorer exist for Windows NT, Windows 3.1, and Macintosh computers.

WinZip: A Windows version of the popular PKZIP compression program.

World Wide Web: Also referred to as *the Web*. This relatively new part of the Internet displays information using fancy graphics. The Web is based on *links,* which allow the user to travel quickly from one Web server to another.

zipped file: A file that has been compressed using the PKZIP or WinZip programs.

Index

(continued)

• N •

The Internet For Macs® For Dummies® 2nd Edition	by Charles Seiter	ISBN: 1-56884-371-2	$19.99 USA/$26.99 Canada
The Internet For Macs® For Dummies® Starter Kit	by Charles Seiter	ISBN: 1-56884-244-9	$29.99 USA/$39.99 Canada
The Internet For Macs® For Dummies® Starter Kit Bestseller Edition	by Charles Seiter	ISBN: 1-56884-245-7	$39.99 USA/$54.99 Canada
The Internet For Windows® For Dummies® Starter Kit	by John R. Levine & Margaret Levine Young	ISBN: 1-56884-237-6	$34.99 USA/$44.99 Canada
The Internet For Windows® For Dummies® Starter Kit, Bestseller Edition	by John R. Levine & Margaret Levine Young	ISBN: 1-56884-246-5	$39.99 USA/$54.99 Canada

MACINTOSH

Mac® Programming For Dummies®	by Dan Parks Sydow	ISBN: 1-56884-173-6	$19.95 USA/$26.95 Canada
Macintosh® System 7.5 For Dummies®	by Bob LeVitus	ISBN: 1-56884-197-3	$19.95 USA/$26.95 Canada
MORE Macs® For Dummies®	by David Pogue	ISBN: 1-56884-087-X	$19.95 USA/$26.95 Canada
PageMaker 5 For Macs® For Dummies®	by Galen Gruman & Deke McClelland	ISBN: 1-56884-178-7	$19.95 USA/$26.95 Canada
QuarkXPress 3.3 For Dummies®	by Galen Gruman & Barbara Assadi	ISBN: 1-56884-217-1	$19.99 USA/$26.99 Canada
Upgrading and Fixing Macs® For Dummies®	by Kearney Rietmann & Frank Higgins	ISBN: 1-56884-189-2	$19.95 USA/$26.95 Canada

MULTIMEDIA

Multimedia & CD-ROMs For Dummies® 2nd Edition	by Andy Rathbone	ISBN: 1-56884-907-9	$19.99 USA/$26.99 Canada
Multimedia & CD-ROMs For Dummies® Interactive Multimedia Value Pack, 2nd Edition	by Andy Rathbone	ISBN: 1-56884-909-5	$29.99 USA/$39.99 Canada

OPERATING SYSTEMS:

DOS

MORE DOS For Dummies®	by Dan Gookin	ISBN: 1-56884-046-2	$19.95 USA/$26.95 Canada
OS/2® Warp For Dummies® 2nd Edition	by Andy Rathbone	ISBN: 1-56884-205-8	$19.99 USA/$26.99 Canada

UNIX

MORE UNIX® For Dummies®	by John R. Levine & Margaret Levine Young	ISBN: 1-56884-361-5	$19.99 USA/$26.99 Canada
UNIX® For Dummies®	by John R. Levine & Margaret Levine Young	ISBN: 1-878058-58-4	$19.95 USA/$26.95 Canada

WINDOWS

MORE Windows® For Dummies® 2nd Edition	by Andy Rathbone	ISBN: 1-56884-048-9	$19.95 USA/$26.95 Canada
Windows® 95 For Dummies®	by Andy Rathbone	ISBN: 1-56884-240-6	$19.99 USA/$26.99 Canada

PCS/HARDWARE

Illustrated Computer Dictionary For Dummies® 2nd Edition	by Dan Gookin & Wallace Wang	ISBN: 1-56884-218-X	$12.95 USA/$16.95 Canada
Upgrading and Fixing PCs For Dummies® 2nd Edition	by Andy Rathbone	ISBN: 1-56884-903-6	$19.99 USA/$26.99 Canada

PRESENTATION/AUTOCAD

AutoCAD For Dummies®	by Bud Smith	ISBN: 1-56884-191-4	$19.95 USA/$26.95 Canada
PowerPoint 4 For Windows® For Dummies®	by Doug Lowe	ISBN: 1-56884-161-2	$16.99 USA/$22.99 Canada

PROGRAMMING

Borland C++ For Dummies®	by Michael Hyman	ISBN: 1-56884-162-0	$19.95 USA/$26.95 Canada
C For Dummies® Volume 1	by Dan Gookin	ISBN: 1-878058-78-9	$19.95 USA/$26.95 Canada
C++ For Dummies®	by Stephen R. Davis	ISBN: 1-56884-163-9	$19.95 USA/$26.95 Canada
Delphi Programming For Dummies®	by Neil Rubenking	ISBN: 1-56884-200-7	$19.99 USA/$26.99 Canada
Mac® Programming For Dummies®	by Dan Parks Sydow	ISBN: 1-56884-173-6	$19.95 USA/$26.95 Canada
PowerBuilder 4 Programming For Dummies®	by Ted Coombs & Jason Coombs	ISBN: 1-56884-325-9	$19.99 USA/$26.99 Canada
QBasic Programming For Dummies®	by Douglas Hergert	ISBN: 1-56884-093-4	$19.95 USA/$26.95 Canada
Visual Basic 3 For Dummies®	by Wallace Wang	ISBN: 1-56884-076-4	$19.95 USA/$26.95 Canada
Visual Basic "X" For Dummies®	by Wallace Wang	ISBN: 1-56884-230-9	$19.99 USA/$26.99 Canada
Visual C++ 2 For Dummies®	by Michael Hyman & Bob Arnson	ISBN: 1-56884-328-3	$19.99 USA/$26.99 Canada
Windows® 95 Programming For Dummies®	by S. Randy Davis	ISBN: 1-56884-327-5	$19.99 USA/$26.99 Canada

SPREADSHEET

1-2-3 For Dummies®	by Greg Harvey	ISBN: 1-878058-60-6	$16.95 USA/$22.95 Canada
1-2-3 For Windows® 5 For Dummies® 2nd Edition	by John Walkenbach	ISBN: 1-56884-216-3	$16.95 USA/$22.95 Canada
Excel 5 For Macs® For Dummies®	by Greg Harvey	ISBN: 1-56884-186-8	$19.95 USA/$26.95 Canada
Excel For Dummies® 2nd Edition	by Greg Harvey	ISBN: 1-56884-050-0	$16.95 USA/$22.95 Canada
MORE 1-2-3 For DOS For Dummies®	by John Weingarten	ISBN: 1-56884-224-4	$19.99 USA/$26.99 Canada
MORE Excel 5 For Windows® For Dummies®	by Greg Harvey	ISBN: 1-56884-207-4	$19.95 USA/$26.95 Canada
Quattro Pro 6 For Windows® For Dummies®	by John Walkenbach	ISBN: 1-56884-174-4	$19.95 USA/$26.95 Canada
Quattro Pro For DOS For Dummies®	by John Walkenbach	ISBN: 1-56884-023-3	$16.95 USA/$22.95 Canada

UTILITIES

Norton Utilities 8 For Dummies®	by Beth Slick	ISBN: 1-56884-166-3	$19.95 USA/$26.95 Canada

VCRS/CAMCORDERS

VCRs & Camcorders For Dummies™	by Gordon McComb & Andy Rathbone	ISBN: 1-56884-229-5	$14.99 USA/$20.99 Canada

WORD PROCESSING

Ami Pro For Dummies®	by Jim Meade	ISBN: 1-56884-049-7	$19.95 USA/$26.95 Canada
MORE Word For Windows® 6 For Dummies®	by Doug Lowe	ISBN: 1-56884-165-5	$19.95 USA/$26.95 Canada
MORE WordPerfect® 6 For Windows® For Dummies®	by Margaret Levine Young & David C. Kay	ISBN: 1-56884-206-6	$19.95 USA/$26.95 Canada
MORE WordPerfect® 6 For DOS For Dummies®	by Wallace Wang, edited by Dan Gookin	ISBN: 1-56884-047-0	$19.95 USA/$26.95 Canada
Word 6 For Macs® For Dummies®	by Dan Gookin	ISBN: 1-56884-190-6	$19.95 USA/$26.95 Canada
Word For Windows® 6 For Dummies®	by Dan Gookin	ISBN: 1-56884-075-6	$16.95 USA/$22.95 Canada
Word For Windows® For Dummies®	by Dan Gookin & Ray Werner	ISBN: 1-878058-86-X	$16.95 USA/$22.95 Canada
WordPerfect® 6 For DOS For Dummies®	by Dan Gookin	ISBN: 1-878058-77-0	$16.95 USA/$22.95 Canada
WordPerfect® 6.1 For Windows® For Dummies® 2nd Edition	by Margaret Levine Young & David Kay	ISBN: 1-56884-243-0	$16.95 USA/$22.95 Canada
WordPerfect® For Dummies®	by Dan Gookin	ISBN: 1-878058-52-5	$16.95 USA/$22.95 Canada

7/29/96

Fun, Fast, & Cheap!™

NEW!

NEW!

SUPER STAR

SUPER STAR

The Internet For Macs® For Dummies® Quick Reference
by Charles Seiter

ISBN:1-56884-967-2
$9.99 USA/$12.99 Canada

Windows® 95 For Dummies® Quick Reference
by Greg Harvey

ISBN: 1-56884-964-8
$9.99 USA/$12.99 Canada

Photoshop 3 For Macs® For Dummies® Quick Reference
by Deke McClelland

ISBN: 1-56884-968-0
$9.99 USA/$12.99 Canada

WordPerfect® For DOS For Dummies® Quick Reference
by Greg Harvey

ISBN: 1-56884-009-8
$8.95 USA/$12.95 Canada

Title	Author	ISBN	Price
DATABASE			
Access 2 For Dummies® Quick Reference	by Stuart J. Stuple	ISBN: 1-56884-167-1	$8.95 USA/$11.95 Canada
dBASE 5 For DOS For Dummies® Quick Reference	by Barrie Sosinsky	ISBN: 1-56884-954-0	$9.99 USA/$12.99 Canada
dBASE 5 For Windows® For Dummies® Quick Reference	by Stuart J. Stuple	ISBN: 1-56884-953-2	$9.99 USA/$12.99 Canada
Paradox 5 For Windows® For Dummies® Quick Reference	by Scott Palmer	ISBN: 1-56884-960-5	$9.99 USA/$12.99 Canada
DESKTOP PUBLISHING/ILLUSTRATION/GRAPHICS			
CorelDRAW! 5 For Dummies® Quick Reference	by Raymond E. Werner	ISBN: 1-56884-952-4	$9.99 USA/$12.99 Canada
Harvard Graphics For Windows® For Dummies® Quick Reference	by Raymond E. Werner	ISBN: 1-56884-962-1	$9.99 USA/$12.99 Canada
Photoshop 3 For Macs® For Dummies® Quick Reference	by Deke McClelland	ISBN: 1-56884-968-0	$9.99 USA/$12.99 Canada
FINANCE/PERSONAL FINANCE			
Quicken 4 For Windows® For Dummies® Quick Reference	by Stephen L. Nelson	ISBN: 1-56884-950-8	$9.95 USA/$12.95 Canada
GROUPWARE/INTEGRATED			
Microsoft® Office 4 For Windows® For Dummies® Quick Reference	by Doug Lowe	ISBN: 1-56884-958-3	$9.99 USA/$12.99 Canada
Microsoft® Works 3 For Windows® For Dummies® Quick Reference	by Michael Partington	ISBN: 1-56884-959-1	$9.99 USA/$12.99 Canada
INTERNET/COMMUNICATIONS/NETWORKING			
The Internet For Dummies® Quick Reference	by John R. Levine & Margaret Levine Young	ISBN: 1-56884-168-X	$8.95 USA/$11.95 Canada
MACINTOSH			
Macintosh® System 7.5 For Dummies® Quick Reference	by Stuart J. Stuple	ISBN: 1-56884-956-7	$9.99 USA/$12.99 Canada
OPERATING SYSTEMS:			
DOS			
DOS For Dummies® Quick Reference	by Greg Harvey	ISBN: 1-56884-007-1	$8.95 USA/$11.95 Canada
UNIX			
UNIX® For Dummies® Quick Reference	by John R. Levine & Margaret Levine Young	ISBN: 1-56884-094-2	$8.95 USA/$11.95 Canada
WINDOWS			
Windows® 3.1 For Dummies® Quick Reference, 2nd Edition	by Greg Harvey	ISBN: 1-56884-951-6	$8.95 USA/$11.95 Canada
PCs/HARDWARE			
Memory Management For Dummies® Quick Reference	by Doug Lowe	ISBN: 1-56884-362-3	$9.99 USA/$12.99 Canada
PRESENTATION/AUTOCAD			
AutoCAD For Dummies® Quick Reference	by Ellen Finkelstein	ISBN: 1-56884-198-1	$9.95 USA/$12.95 Canada
SPREADSHEET			
1-2-3 For Dummies® Quick Reference	by John Walkenbach	ISBN: 1-56884-027-6	$8.95 USA/$11.95 Canada
1-2-3 For Dummies® 5 For Dummies® Quick Reference	by John Walkenbach	ISBN: 1-56884-957-5	$9.95 USA/$12.95 Canada
Excel For Windows® For Dummies® Quick Reference, 2nd Edition	by John Walkenbach	ISBN: 1-56884-096-9	$8.95 USA/$11.95 Canada
Quattro Pro 6 For Windows® For Dummies® Quick Reference	by Stuart J. Stuple	ISBN: 1-56884-172-8	$9.95 USA/$12.95 Canada
WORD PROCESSING			
Word For Windows® 6 For Dummies® Quick Reference	by George Lynch	ISBN: 1-56884-095-0	$8.95 USA/$11.95 Canada
Word For Windows® For Dummies® Quick Reference	by George Lynch	ISBN: 1-56884-029-2	$8.95 USA/$11.95 Canada
WordPerfect® 6.1 For Windows® For Dummies® Quick Reference, 2nd Edition	by Greg Harvey	ISBN: 1-56884-966-4	$9.99 USA/$12.99/Canada

Order Center: (800) 762-2974 *(24 hours a day, seven days a week)*

Quantity	ISBN	Title	Price	Total

Shipping & Handling Charges

	Description	First book	Each additional book	Total
Domestic	Normal	$4.50	$1.50	$
	Two Day Air	$8.50	$2.50	$
	Overnight	$18.00	$3.00	$
International	Surface	$8.00	$8.00	$
	Airmail	$16.00	$16.00	$
	DHL Air	$17.00	$17.00	$

*For large quantities call for shipping & handling charges.
**Prices are subject to change without notice.

Ship to:

Name _____

Company _____

Address _____

City/State/Zip _____

Daytime Phone _____

Payment: ☐ Check to IDG Books Worldwide (US Funds Only)

      ☐ VISA   ☐ MasterCard   ☐ American Express

Card # _____ Expires _____

Signature _____

Subtotal _____

CA residents add
applicable sales tax _____

IN, MA, and MD
residents add
5% sales tax _____

IL residents add
6.25% sales tax _____

RI residents add
7% sales tax _____

TX residents add
8.25% sales tax _____

Shipping _____

Total _____

Please send this order form to:

**IDG Books Worldwide, Inc.
Attn: Order Entry Dept.
7260 Shadeland Station, Suite 100
Indianapolis, IN 46256**

*Allow up to 3 weeks for delivery.
Thank you!*

IDG BOOKS WORLDWIDE REGISTRATION CARD

Visit our
Web site at
http://www.idgbooks.com

ISBN Number: 0-7645-0160-7

Title of this book: Microsoft® Network For Dummies® , 2nd Edition

My overall rating of this book: ❏ Very good [1] ❏ Good [2] ❏ Satisfactory [3] ❏ Fair [4] ❏ Poor [5]

How I first heard about this book:

❏ Found in bookstore; name: [6] _____

❏ Advertisement: [8]

❏ Word of mouth; heard about book from friend, co-worker, etc.: [10]

❏ Book review: [7] _____

❏ Catalog: [9]

❏ Other: [11]

What I liked most about this book: _____

_____

_____

What I would change, add, delete, etc., in future editions of this book: _____

_____

_____

Other comments: _____

_____

Number of computer books I purchase in a year: ❏ 1 [12] ❏ 2-5 [13] ❏ 6-10 [14] ❏ More than 10 [15]

I would characterize my computer skills as: ❏ Beginner [16] ❏ Intermediate [17] ❏ Advanced [18] ❏ Professional [19]

I use ❏ DOS [20] ❏ Windows [21] ❏ OS/2 [22] ❏ Unix [23] ❏ Macintosh [24] ❏ Other: [25]_____

(please specify)

I would be interested in new books on the following subjects:

(please check all that apply, and use the spaces provided to identify specific software)

❏ Word processing: [26] _____

❏ Data bases: [28]

❏ File Utilities: [30]

❏ Networking: [32]

❏ Other: [34]

❏ Spreadsheets: [27] _____

❏ Desktop publishing: [29]

❏ Money management: [31]

❏ Programming languages: [33]

I use a PC at (please check all that apply): ❏ home [35] ❏ work [36] ❏ school [37] ❏ other: [38] _____

The disks I prefer to use are ❏ 5.25 [39] ❏ 3.5 [40] ❏ other: [41]_____

I have a CD ROM: ❏ yes [42] ❏ no [43]

I plan to buy or upgrade computer hardware this year: ❏ yes [44] ❏ no [45]

I plan to buy or upgrade computer software this year: ❏ yes [46] ❏ no [47]

Name: _____ Business title: [48] _____ Type of Business: [49] _____

Address (❏ home [50] ❏ work [51]/Company name: _____)

Street/Suite# _____

City [52]/State [53]/Zip code [54]: _____ Country [55] _____

❏ **I liked this book!** You may quote me by name in future
IDG Books Worldwide promotional materials.

My daytime phone number is _____

™

IDG
BOOKS
WORLDWIDE

**THE WORLD OF
COMPUTER
KNOWLEDGE®**

❑ YES!

Please keep me informed about IDG Books Worldwide's World of Computer Knowledge. Send me your latest catalog.